# Narrative Semiotics
in the
Epic Tradition

# Narrative Semiotics in the Epic Tradition: The Simile

Stephen A. Nimis

INDIANA UNIVERSITY PRESS
Bloomington & Indianapolis

Manufactured in the United States of America

Library of Congress Cataloging-in-Publication Data

Nimis, Stephen A.
    Narrative semiotics in the epic tradition.

    Bibliography: pp. 200-8
    Includes Index.
    1. Epic literature--History and criticism.
2. Semiotics and literature. 3. Simile. I. Title.
PN56.E65N56  1987  809.1'3  87-45323
ISBN 0-253-33997-9
1 2 3 4 5 92 91 90 89 88 87

To my very best friend,

Maureen Rose Nimis

# Contents

# Acknowledgments

Many people read various versions of this manuscript, and their criticism and encouragement helped me enormously. I would therefore like to acknowledge gratefully Kathleen Brady, Terry Cochran, Eleanor Leach, Gregory Nagy, Walter Nichipor, Jack Peradotto, Peter W. Rose, Ronald Sousa, Jim Sosnoski, and especially Wlad Godzich.

In the preparation of camera-ready copy I was assisted by the following staff and faculty at Miami University: Marina Faraguna and Shirley Jones (Classics), Joe Simpson (Academic Computing Services), Eileen Gill and Len Simutis (Research and Development Office), Mark Soupene (Learning Technology Center), Richard Smith (College of Arts and Science).

# Narrative Semiotics
in the
Epic Tradition

# INTRODUCTION

## Scope and Aims of the Work

This study focuses on the transformations of textual strategies and devices in a selection of literary works from Homer to Milton. The works to be looked at are all of "epic proportion," in the sense that they try to produce some sort of master narrative about serious matters. They are also epics in the sense that they share numerous characteristics and devices traditionally identified with the historical genre of epic. One of these devices, the epic simile, will serve as the main signpost for the investigation of the various works. Unlike other studies of the epic simile, however, the focus here will be on the *semiotics* of this traditional device, on *how* texts signify rather than on *what* they signify. The analysis of the similes will be a sort of symptomology opening out into more general issues of textual production in different historical contexts. The purpose is twofold: to bring to bear on these individual narratives the insights and preoccupations of semiotics; and, at the same time, to make a contribution to semiotics by bringing to bear on it the singularity of these various texts. That is, what follows is not only an application of semiotics to literary works, but also an application of literary works to our current understanding of signifying practices. For this reason, the theoretical framework for the textual analyses will itself be evolved in the course of making those analyses.

I begin by placing the problem of Homer's similes in the context of reading in general. I then outline a theoretical framework and preliminary terminology for the whole work, including a précis of Umberto Eco's theory of codes and of Michael Riffaterre's theory of intertextuality. The work of Eco and Riffaterre will form the basis for discussion of more specific theoretical issues to be taken up as they arise. I then turn to Homer's *Iliad*, for us the beginning of the epic tradition in the west. In approaching Homer's similes, I emphasize their *productive* character rather than their representational function. The similes of the *Iliad*, I argue, perform a whole range of roles in propelling the narrative of the poem forward. In fact, they often turn out to be solutions to specific textual complexities and are thus privileged places to see Homer's poetics at work. As such, Homer's similes go beyond the ornamental role usually attributed to them and can serve as an index of the textual and thematic problems that the poem tries to overcome.

Subsequent chapters take up the reorientation and redeployment of the simile in the *Argonautica* of Apollonius of Rhodes, the *Aeneid* of Vergil, Dante's *Divine Comedy*, and Milton's *Paradise Lost*, with discussion of other texts wherever that seemed necessary to clarify a context. These texts hardly exhaust the possibilities of discussing the epic simile, but they do make up a series with a rich range of similarities and differences, and they all stand in a tradition of conscious imitation of predecessors which begins with Homer. A close structural and theoretical reading of the similes of these texts will provide a means of explaining how each text relates to its textual tradition and how changing cultural contexts produce different ways of conceiving and constructing meaning. These transformations in the process of meaning formation are traced as the culture in which the epic occurs changes from an integrated warrior culture, to the more heterogeneous and widely diffused culture of the Hellenistic era, to the Roman context, with its universal pretensions, to late medieval Christian culture and finally to a culture which can no longer sustain the epic.

## Reading Homer

Since Hellenistic times the epic similes of Homer have been viewed basically as ornamental, for like many aspects of the *Iliad* and *Odyssey*, they often seemed to critics of the post-Aristotelian era to add little to the advance of the narrative itself.[1] These critics had the word of Aristotle (*AP* 1459a) that an epic should present a unified action, with all its parts correlated like a living organism. Indeed, the meandering similes of Homer, often scandalously inapposite to the narrative situation they ostensibly elucidate, have presented Homeric scholars with the same problem raised by the texts as a whole: namely, that they seem to be diffuse, loosely constructed and full of digressions and illogic. Given their presuppositions about what constitutes a proper epic, ancient commentators on Homer divided their activities between, on the one hand, emending, excising and otherwise reconstructing the poems to fit their own expectations for a work of art; and on the other, seeking an underlying unity in the form of allegorical interpretations.[2] The activity of nineteenth-century critics showed similar concerns: the "analysts" attempted to reconstitute the original text of Homer from the lamentably incoherent one transmitted to us; the "unitarians" to show that the *Iliad* and *Odyssey* were indeed unified in their received form if one considered them with sufficient subtlety.[3] It is well known how the work of Milman Parry radically changed the terms of this controversy. Parry showed that Homeric diction was a traditional medium and that the inclusion of words and phrases from different dialects and different historical strata was the result of a long process of development ruled by the constraints of "economy of expression." He concluded that the language of Homer was that of an oral tradition and that the use of noun-epithet combinations exhibited a traditional and unified composition technique.

A great deal of subsequent scholarship has attempted to enlarge on Parry's findings, assuming in varying degrees that the *Iliad* and *Odyssey* cannot be properly understood in terms of the Aristotelian notion of a "well-made story." Rather, the diffuse and loosely constructed poetic surface of Homer results from the circumstance that oral poetic production is governed by the logic of traditional patterns which underlie that surface.[4] Numerous studies have tried to identify these underlying patterns in the form of "typical scenes," usually coupled with the purpose of reconciling narrative inconsistency with unity of authorship by showing the underlying compositional habits of the poet. Thus, Hansen's work on the "conference sequence" answers the objections of Kirk and Page to certain irrelevancies in the plot of the *Odyssey* by showing a deeper regularity in the poet's composition of such scenes.[5] Fenik challenges not only analyst claims of interpolation, but also the "neo-analytic" position that some motifs of the *Iliad* must be borrowings from *antehomerica*, by showing the typicality of most of those motifs throughout the *Iliad*.[6] Again, W. C. Scott counters the thesis of Lee and Shipp that many of the similes of the *Iliad* are late interpolations by showing underlying regularities which characterize their use throughout the poem.[7]

The object of these studies, however, is limited to showing that the poems are the product of a single poet, a single tradition or a single oral poet. Hence the criteria consistently invoked are compositional economy and the autonomy of narrative patterns. What seems to be an inconsistency in the narrative surface is resolved once one has grasped the underlying motivation. The exigencies of oral composition and the pressure exerted by compositional habits combine to account for the inclusion of elements inappropriate to a specific context as well as other types of apparent anomaly. These studies, therefore, tend to treat the problem of Homeric composition negatively: compositional economy and the autonomy of narrative patterns, after all, provide apologies for the poet's petty failings rather than than explanations of his poetic purpose. "It has gradually become obvious," writes Nagler, "that even if one could view oral-traditional language as embodying a repertoire of 'stock formulas' this would offer no automatic solution to the problem of denotative, to say nothing of poetic meanings in Homeric diction...[and] the problem has been the same on the level of the motif." [8]

In response to this problem Nagler proposed a generative approach to Homer's language, replacing the notion of formula with a more open-ended "family" of phrases and words related to each other by poetic signification. Thus, for example, Nagler suggests that the explicit mention of attendants following a character conveyed to the properly cued audience significant information about the status of that individual. But various related accoutrements and activities (veils, ascending and descending, chambers, etc.), as well as certain key syntagms (καὶ ἁμὰ τῷ, ἁμ' ἕπονται, etc.) can refer to the same nuclear event of attendance. Moreover, the related accoutrements and activities can be realized by a number of "allomorphs" (e.g., "wave" for "veil"), all of which adds up to an extensive family of associated diction referring to the nuclear event of attendance with its poetic signification of conferring τίμη on the principal. The various realizations of this dictional family are generated, according to Nagler, by a "pre-verbal template" or "Gestalt"; that is, each verbal realization is a derivative "not of any other phrase but of some pre-verbal, mental, but quite real entity underlying all such phrases at a more abstract level" (*Spontaneity*, 12).

For the nature of these pre-verbal templates, Nagler adopts the framework of certain Sanskrit grammarians whose theory of meaning revolved around the concept of *sphota* (*Spontaneity*, 13-14):

> The term, *sphota*, is derived from an onomatopoetic root *sput* "to burst," its application to language being the intuitive perception of meaning which in our idiom also "bursts" upon the mind in some unknown way either spontaneously or when triggered by a linguistic symbol: word, phrase of sentence. The concept of *sphota* was defined from two points of view, both of which are

useful for my purposes: (a) "that from which the meaning bursts forth," "the linguistic sign in its aspect of meaning bearer," and (b) as an entity which itself is (at least partially) manifested by speech. But any one Gestalt or *sphota* beggars definition, for it is itself undifferentiated with respect to any describable phonological feature. The given word, phrase or sentence is only a kind of hypostasis of this entity--an allomorph, as I have been using the term--as a particular geometric shape is a hypostasis of its Platonic Form.

Between this "timeless, undefinable" *sphota* and the surface structures of actual utterance lies an intermediate stage consisting of patterns of phonological and syntactic norms imperfectly revealed by individual speech acts. Nagler analyzes Homer's text by abstracting from a number of examples a pattern of syntactic and semantic archetypes. These ideal configurations make up a sort of grammar by which the underlying *sphota* is transformed into verbal utterance. For Nagler this process of transformation into poetic utterance is *hierarchical*: from these pre-verbal templates to textual surface, from an inherent "meaning," which is ontologically prior to linguistic expression, to individual utterances which manifest, darkly, the presence of meaning.

The crucial issue raised by Nagler's theory is whether meaning is immanent or produced: whether there is a single meaning in all languages or whether meaning is context dependent. The Indian model adopted by Nagler is a radical example of a "universalist" theory of language, in which every utterance derives its meaning by virtue of being a manifestation of some underlying Gestalt which is ontologically prior to its articulation.[9] The *sphota* is "eternal and partless, manifested in time but not affected by time" (*Spontaneity*, 16); it is located so deep in consciousness "that one cannot properly speak of it as pertaining to, or affected by, a particular tradition" (*Spontaneity*, 26). Thus, for example, a child learning a language will develop an "intuitive feel" for an underlying Gestalt by hearing a number of its manifestations (*Spontaneity*, 17). The process of language acquisition is therefore a matter of giving particular form to a predetermined content, *Widererzeugung* to use Humboldt's term.[10] The implication of this model is that a text such as the *Iliad* articulates the same basic meaning articulated by all texts, variations occurring only at a number of more superficial levels of linguistic organization. Thus Nagler feels free to corroborate the identity of a Gestalt from any number of other cultural traditions (Near Eastern texts, *Beowulf*, etc.) for it is basically the same for all people in all times.

Nagler's explicitly Platonic theory is a straightforward example of an "essentialist" theory of meaning. Nagler's theory takes to its logical conclusion the tendency to project from various regularities in a text an ontologically prior generative mechanism, whether one is speaking of formulae, type scenes or mythic paradigms. It is worth giving some scope to his theory because Nagler lays out the assumptions which are usually tacit in essentialist interpretive strategies: namely, the undialectical separation of form and content so that language becomes treated as an instrument which we merely take up and use in order to convey information or feelings which existed prior to the act of communication. Interpretive strategies based on such a notion of language focus on finding meaning "in" the text or "under" the text, and generally end up minimizing the historical determinants of the process of meaning production and conferring some more abstract and ahistorical significance on works of literature. Thus, for example, James Redfield, Cedric Whitman and Nagler all end their studies of the *Iliad* with a version of Achilles as an "existential" hero who experiences the "true meaning of life." Such readings, however, are based on an ideology of language which views literature as embodiments of eternal verities still accessible to us today as such.[11]

To say that a text "has" a meaning is the hallmark of an essentialist theory of language. Meaning, as it will be defined below, must be meaning to someone in some place at some time in some context. This is not to say that essentialist readings such as Nagler's are useless, but that they are critically incomplete and must be supplemented by an inquiry which takes seriously a fuller range of factors of meaning production. Although clearly the "universal limitation of death"[12] has something to do with the *Iliad*, to foreground such matters cannot but reduce the poem to a repetition of our own most general anxieties. In the following section, I will outline Umberto Eco's theory of codes, which deals with the problem of signification within a communicational framework. Having dealt with the notion of the "essence" of meaning, it will be necessary to turn to the problem of the "reader." Then, in the final section of this introduction, it will be possible to outline an "intertextual" approach to meaning production.

## Eco's Theory of Codes

Semiotics is the unified study of all phenomena of signification and/or communication.[13] The need for such a discipline became explicit in the last century when the term "language" became extended to include a number of non-verbal communication systems (photography, film, painting, etc.) and to a number of "languages within language" (the language of myth, of dreams, of narrative codes, etc.). The idea that verbal language should serve as the model for the study of all types of signification systems led to a number of false expectations and far-fetched metaphors in these areas of research. It therefore seemed desirable to establish a more broadly based study of signifying systems without assuming that verbal language would be the privileged model. One of the most important and thorough responses to this imperative is Umberto Eco's *A Theory of Semiotics* (Bloomington, 1976). In his treatment of semiotic phenomena, Eco centralizes the notion of code. Communication occurs when a system of signification exists, and such a system relies on the functioning of a code for the production of an interpretive response in an addressee. Eco distinguishes four types of code (Eco, 36-37):

(a) "A set of *signals* ruled by internal combinatory laws." The signals can have many forms: gestures, graphic symbols, sounds, etc. They can be considered as a "pure combinational structure...an interplay of empty positions." It is a *syntactic* system.

(b) "A set of possible communicative contents" comprised of "*notions*" about something, able to be conveyed by a variety of signals and thus independent of any given system of signals. This is a *semantic* system.

(c) "A set of possible *behavioral responses* on the part of the destination." This is a *pragmatic* system, and most behaviorists define meaning in terms of such responses.

(d) "A rule coupling some items from the (a) system with some from the (b) or (c) system."

Only this last is properly a code, and Eco calls the other three system-codes, or s-codes for short. The function of a code, then, is to apportion the elements of a conveying system, an s-code of type (a), to the elements of a conveyed system, an s-code of type (b) or (c). The result of such an apportioning is a sign, or a sign-function as Eco calls it to emphasize its operational status (Eco, 49):

> Signs are the provisional result of coding rules which establish transitory correlations of elements, each of these elements being able to enter--under given coded circumstances--into another correlation and thus form a new sign.
> Take for instance the expression /plane/: the English language provides many content items for it, i.e. "carpentry tool" or "level" or "aircraft." In this sense we are faced with three sign-functions: plane=X, plane=Y, plane=K.

Such a conception of codes and their operation emphasizes the conventional nature of signification and communication. Not only are the coupling rules culturally defined, but the s-codes themselves are cultural constructs and eminently open to change. The s-codes are systems or structures

> that can also subsist independently of any sort of significant or communicative purpose, and as such may be studied by information theory or by various types of generative grammar. They are made up of finite sets of elements oppositionally structured and governed by combinational rules that can generate both finite and infinite strings or chains of these elements (38).

This structuredness allows s-codes to enter into correlation with one another and is a necessary condition for their semiotic functioning. This is so not only for syntactic systems, like algebraic or phonological systems, but also for semantic systems, which must be thought of as cultural constructs with the same ontological status as any other system-code.

The "content" of an expression must be distinguished from its possible referents (Eco, 58-68). The content of an expression such as the word /dog/ is not this or that particular dog, but a culturally defined class of objects which can be conveniently labeled a "cultural unit." A cultural unit is anything culturally defined and distinguished as an entity, but it is defined inasmuch as it is *placed* in a system of other cultural units which are opposed to it and circumscribe it. A cultural unit "exists" and is recognized insofar as there exists another one which is opposed to it. It is the relationship between the various terms of cultural units which subtracts from each of the terms what is conveyed by the others (Eco, 73).

If then the phenomenal world can be thought of as an undifferentiated continuum of raw data, it is culture which segments that continuum and assigns value to the discrete units by placing them in opposition to each other. The value of the various units can thus be thought of as differential. Taxonomic classification systems are the clearest examples of this process, since they define their objects in terms of specific and generic *differences*. But the same mechanism operates in any semantic system; any definition according to "essential" qualities is in reality a definition according to differences.

A sign is thus the result of a correlation of elements from two systems of differences. Human language, however, is much too complex to be thought of in terms of a series of binary correlations. Language is best viewed as a number of systems and subsystems, all intricately related by a vast complex of codes. The theory of codes makes it possible to rethink certain notions about language, such as the distinction between connotation and denotation. Although both denotation and connotation rely on codes, a connotative code can be said to rely on another code. Thus, for example, the word /dog/ is correlated by one code to the cultural unit *canis familiaris*. But that cultural unit, along with its expression unit, is further correlated with the cultural unit "fidelity." Such a "super-elevation of codes" can be extremely complex and can take place among units of any magnitude. Thus a pastoral setting can be correlated by a connotative code with "setting for love" or "blissful state." Such connotative codes can be conveniently called "subcodes" or "secondary codes" since they are perceived as being dependent on a prior code. But the distinction between codes and subcodes, denotation and connotation, is not an ontological one, since from a semiotic perspective it is impossible to make an appeal to the referent for such a distinction; that is, *canis familiaris* is not a more real content than "fidelity." Out of a complex of interdependent codes, however, a culture will inevitably specify one as more real, "natural" and transparent than others. Denotative codes are established by culture and recognized as such by a semiotics of the code. Any given expression will usually convey a number of intertwined contents and will thus not be a simple message, but a *text* whose content is a multi-leveled *discourse*.

The conception of the semantic plane as a system of differences allows us to define meaning without any reference to "objects" or Platonic entities. And although a system-code can be an object of study as such, it is of interest to semiotics only in terms of its dialectical relationship with another system-code and a set of coding rules which constitutes them into semantic plane and expression plane (Eco, 40-46). Thus, a cultural unit can be thought of as the focal point of a system of signs. Various coding correlations can put a cultural unit into relationship with any number of semantic axes. So, for example, the oppositions dark vs. bright, bad vs. good, stupid vs. smart, are interconnected by such expressions as "bright student," "dark purposes," etc. A cultural unit can be analyzed into more elementary components based on the various readings it has in different contexts. These elementary components are called semantic markers, or semic components or semes.[14] Whatever their nomenclature, they must be thought of as differential--that is, they are values issuing from systematic oppositions. A cultural unit is a *nodal point* arising from a series of criss-crossings of numerous oppositional axes.

A cultural unit conceived of as the inventory of a set of semantic markers is called a "sememe." The format of a sememe would be, Eco notes, that of an encyclopaedia, specifying all the coding information necessary to establish the correct "reading" in a given circumstance. Since every semantic marker, moreover, is itself a sememe to be explained by its own componential analysis, a complete semantic structure of any but the most simple units would be virtually infinite and hence must remain a "regulative hypothesis" (Eco, 128-29):

> There must be a methodological principle of semantic research whereby, in almost all cases, the description of fields and semantic branches can only be achieved *when studying the conditions of signification of a given message*.... A semiotics of the code can be established--if only partially--when the existence of a message *postulates* it as an explanatory condition.

This practical limitation will be frustrating to the linguist trying to generalize about semantic facts--particularly if he seeks to identify a limited number of semantic universals, as Chomsky proposed.[15] But for the literary critic, the transitory, unstable nature of the semantic system, the fact that it can be manipulated and changed by new messages which propose unforeseen coding correlations, all this is of utmost interest.

The workings of the process of accommodating new messages Eco explains in part by developing Peirce's notion of the interpretant. Peirce defined the term as the idea to which a sign gives rise in an addressee.[16] Thus it is some sort of equivalence by which an addressee interprets a sign. An interpretant can be a definition, an emotive response, a synonym or a translation into another semiotic system. Eco defines it simply as *"another representation which is referred to the same 'object.'* In other words, in order to establish what the interpretant of a sign is, it is necessary to name it by means of another interpretant to be named by another sign and so on" (Eco, 68). The notion of the interpretant shows again the inherent circularity of the communicative process, which "by means of continual shiftings which refer a sign back to another sign or string of signs circumscribes cultural units in an asymptotic fashion, without ever allowing one to touch them directly, but making them accessible through other units" (Eco, 71). Given a particular message, an addressee will approach it by proposing various interpretants. It is by this process of circumscribing a new message with a *sequence of interpretants* that an addressee constitutes a meaning for that message.

The theory of codes outlined here is but a small part of Eco's semiotic theory. This and other parts of Eco's work will be expanded later in suitable contexts. For the time it will be sufficient to review the basic points and terminology introduced so far. A *code* is a set of rules correlating elements of a conveying system with elements of a conveyed system. Considered separately, the conveying system and conveyed system are structures of relationships among a series of elements. These structures Eco calls *s-codes*, and their elements have value in terms of their opposition to other elements in the same system. A correlation of elements from two s-codes is a *sign* or *sign-function.* The elements of a semantic system are called *cultural units* and, as in any s-code, their value is defined differentially. A cultural unit viewed in terms of its manifold coding correlations is called a *sememe.* A sememe is thus a cultural unit considered as the locus of a system of signs. A sememe can be analyzed into more elementary components (*semes* or *semantic markers*) which are themselves loci of other systems of signs. The *interpretant* can be defined broadly as that which an addressee brings to a message in order to interpret it. So defined the interpretant may seem to be a rather uninteresting tautology, but it will be more useful in the context of specific messages. Eco's theory of codes is basically quite simple, yet it is capable of unlimited complication in its own terms whenever a system of signification or a communicative act requires such a complication. The theory of codes lays the groundwork for a theory of meaning production as the production of signs (interpretants); and the second half of Eco's book examines various *modes of producing signs*, understanding such modes to encompass both the composition and the interpretation of texts.

### Reading and the Reader

Eco's theory implies that a message does not have an intrinsic meaning, but can give rise to any number of meanings. For this reason, a formal analysis of a text must be supplemented by a consideration of the text in a communicational framework in order to take account of the function of the "addressee." This notion, now a commonplace in literary criticism, has led to an ever growing literature on "the role of the reader" as the one who activates the play between text and interpretant.[17] Studies with such a focus have as their common denominator the intent of deflecting attention away from the literary work as "object" with intrinsic meaning toward the relationship between text and reader. Studies of the act of reading, however, deserve scrutiny to assure that an essentialism which valorizes the text or author as locus of meaning has not been replaced by one which valorizes the "Reader" as locus of meaning.

Norman Holland, for example, notes that individuals bring certain obsessions to their reading activity.[18] He then examines a number of responses to particular works and shows how each reader recreates the work according to his or her own psychological makeup. The object of literary criticism, however, is not to be found in the psychological properties of particular readers, but in the properties of reading as a cultural activity. To use literary artifacts as a sort of Rorschach test has legitimate implications for the psychology of individuals, but criticism is interested in the public reference of the act of reading, not the individual or pathological.

Stanley Fish is also interested in the response a literary work evokes in its readers.[19] Since meaning for Fish is an "event," a process involving text and reader, he insists that the proper focus for the critic's attention is the "developing response of the reader in relation to the words as they succeed one another in time." Thus, in his essays on seventeenth century texts, Fish poses the question "what does this text do?" and explains the affective consequences of the linear unfolding of the sentences. Unlike Holland, Fish is not interested in the particulars of idiosyncratic readings, but in the response a text would ideally evoke from an ideal reader--a reader capable of responding to a text in the way structured by the author's conscious or unconscious intent. How do we assess an ideal reader's response? Fish proposes to "become" this ideal reader, or "informed reader," as much as possible by finding out everything he can about a work's context. He explains it in this way (407):

> The reader, of whose responses I speak, then, is this informed reader, neither an abstraction, nor an actual living reader, but a hybrid--a real reader (me) who does everything within his power to make himself informed. That is, I can with some justification project my responses into those of "the" reader because they have been modified by the constraints placed on me by the assumptions and operations of the method: (1) the conscious attempt to become the informed reader by making myself the repository of the (potential) responses a given text might call out and (2) the attendant suppressing, insofar as that is possible, of what is personal and 1970ish in my response.

Holland would no doubt object that Fish cannot "suppress what is idiosyncratic and 1970ish" in his response; indeed, it is difficult to imagine how one would go about becoming *the* seventeenth century (if there is such a thing) and then reporting one's responses. In fact, Fish's method is more of a means for explaining an interpretation *ex post facto* than an approach to texts. Since the "potential responses a given text might call out" are virtually infinite, Fish's theory is really a "subjective" version of the traditional "objectivity" of the literary critic. It is, in short, a theory of well-informed impressionism; and although the interpretations of outstanding readers will always be valuable heuristically, a theory such as Fish's has not gotten us far beyond the problem posed by more strictly formalist approaches.[20]

The problem raised by Fish and Holland is the possible scope of a theory of reading. Out of the totality of any given reader's response, what part can be subjected to an analysis which would bring out the cultural functioning of literary artifacts? The limiting case for generalizing out of the scope of literary criticism all that is "idiosyncratic" is the notion of a *literary competence* analogous to linguistic competence. The notion is linked to the idea of an "ideal reader" somewhat more disembodied than Fish's informed reader. Jonathan Culler, for example, refers to Frye's call for a "coherent and comprehensive theory of literature, logically and scientifically organized, some of which the student learns as he goes on, but the main principles of which are as yet unknown to us."[21] Culler then proposes the linguistic analogy:

> It is easy to see why, from this perspective, linguistics offers an attractive methodological analogy: a grammar, as Chomsky says, "can be regarded as a theory of language," and the theory of literature of which Frye speaks can be regarded as the "grammar" or literary competence which readers have assimilated but of which they may not be consciously aware. To make the implicit explicit is the task of both linguistics and poetics; and generative grammar has placed renewed emphasis on two fundamental requirements for theories of this kind: that they state their rules as formal operations (since what they are investigating is a kind of intelligence they cannot take for granted intelligence used in applying rules but must make them as explicit as possible) and that they be testable (they must reproduce, as it were, attested facts about semiotic competence).

Culler explicitly connects the notion of literary competence with linguistic competence as developed by transformational grammarians, and this analogy requires some scrutiny.

Chomsky's opposition of competence and performance, the latter being "almost useless as it stands for linguistic analysis of any but the most superficial kind,"[22] the former being the implicit generative rules underlying all human language which are the proper object for a science of linguistics, purifies his linguistic theory of all the messy exigencies of actual language. It is for this reason that George Steiner characterizes transformational grammar as a "meta-mathematical ideal of considerable intellectual elegance, but not a true picture of human language at all."[23] An analogous opposition of competence and performance with regard to literature seems even more problematic, for there is even less evidence that there are implicit generative rules underlying "human literature" as a whole which could be described as a general literary competence. As it turns out, the only formal reading operation that Culler discusses is "naturalization," "the intent at totality of the interpretive process" (*Structuralist Poetics*, 127), a principle, however, not peculiar to reading, but to cognition in general. Again, hypothesizing generative rules has great heuristic value; indeed, such hypothesizing is a necessary preliminary step in any analysis of literary texts. But the objectification of such rules into a "deep structure" of interpretive rules leads to an essentialist poetics like that of Nagler.

A theory of reading which would avoid the Scylla of essentialist notions like literary competence and the Charybdis of impressionism (whether idiosyncratic, well-informed or from "interpretive communities") is suggested by Eco's theory of codes. Meaning, as defined by the theory of codes, is differential. The reader does indeed constitute the meaning of a text, but s/he does so in part by bringing together a newly encountered text with other texts or fragments of texts which s/he has read before. In the terms introduced above, these texts act as interpretants. Since all literary texts belong to a tradition in one way or another, a study of the "intertextual" relationships of a work will bring to the fore aspects of its functioning as a cultural artifact. The question will not be how particular readers or ideal readers did or do respond to a text, but how a text, by being put into relationship with other texts, produces meaning in this "intertext." Generally, texts will privilege in various ways the texts to which they can be most fruitfully related (traditional notions of genre, theme, period, etc., recount these privileged connections) and the epics to be considered in the present study give ample testimony to this fact.

An intertextual approach will not entirely avoid the pitfalls of impressionism, on the one hand, and on the other, the objectification of generative rules. Nevertheless, by focusing on textually established interpretants, it is possible to relegate hypothetical "rules" and individual responses to their proper role as heuristic devices. This delimitation is stated in Eco's definition of the reader as a "*textually established* set of felicity conditions to be met in order to have a macro-speech act (such as a text is) fully actualized."[24] Such a notion is intimately bound up with historical specificity, with placing a literary work in an historical context. A reading produced by an intertextual focus will not necessarily be one ever ascribed to a work by its historical audience; it is not necessarily one "intended" by its author; such a reading certainly will not be the meaning which is "in" the text. It will rather be a meaning which *can* be produced by inserting a text into a certain system. Given the level of generality of Eco's semiotic theory, it will be useful, before going on to the *Iliad*, to consider the intertextual reading model of Michael Riffaterre, which, although not without problems, does provide a more specific set of terminology and indicates ways in which Eco's semiotic can be applied to literary works.

## Intertextuality

In his studies of intertextual relationships in literary texts, Michael Riffaterre identifies *indirection* as the fundamental characteristic of poetry; that is, a poem says one thing and means another.[25] He therefore distinguishes the *meaning* of a poem from its *significance*. The meaning is the "mimetic" content of a text, its attempt to *represent* some sort of reality. The significance is the content of a text which is articulated indirectly. The act of reading a poem involves, according to Riffaterre, a transformation from meaning to significance, a process carried out by the reader retroactively: one initially reads a poem for its "meaning," its reference. Such a reading will always be unsatisfactory in a poem, leading the reader to make another attempt to comprehend the poem on a different level of organization. The path which will lead to the *significance* of the poem is made manifest by some sort of "ungrammaticality," some element or feature which does not seem to fit into the mimetic level of the poem's structure. The shift from meaning to significance is made possible by the reader's intervention, but Riffaterre asserts that such a shift is implied by the organization of the poem, its indirection.

A poem is comprised, according to Riffaterre, of a set of lexical transformations of a "semantic given," which he calls the *matrix*. The matrix is expressed in the poem by a series of variants determined by a *model*, which is the first or primary actualization of the matrix in the poem. The organization of a poem at the level of significance is thus a set of lexical sequences circumscribing a semantic nucleus. Now it should be clear from our discussion of cultural units that a semantic element can be displayed in the scope of verbal language only through a series of representations, which we have called the sequence of interpretants. The set of lexical transformations of a semantic given, then, is in Eco's terms the *sequence of verbal interpretants* of a cultural unit. Riffaterre calls such a lexical sequence, whether it is part of a poem or not, a *hypogram*.[26] Hypograms are themselves systems of signs related to a "semantic given" (i.e., a content). In semiotic terms, the semantic given is the focal point of a series of coded relations which make up the sememe of a cultural unit. Sememe, sequence of interpretants, lexical transformations of a semantic given, are all terms for the same theoretical concept (its interpretants).

A hypogram can be either "potential, therefore observable in language, or actual, therefore observable in another text" (*Semiotics of Poetry*, 23). That is, a hypogram outside of poetic discourse is simply the sequence of verbal interpretants of a cultural unit. A hypogram is poeticized, according to Riffaterre, when its semantic nucleus becomes the matrix of a poem. Since the semantic nucleus has no status outside of its hypogrammatic representation, one can say that poetic discourse sets up an equivalence between two sets of verbal sequences (of whatever scope): one is the poem itself, the other is the hypogram as it exists in language or in other texts. It is in this sense that Riffaterre's approach is intertextual:  there is a relationship between a poem and another verbal sequence, which can be summarized as a word, which can be a cliché or a whole text. If a reader does not recognize the "other" verbal sequence around which a text is built, s/he will no doubt constitute some meaning or other in reading the text; but it is basic to Riffaterre's method that there is *one* verbal sequence which will give the fullest account of a poem's production.

An example will perhaps illustrate the matter better.  Consider the following poem by Emily Dickinson:[27]

1. Ended ere it begun--
2. The title was scarcely told
3. When the preface perished from consciousness
4. The story, unrevealed

5. Had it been mine, to print!
6. Had it been yours, to read!`
7. That it was not our privilege
8. The interdict of God

There are two hypograms poeticized here: "book" and "lovestory." The word "book" is not used in the poem but suggested by *semic actualization*.[28] Semantic markers (semes) of the word "book" are present in each line. The most obvious ones are "title," "preface," "story," "to print" and "to read" (lines 2-6), so that the "it" of these lines must be a book. But a book also has a beginning and an end (line 1) and often has an *imprimatur*, which is its privilege (line 7) to be printed and read. This privilege can be abrogated by an interdict (line 8). The poem then is an articulation of semes of the word "book," and in each line the seme is negated (scarcely told title, perished preface, unrevealed story, etc.). The second hypogram is "lovestory." The collocation of "mine," "yours," "ours" (lines 5-7) suggests a sort of mutuality between people. The text is formally a lyric poem, a traditional genre for love themes, suggesting that this mutuality is one of love. Specifically, it is a love represented as a lovestory--a story of love which is, moreover, unauthorized, forbidden. The matrix of the poem, its "semantic given," can be represented by some such statement as "our love is forbidden." The model of the poem, the determinant of the derivation of the matrix, is something like "the book which is unauthorized." Forbidden love is presented as an unauthorized book.

This example shows clearly Riffaterre's distinction between matrix, model and hypogram. It also pinpoints what it is that is "outside" of the text which must be brought to bear on the poem to establish its significance. The two hypograms, book and lovestory, are sign systems which are prior to the poem, or more accurately, their prior existence is implied by the poem. They are coded systems. The fact that the sememe of the word "book" includes such semes as preface, story, title, etc., implies a complex of coded relationships which is already actual or potential in language. Lovestory is also a notion which implies a complex of coded relationships involving lovers, trysts, etc., among which is "love is often thematized in lyric verse." The handling of these hypograms in the poem (i.e., their negation) allows us to formulate the model and the matrix, which are also conventional.

Riffaterre's method involves the reader as the participant who must actualize the *process* of signification. The analysis makes explicit certain operations which are possible in terms of the available codes. It is conceivable that in the future, the eight line stanza will come to be used only for challenges to do battle. In that case, a reader unaware of the historical determinants of Dickinson's poem might assume that it was the musings of a frustrated general unable to do battle with a hated enemy because of politics. No doubt the poem is capable of eliciting a number of responses from a number of readers. Riffaterre's method focuses on the cultural codes which can be reconstructed on the basis of texts.

The remarkable thing about Riffaterre's approach is that poems are mere proliferations of signifiers, periphrases of rather common verbal sequences. Although the process takes place in terms of codes, the poeticizing of verbal sequences--in stark contrast to Nagler's hierarchical theory--is entirely *lateral*. A hypogram is not an ideal configuration existing on a higher ontological plane than any of its "realizations"; it is itself a system of signs whose poetic transformation results in the generation of variants of itself. As an extreme example of this, Riffaterre offers the following poem by Athanasius Kircher (*Semiotics of Poetry*, 20):

Tibi vero gratias agam quo clamore? Amore, more, ore, re.

The matrix here is "thanksgiving," the model "crying out" (*clamore*), both standard Christian themes.[29] The peculiar thing about this poem is that the various ways of crying out (love, habit, word, deed) are, by a happy coincidence in Latin, all physical (phonological and graphic) as well as grammatical proliferations of the model. Although such a text cannot be taken as typical of poetic discourse, it does show the generative power of the signifier, a power completely ignored in the more abstract approach of Nagler. One need only recall that Nagler uses Latin words (*procedo, non sola*, etc.) to "avoid confusion of the thing itself with any of its allomorphs" (*Spontaneity*, 68). For Riffaterre, there are only "allomorphs," a series of variants derived not from some underlying "thing itself," but from each other.

The difference between the approaches of Nagler and Riffaterre is a function of their assumptions about the status of meaning and its relationship to culture. For Nagler, to repeat, meaning is inherent and prior to culture. For Riffaterre, meaning is above all a product of cultural dynamics: the process of "defining" in its literal sense of "setting down boundaries," segmenting the continuum of experience into discrete units which have value by their insertion into a system of oppositions. To name something is to establish that it is significant to someone in some way. To a group of people for whom communication is necessary or desirable, the set of significant units defined by their common needs and interests will become articulated into the semantic plane of a signifying system by means of some set of signals organized into a syntactic system. This is the basic model of a *culture*. The expanding, changing character of signifying systems is the concomitant of an expanding, changing culture ("concomitant" because the relationship is *dialectical*).

The workings of this process is the subject of semiotics. Riffaterre's literary analyses pose the question, what coding correlations are implied as an explanatory condition for this poem? The answer to this question lies in the concrete communicative acts which establish the configuration of the semantic plane and the coding correlations which constitute it into a signifying system. The question Riffaterre asks could be posed for any message, and it is in fact the question which users of a signifying system pose in order to interpret any message. For this reason, Riffaterre's claim that "indirection" is the proprium of poetry seems rather curious. All messages require an addressee to produce a sequence of interpretants which are variants of the message and circumscribe the content unit of the message. Riffaterre's insistence on this point is, in fact, indicative of a residual essentialism in his theory. Just as Eco replaces Peirce's typology of *signs* with a typology of *modes of sign production* (Eco, 216-17), we should give up the opposition between poems and non-poems (except as an approximation), and speak of the *poetic functioning* of a message. Hence Eco notes that a message "assumes a poetic function when it is ambiguous and self-focussing" (262); and we should add that any message can assume such a function given an appropriate context. A complex message will always be produced and interpreted by a variety of modes of sign-production. The "aesthetic" function traditionally associated with poetry and to which Riffaterre gives the name "indirection" will be rethought below in terms of Eco's notion of *ratio difficilis* (Eco, 183-89; 217-60).

The problematic nature of Riffaterre's definition of indirection is somewhat masked by the scope of his study: all his examples are from modern poems of brief compass with little or no interest at the "mimetic" level. They are thus somewhat prejudicial to the clear-cut distinction between meaning (mimesis) and significance, to the notion of "ungrammaticalities" as the motivating force for the shift from meaning to significance, and to the necessity of a second retroactive reading (which must strike the Homeric scholar as decidedly problematic). These notions reflect Riffaterre's interest in describing the literary phenomenon as a "dialectic between text and reader" and in formulating rules "governing this dialectic" (*Semiotics of Poetry*, 1). Thus, it is not surprising that Riffaterre introduces the term *literary competence*, the reader's "familiarity with descriptive systems,[30] with themes, with his society's mythologies, and above all with other texts" (*Semiotics of Poetry*, 5). Riffaterre means by literary competence the encyclopedic knowledge which enables one to produce appropriate interpretants, a much more culture-specific notion than that of Culler. Nevertheless, his use of the term and his tendency to describe how *the* reader recognizes "ungrammaticalities" and becomes frustrated by a mimetic reading, etc., show that Riffaterre has not entirely left behind certain essentialist assumptions. *The Reader*, as "he" emerges as a textual function in a communicational model is still a formalist fiction, and reader-response criticism has taught us that real readers always exceed in various ways the position a text provides for them. Readers are "addressees," but they are also more than that; and messages are not only utilizations of a communicational channel in order to convey information or feelings, but also can be exercises of and submissions to power.[31]

In the semiotic approach to be developed below, both author and audience enter the analysis as *textually established* entities. That is, they are part of the complex of coded relationships postulated by a message as an explanatory condition for its interpretation. A historical person adopts a certain textual strategy in order to communicate something. At the same time, the adoption of a textual strategy is modulated by consideration of the potential audience (beginning with the choice of a language, genre, style, etc.). The textual strategy of the *Iliad* and the interpretive apparatus implied as an explanatory condition for it are available to us as examples of various discursive processes,[32] and as such are able to be subjected to a semiotic analysis. At the same time, a historical person adopts a certain textual strategy in order to *do* something; that is, as a kind of *social practice*. Just as a formalist analysis must give way to a consideration of communicational factors, so too, Riffaterre's intertextual approach must be supplemented by a more "material" cultural analysis. These are not, however, options from which one can choose beforehand, but different moments on an methodological continuum.[33]

It will be useful at this point to draw attention to two complementary forms of investigation: *poetics*, which studies textual processes, the way texts are built up; and *reading*, which studies the pragmatic implications of these processes in textual realizations. The emphasis in this study will be on the former, but that will inevitably lead to the latter within the constraints outlined above. The inextricable link between poetics and reading lies in the fact that they are both forms of sign production. One of the unfortunate consequences of Parry's theory of the formula, as well as the type scene studies based on it, is that they tend to separate these two concerns, resulting in a rather static view of Homer's poetics.[34] Scholars who take exception to this tendency, such as Nagler, have described a more flexible poetics, but one based on a rather static notion of meaning production.[35]

Riffaterre's intertextual approach posits that texts are produced from other texts and that meaning is produced not by substance (e.g., *sphota*) but by *difference*. What will be useful for us in the method of Riffaterre will be the various types of poetic mechanisms that he discusses. The notion of hypogrammatic derivation, for example, a concept derived from and especially appropriate to short poems, will provide a starting point for the study of

Homer's similes, themselves formally discrete from their narrative context. The continuity of the similes with the rest of the narrative, however, will necessitate an extension of Riffaterre's terms and the evolution of broader concepts of textual poetics. At the same time, Eco's semiotic theory will provide a conceptual basis for extending a purely communicational analysis to an analysis of signifying practices as *social practices*, specifically as examples of *ideological production*. The investigation of the similes in Homer and his imitators will try to see how they function in the "linguistic economies" which articulate and are articulated by these texts in their various historical contexts.

# HOMER

## The Simile as Textual Stratagem

In Book Sixteen of the *Iliad*, as the Myrmidons are preparing themselves for battle, they are compared to wolves in a most befuddling simile (Π 155-65):

Μυρμιδόνας δ' ἄρ' ἐποιχόμενος θώρηξεν Ἀχιλλεὺς,
πάντας ἀνὰ κλισίας σὺν τεύχεσιν· οἱ δὲ λύκοι ὣς
ὠμοφάγοι, τοῖσίν τε περὶ φρεσὶν ἄσπετος ἀλκή,
οἵ τ' ἔλαφον κεραὸν μέγαν οὔρεσι δῃώσαντες
δάπτουσιν· πᾶσιν δὲ παρήϊον αἵματι φοινόν·
καί τ' ἀγεληδὸν ἴασιν ἀπὸ κρήνης μελανύδρου
λάψοντες γλώσσῃσιν ἀραιῇσιν μέλαν ὕδωρ
ἄκρον, ἐρευγόμενοι φόνον αἵματος· ἐν δέ τε θυμὸς
στήθεσιν ἄτρομός ἐστι, περιστένεται δέ τε γαστήρ.
τοῖοι Μυρμιδόνων ἡγήτορες ἠδὲ μέδοντες
ἀμφ' ἀγαθὸν θεράποντα ποδώκεος Αἰακίδαο.

But Achilles went meanwhile to the Myrmidons, and arrayed them
all in their war gear along the shelters. And they, as wolves
who eat flesh raw, in whose hearts the battle fury is endless,
who, having brought down a great horned stag in the mountains,
devour him, till all their jowls run blood;
and then go all in a pack to drink from a spring of dark water,
lapping with their lean tongues along the top of the dark water,
belching up the clotted blood; in the heart of each one
is a spirit untremulous, but their bellies are full and groaning;
just so the lords of the Myrmidons and their men of council [swarmed]
around the brave henchmen of swift-footed Aiakides.

From the standpoint of "mimesis" (in Riffaterre's sense), the simile is particularly confusing, and Leaf's analysis is typical of scholarly commentary on the passage:

> The following elaborate simile is unique as presenting two distinct scenes, first the rending of the body, and then the rush to the spring. The second part, 160-63, contains several strange expressions, and is quite unsuited to its place; for although the eager Myrmidons may be compared to wolves tearing a deer (although even this is premature while they are only arming), there is less than no point in comparing them to *glutted* wolves going off for a drink.
>
> The epic poet often expands a simile with touches that do not bear directly on the main point of the comparison, but not with a further development directly contradicting it. The natural history of 163 is wrong, for a glutted wolf is a thorough coward.... In spite, therefore, of the vigorous character of the four lines, we must condemn them with Hentze. They may be interpolated from some poem where they were more appropriately applied to an army returning from battle.[1]

Leaf notes that the simile of the wolves does not cohere mimetically in two ways: first, it does not cohere in terms of the referent (the natural history is wrong); and secondly, the actions of the wolves are not similar to the actions of the Myrmidons (are not a good "imitation" of those actions). Attempts to reconcile these apparent "ungrammaticalities" try to salvage some notion of similarity between the two situations. Wilamowitz, for example, suggests that the simile shows the Myrmidons are *kampflustig* after being overfed on inactivity, which is virtually a *lucus a non lucendo*.[2] Fraenkel suggests that the point of the simile is how the Myrmidons hasten around Patroklos (Wie die Wölfe zur Quelle, so trotte die Myrmidonenhaufe zu Patroklos hin), and that the first part of the simile emphasizes how quickly they respond (an Waschen denkt keiner).[3] This explanation also seems to stretch the comparison by denying the whole thrust of the picture: a herd of wolves devouring a deer, drinking and then lolling around bloated and belching. The simile is, in fact, quite "ungrammatical" as a representation of the mustering of the Myrmidons. There is no particular identity in terms of *Stimmungsbild*, nor any "immediate visual relevance" or "existential identity"; there is not even a clear *tertium comparationis*.[4]

Such a simile presents the reader of Homer with a direct challenge, and the methodology of Riffaterre offers itself as a remedy to the problem posed by this "dissimilar simile." As a clearly defined swathe of text, the wolf simile can be studied in its own terms as an example of hypogrammatic derivation. The single dominating element in the simile is the notion of eating a meal, from ὠμοφάγοι to γαστήρ. Since feasting is a nuclear event of some prominence in Homer, it is possible to compare the wolf simile with other eating *loci* and determine the precise character of the hypogram which gives unity to the simile, and to the nature of the transformation that hypogram has undergone. We will thus have to bracket our common sense notion of "similarity," and work our way toward a more semiotic conception of the narrative function of this simile.

Many meals are described in the Homeric poems and Walter Arend has collected all the examples and considered their relationships to one another.[5] Like many of the typical scenes Arend discusses, the descriptions of meals contain a host of repeated formulas and elements, such as αὐτὰρ ἐπεὶ πόσιος καὶ ἐδητύος ἐξ ἔρον ἕντο, which marks the end of nearly every detailed meal. The meals of the heroes, therefore, along with a number of other related activities (libations, entertainment, etc.) comprise what Riffaterre calls a "descriptive system"--a network of verbal sequences associated with one another around a kernel word in accordance with that word's sememe, but "already actualized in set form within the reader's mind" (*Semiotics of Poetry*, p. 39); or, less mentalistically, already actualized in set form in some locatable texts. A descriptive system is not an abstract template which is instantiated in a series of "multiforms," but is the set of words themselves. This is important because the wolf simile is not generated by the general idea of a feast, but by the words themselves used to describe meals elsewhere. That is, the relationship is *intertextual*.

The operation which gives internal coherence to the wolf simile is its consistent *conversion*[6] of the positive aspects of human feasts into negative aspects. The word ὠμοφάγοι names this conversion most clearly: men roast their meat, not only the meat which they eat, but also the meat they prepare as offerings before the meal. The word ὠμοφάγοι establishes the opposition human vs. savage, and the rest of the simile describes the wolves in a way that calls attention to that opposition by standing the descriptive system of heroic feasts on its head. Here is the scene from B 421-33, which contains numerous repetitions from A 458ff., H 314ff., and many others:

αὐτὰρ ἐπεί ῥ' εὔξαντο καὶ οὐλοχύτας προβάλοντο,
αὐέρυσαν μὲν πρῶτα καὶ ἔσφαξαν καὶ ἔδειραν,
μηρούς τ' ἐξέταμον κατά τε κνίσῃ ἐκάλυψαν
δίπτυχα ποιήσαντες, ἐπ' αὐτῶν δ' ὠμοθέτησαν.
καὶ τὰ μὲν ἄρ σχίζῃσιν ἀφύλλοισιν κατέκαιον,
σπλάγχνα δ' ἄρ' ἀμπείραντες ὑπείρεχον Ἡφαίστοιο.
αὐτὰρ ἐπεὶ κατὰ μῆρ' ἐκάη καὶ σπλάγχνα πάσαντο,
μίστυλλόν τ' ἄρα τἆλλα καὶ ἀμφ' ὀβελοῖσιν ἔπειραν,
ὤπτησάν τε περιφραδέως, ἐρύσαντό τε πάντα.
αὐτὰρ ἐπεὶ παύσαντο πόνου τετύκοντό τε δαῖτα,
δαίνυντ', οὐδέ τι θυμὸς ἐδεύετο δαιτὸς ἐΐσης.
αὐτὰρ ἐπεὶ πόσιος καὶ ἐδητύος ἐξ ἔρον ἔντο,
τοῖς ἄρα μύθων ἦρχε Γερήνιος ἱππότα Νέστωρ.

Now when all had prayed and flung down the scattered barley,
first they drew back the victim's head, cut his throat and skinned him,
and cut away the meat from the thighs and wrapped them in fat,
making a double fold, and laid shreds of flesh above them.
Placing these on sticks cleft and peeled, they burned them,
and spitted the vitals and held them over the flame of Hephaistos.
But when they had burned the thigh pieces and tasted the vitals,
they cut all the remainder into pieces and spitted them
and roasted them carefully and took off the pieces.
Then after they had finished the work and got ready the feast
they ate, nor was any man's hunger denied a fair portion.
But when they had put away their desire for eating and drinking,
the Gerenian horseman Nestor began speaking among them.

To begin with, it is noteworthy that ὠμοφάγοι and ὤπτησαν are equivalent metrically and in word position. Indeed, Π 157 can be compared in detail with Β 429. The adjective ἄσπετος, "boundless," "without limits," inverts the meaning of περιφραδέως, "circumspectly," "in a measured way," a word that occurs in Homer only with ὤπτησάν τε in the meal formula. There is even a slight verbal echo between περὶ φρέσιν and περιφραδέως. The word ἀλκή is generally confined to military contexts, but is also found in eating contexts as that which one eats in order to attain (I 705-6; cf. T 160-61):

νῦν μὲν κοιμήσασθε τεταρπόμενοι φίλον ἦτορ
σίτου καὶ οἴνοιο· τὸ γὰρ μένος ἐστὶ καὶ ἀλκή.

Go to sleep now that the inward heart is made happy with food and drink, for these are the strength and *courage* within us.

The word ἀλκή is thus doubly pertinent in the simile. The narrative context describes the arming of the Myrmidons (cf. the phrase δύμεναι ἀλκήν, "to put on one's valor," as in I 231); but part of the preparation for battle is eating, whence one derives ἀλκή. The wolves reverse this sequence, having ἀλκή to begin with and, as we shall see, losing it after the meal.

The next line of the simile, οἵ τ' ἔλαφον κεραὸν μέγαν οὔρεσι δηώσαντες, can be summarized as the "preparation" of the wolves' meal. The singularly simple mode of preparation, δηώσαντες, "cut down," is generated in part by the numerous verbs used to describe the elaborate ritual of killing and cutting up the meat by the heroes: ἔσφαξαν, ἔδειραν, ἐξέταμον, μίστυλλον. Usually the sacrificial beast is a bull, but it is always a domestic animal; the wolves attack a wild beast. The mention of οὔρεσι seems to correspond to the occasional mention of the place of the sacrifice made by the heroes, such as the ἐΰδμητον βωμόν ("well-polished altar") of A 448; for mountains are often mentioned as the place where all sorts of natural disasters take place: forest fires rage there; swollen rivers crash down from the mountains; particularly ferocious animals are often ὀρεσίτροφος, "bred in the mountains." Mountains are thus emblematic of the untamed and undomesticated aspects of the world, as opposed to an altar or even the hearth of Eumaios where he slaughters a pig for Odysseus (ξ 420).

The end of the preparation of a meal is usually capped off with the Abschlussvers αὐτὰρ ἐπεὶ παύσαντο πόνου τετύκοντό τε δαῖτα (B 430 = A 467 = H 319, etc.): "After they had finished the work and got ready the meal." This line is always followed by δαίνυντ', οὐδέ τι θυμὸς ἐδεύετο δαιτὸς ἐΐσης, "they ate, nor was anyone lacking a fair portion." These two lines are inverted in a striking way by Π 158-59:

οἵ τ' ἔλαφον κεραὸν μέγαν οὔρεσι δηώσαντες
δάπτουσιν· πᾶσιν δὲ παρήϊον αἵματι φοινόν.

who, having cut down a great horned stag in the mountains,
devour him, till all their jowls run blood.

The substitution of the verb δάπτουσι (devour) for δαίνυντ' is, like ὠμοφάγοι, especially indicative of the opposition human vs. savage; for δάπτω is, like the German *fressen*, used only for beasts; whereas δαίνυμι is a euphemism for eating, its literal meaning being "divide" or "distribute." The word for meal at the end of B 430, δαῖτα, is a related word: literally, "a thing divided up," "a portion." Another related word is δαίω, "to divide," used also in meal contexts (ο 140: κρέα δαίετο). But δαίω has a homophone meaning "to burn," and then "to destroy" from which the verb δηιόω is derived, of which we have the participial form δηώσαντες at the end of Π 159. By its position and meaning this participle is most closely compared to the ending of the *Abschlussvers*, τετύκοντό τε δαῖτα (literally, "when they had got ready the thing divided up"), which has thus generated a verb which not only negates the notion of careful division, but calls attention to the switching of semantic fields (eating and destroying). The verb δηιόω has numerous uses in battle contexts: it frequently occurs meaning to wound by cutting (e.g., Θ 534, Ε 452), used often with an instrumental like χαλκῷ. Like ἀλκή, δηώσαντες is especially pertinent because of its dual connection to both military "cutting" and the "division" of heroic meals.

The end of Β 431, οὐδέ τι θυμὸς ἐδεύετο δαιτὸς ἐίσης, restates the notion of equal division. This phrase generates the end of Π 159: πᾶσιν δὲ παρήϊον αἵματι φοινόν, "and the cheeks of all were red with blood." Note that the litotes οὐδέ...ἐδεύετο is resolved to πᾶσιν in the simile. Alongside the lexical conversions (ὤπτησαν / ὠμοφάγοι, περιφραδέως / ἄσπετος), therefore, we can speak of formal conversions: a litotes in heroic meals generates a hyperbole in the simile. Such an operation is quite appropriate thematically, since the basis of the opposition is the *ritual* behavior of the heroes versus the unrestrained behavior of the wolves. The word φοινόν is another example of military language used to describe the wolves' eating: φοινός means "blood-red," connected to φόνον, "slaughter." In a particularly relevant passage, Achilles uses the word φόνος when he explicitly contrasts the spheres of eating and fighting (Τ 213-4):

> τό μοι οὔ τι μετὰ φρεσὶ ταῦτα μέμηλεν,
> ἀλλὰ φόνος τε καὶ αἷμα καὶ ἀργαλέος στόνος ἀνδρῶν.

> Food and drink are not a care to my heart,
> but slaughter, blood and the hard groaning of men.

Characteristic of the wolves in the simile is the confounding of the conventional separation of the spheres of eating and fighting.

The next phase of the simile is the movement of the herd to the spring for a drink.[7] Drinking is not always specifically mentioned in Homeric meals, except for the libation which sometimes follows. We have the repeated lines (Α 470-71):

κοῦροι μὲν κρητῆρας ἐπεστέψαντο ποτοῖο
νώμησαν δ' ἄρα πᾶσιν ἐπαρξάμενοι δεπαέσσιν.

The young men filled the mixing bowls with pure wine, passing
a portion to all, having poured out a libation from the goblets.

Here the ritual word ἐπαρξάμενοι indicates the most important part of the
drinking: the libation. Obviously there can be no question of the wolves
pouring a libation, but the simile adds details which seem to function only to
invert details of human feasts. It is specifically stated, for example, that the
wolves drink off the top (ἄκρον) of the water--the portion of a drink poured
out to the gods in a libation. The cups with which the men drink, like other
utensils, are often described by ameliorative epithets, such as "golden" (γ
472, ο 149; see especially the cup of Nestor, Λ 632-35). This generates the
pejorative ἀραιῆσιν to modify the tongues of the wolves, used twice of
Hephaistos' lame leg (Σ 411=Υ 37) and once of Aphrodite's hand in a deroga-
tory remark by Athena (Ε 425).[8]

Similarly, the epithet μέλαν is a conversion of the ameliorative epithets of wine: μελίφρονα, μελιήδεα, but, especially αἴθοπα, "gleaming,"
used of heavenly bodies, the *aether* and very commonly of wine. The verb
λάψοντες, a hapax, inverts the very word for libation, λείβειν, particularly
in the repeated phrase (Α 462-63, γ 459-60):

ἐπὶ δ' αἴθοπα οἶνον/ λεῖβε

And over them the gleaming wine/ he poured

Compare this with Π 160-61:

ἀπὸ κρήνης μελανύδρου/ λάψοντες.

Instead of *pouring gleaming wine on* the offerings, the wolves *lap out of* a
*dark-watered* spring. The most meaningful interpretant of this passage is Ζ
266-68:

χερσὶ δ' ἀνίπτοισιν Διὶ λείβειν αἴθοπα οἶνον
ἅζομαι· οὐδέ πη ἔστι κελαινεφέϊ Κρονίωνι
αἵματι καὶ λύθρῳ πεπαλαγμένον εὐχετάασθαι.

I fear to pour out the gleaming wine to Zeus with unwashed

hands; nor is it permissible to pray to the son of Kronos
who is shrouded in the clouds when spattered with blood and gore.

The *aidos* of Hector in this scene, indeed, the *aidos* of Homeric feasters in general, is not simply absent in the wolf simile, but dramatically negated. The vomiting of the wolves also seems to be added simply to make the scene more repulsive. It is perhaps also a travesty of the libation--a pouring out of the "last" portion instead of the first. The only other example of vomiting in the Homeric poems is by that most discourteous host and unceremonious feaster, the Cyclops (ι 373-74). The vomiting, however, is also linked to the next phase of the simile, the repletion of the wolves (Π 162-63):

$$\text{ἐν δέ τε θυμὸς}$$
$$\text{στήθεσιν ἄτρομός ἐστι, περιστένεται δέ τε γαστήρ.}$$

This should be compared to a line repeated some twenty times in Homer marking the end of a meal:[9]

$$\text{αὐτὰρ ἐπεὶ πόσιος καὶ ἐδητύος ἐξ ἔρον ἕντο.}$$

But after they had put away their desire for eating and drinking.

This line caps off a proper Homeric meal and even its simple absence, as in the eating of the sun's cattle in *Odyssey* 12, probably constitutes a significant variation.[10] Whereas the heroes' repletion is described by euphemistic understatement (they "set aside their desire" for food), that of the wolves is described by a hyperbole (they stuff themselves until their stomachs groan). The word ἄτρομος is an ambiguous word. A τρόμος is a trembling motion which afflicts the limbs when one is afraid. Hence the two other occurrences of ἄτρομος in Homer mean "fearless" (E 124, P 157). But the various forms of τρεμ-/ τρομ- retain their connection with physical motion, as is shown by the adverb ἄτρεμας which means "still" (used of Zeus' sleep in Ξ 352, of clouds in E 524, etc.) and by Hesiod's use of the verb ἀτρεμέω to describe the stiffening of hair in the cold (*Erga* 539). If the θυμός is, as Snell has argued,[11] "the generator of motion or agitation," then to have an ἄτρομος θυμός may well mean to be fearless in a military context; but after a gluttonous feast such as the wolves have just indulged in, it could suggest that they are too stuffed to move. The progression of the simile reverses the sequence of a human feast. Heroes eat in order to restore their ἀλκή, but the wolves have boundless ἀλκή to begin with. A heroic feast is a preparation for some action; but the wolves have been rendered incapable of action: ἄτρομος.

The θυμός is also the generator of speech and as such provides a contrast with the γαστήρ of the wolves, which "groans" (περιστένεται). A communal meal is a ritual action, a form of communal language signifying the identity of the participants in respect to a community. Meals are often followed by a speech rousing the heroes to some action for which the meal was a preparation (as in B 433). The wolves' meal, however, has no ritual significance and is clearly not a preparation for any action. A groan is an undifferentiated, unarticulated expression unit. As such, it is correlated to an undifferentiated, unarticulated, and hence undefined content. In short, it is non-significant. The unarticulated, non-significant "groaning" of the wolves' stomachs at the end of the simile negates the signifying function of the ritual action of sharing a meal, as well as the arousal to action which follows meals.

A similar opposition of sharing a meal and "groaning" is implied in the line cited above (T 214): Achilles cares not for food and drink, but for φόνος τε καὶ αἷμα καὶ ἀργαλέος στόνος ἀνδρῶν, "slaughter, blood and the hard *groaning* of men." Even more pertinent is Gaia's reaction in the *Theogony* to the ghastly meal[12] that Ouranos imposes on her. After being forced to reingest her children, Gaia groans (*Theo.* 159-60):

ἥ δ' ἐντὸς στοναχίζετο Γαῖα πελώρη/ στεινομένη

But the wide earth *groaned* inwardly/ being *stuffed*.

Hesiod apparently plays on two sets of words grouped around στείνω, "to crowd" or "make narrow," and στένω, "to groan."[13] Nor is it a gratuitous connection. The stuffing of the earth with her own children is a most uncultural act, and the groaning which is caused by it is the obverse of the signifying function of a communal meal. Lattimore's translation of Π 164 as "their bellies were *full* and *groaning*" catches both the semantic connections of περιστένεται. We could rephrase the line, perhaps, as "their bellies were stuffed, instead of being apportioned a fair division, and therefore groaned, instead of making a culturally coded communicative act." It is the communal language of a proper meal which is negated by the wolves' actions as well as their "words."

The wolf simile, therefore, does not present an action which "represents" the narrative event of mustering. As a discrete textual swathe, however, the simile does articulate a single hypogram: a savage meal. Actually, we should say a non-heroic meal; for it is not on a par with descriptions of other meals of animals. The simile represents a coherent picture not in terms of the "natural history" of wolves, but in terms of how heroes conduct a feast. The simile is a conversion of the descriptive system of the meals of heroes. Nevertheless, the wolf simile is not a separate poem; neither its generation here nor its pragmatic consequences are independent of the narrative context of Book 16. Thus, to account more fully for the simile's role in the text, it will be necessary to consider that narrative context in order to pose the question, why was an anti-heroic meal generated at this particular point? In doing so, we will be going beyond the scope of Riffaterre's "semiotics of poetry": that is, the semiotics of relatively short poems in which the unit of significance is the whole text. But this will not entail a qualitative leap from a theoretical standpoint, despite the fact that narrative has a number of special problems. If we can characterize narrative in a preliminary fashion as a succession of textual swathes, the interrelationships among these various units and the flow from one textual unit to another will be determined by a number of coded factors. Notions of narrative "sequences," "motifs," "patterns," etc., are common interpretative devices which are used to account for these interrelationships.

Interpretive devices such as narrative patterns or sequences enter a semiotic analysis as what Eco calls "overcoding": "given a code assigning meaning to certain minimal expressions, overcoding will assign additional meaning to more macroscopic strings of these expressions" (Eco, 134). This grouping together of a series of actions into a single "scene" which has a significance beyond its discrete components is an important part of the interpretive process by which readers produce meaning. Since a textual strategy always attempts to determine in some degree interpretive responses, a narrative tradition assimilates the results of overcoding in the form of narrative rules. Thus, for example, Vladimir Propp identified a number of narrative functions organized by certain plot rules in a series of Russian fairy tales.[14] These rules are the result of the "super-elevation of codes" introduced above in the discussion of connotation (p. 9) producing thereby a *narrative subcode*. This notion will be elaborated more fully in an appropriate context, but for now it will be sufficient to note that narrative subcodes are textually established: they are produced by the dialectics of the communicative process. Innovative texts can propose unforeseen coding correlations, and if they are accepted, can modify the narrative rules.[15] In order to assess the pragmatic implications of the wolf simile of *Iliad* 16, as well as the textual dynamics which generated it there, it will be necessary to consider the narrative function of the cultural unit of a communal meal, particularly in the context of preparation for battle, which I will argue makes up a narrative subcode.

## The Meal as Communal Language

In Book 16 of the *Iliad*, Achilles and Patroklos meet and decide that Patroklos should lead out the Myrmidons. Patroklos arms himself while Achilles marshals the troops. There is a catalogue, an arousal speech and then the Myrmidons set out. The scene thus resembles Book 2, where there is a similar sequence of events, except for the full description of a preparatory meal in Book 2. At the beginning of the other three days of battle (Books 8, 11 and 19), the preparation is varied. In Book 8 there is a divine assembly and the preparation of the Greeks is compressed into only two lines (Θ 53-54):

οἱ δ' ἄρα δεῖπνον ἕλοντο κάρη κομόωντες Ἀχαιοὶ
ῥίμφα κατὰ κλισίας ἀπὸ δ' αὐτοῦ θωρήσσαντο.

Now the flowing-haired Achaeans had taken their dinner
hastily among the shelters, and then put on their armor.

At the beginning of Book 11, there is an impressive arousal, the arming of Agamemnon is described at length, but no preparatory meal is taken. In Book 19, however, after Achilles assembles the Greeks and urges an immediate encounter, there is a long debate about the wisdom of fighting before the Greeks have eaten. It is this debate and the other references to eating, rather than any strict parallelism of the various preparation scenes, which shows clearly the importance of a meal in the narrative context of preparation for battle.

In Homer, as in many other contexts, sharing a meal functions as an expression of social harmony, the physical and spiritual continuity of a group which is dedicated to some concerted action. In Homer a feast regularly

precedes and concludes important actions and decisions, to the point that
Odysseus has three meals during the course of the evening of Books 9-10.
The social cohesion that feasts exemplify and confirm is put into question by
the quarrel of Achilles and Agamemnon; and the consequences of that fissure
are portrayed in the subsequent defeats of the Greeks. When Achilles finally
returns in Book 19, his actions are ambivalent. Although he has returned to
battle and the aid of the Greeks, he is less interested in patching things up
than in exacting revenge; and this is indicated by, among other things, his
refusal to share a meal before going to battle. Achilles shows no interest in
Agamemnon's conciliatory gesture (T 146-7) and is all for setting out
immediately. Odysseus reprimands him for this, reminding him of the
necessity of food and insisting on a public reconciliation. Here are some of
the pertinent lines (T 160-3; 171-4; 179-80):

ἀλλὰ πάσασθαι ἄνωχθι θοῇς ἐπὶ νηυσὶν Ἀχαιοὺς
σίτου καὶ οἴνοιο· τὸ γὰρ μένος ἐστὶ καὶ ἀλκή.
οὐ γὰρ ἀνὴρ πρόπαν ἦμαρ ἐς ἠέλιον καταδύντα
ἄκμηνος σίτοιο δυνήσεται ἄντα μάχεσθαι....
ἀλλ' ἄγε λαὸν μὲν σκέδασον καὶ δεῖπνον ἄνωχθι
ὅπλεσθαι· τὰ δὲ δῶρα ἄναξ ἀνδρῶν Ἀγαμέμνων
οἰσέτω ἐς μέσσην ἀγορήν, ἵνα πάντες Ἀχαιοὶ
ὀφθαλμοῖσιν ἴδωσι, σὺ δὲ φρεσὶ σῇσιν ἰανθῇς....
αὐτὰρ ἔπειτά σε δαιτὶ ἐνὶ κλισίης ἀρεσάσθω
πιείρῃ, ἵνα μή τι δίκης ἐπιδευὲς ἔχησθα.

Rather tell the Achaeans here by their swift ships
to take food and wine, since these make for strength and courage.
For a man cannot fight his way forward all day
long until the sun goes down if he is starved for food....
Come then, tell your men to scatter and bid them get ready
a meal; and as for the gifts, let the lord of men Agamemnon
bring them into the middle of the assembly so all the Achaeans
can see them before their eyes and your own heart may be pleased....
After that in his own tent let him appease you
with a generous meal, so that you will lack nothing of your due.

Odysseus refers first to the physical necessity of food, but this is only a pre-
text for engineering a public affirmation of communal bonds. The call for a
meal is immediately followed by a call for a formal reconciliation. Achilles
must accept Agamemnon's gifts and be reconciled, and then Agamemnon

must appease Achilles with a meal. The ending of line 180, ἵνα μή τι δίκης ἐπιδευὲς ἔχησθα, is clearly a call for a return to the social harmony reflected in the fair division of a meal: οὐδέ τι θυμὸς ἐδεύετο δαιτὸς ἐίσης.[16] Agamemnon agrees, but Achilles will have none of it (T 205-14):

> ἦ τ' ἂν ἔγωγε
> νῦν μὲν ἀνώγοιμι πτολεμίζειν υἷας Ἀχαιῶν
> νήστιας ἀκμήνους, ἅμα δ' ἠελίῳ καταδύντι
> τεύξεσθαι μέγα δόρπον, ἐπὴν τεισαίμεθα λώβην.
> πρὶν δ' οὔ πως ἂν ἔμοιγε φίλον κατὰ λαιμὸν ἰείη
> οὐ πόσις οὐδὲ βρῶσις, ἑταίρου τεθνηῶτος,
> ὅς μοι ἐνὶ κλισίῃ δεδαϊγμένος ὀξέϊ χαλκῷ
> κεῖται ἀνὰ πρόθυρον τετραμμένος, ἀμφὶ δ' ἑταῖροι
> μύρονται· τό μοι οὔ τι μετὰ φρεσὶ ταῦτα μέμηλεν,
> ἀλλὰ φόνος τε καὶ αἷμα καὶ ἀργαλέος στόνος ἀνδρῶν.

No, but I would now
drive forward the sons of the Achaeans into the fighting
starving and unfed, and after the sun goes down
make ready a great feast, when we have paid off our defilement.
But before this, for me at least, neither food nor drink
shall go down my very throat, since my companion has perished
and lies inside my shelter torn about with the cutting bronze,
and turned against the forecourt while my companions mourn
about him. Food and drink are not a care to my heart,
but slaughter, blood and the hard groaning of men.

Achilles is no more interested in patching things up with Agamemnon now than he was in Book 16 or in Book 9. His only motivation for "returning" is vengeance against Hector. In particular, Odysseus' call for a public ritual reaffirming communal bonds between Achilles and the other Greeks is opposed by Achilles to the "groaning of men" (στόνος ἀνδρῶν). It is not simply that Achilles is in a hurry to get after Hector; what is emphasized in the whole passage is Achilles' pointed refusal to play according to the rules of the game. This draws a second rebuke from the ever-decorous Odysseus. This time Odysseus links a communal meal with giving over one's attachment to the dead and going on with life (T 225; 228-31):

> γαστέρι δ' οὔ πως ἔστι νέκυν πενθῆσαι Ἀχαιούς....
> ἀλλὰ χρὴ τὸν μὲν καταθάπτειν ὅς κε θάνῃσι,
> νηλέα θυμὸν ἔχοντας, ἐπ' ἤματι δακρύσαντας·
> ὅσσοι δ' ἂν πολέμοιο περὶ στυγεροῖο λίπωνται,

μεμνῆσθαι πόσιος καὶ ἐδητύος, ὄφρ᾽ ἔτι μᾶλλον κτλ.

The Achaeans cannot mourn a dead man by denying the belly....
No, but we must harden our hearts and bury the man who
dies, when we have wept over him for a day, and all those
who are left about from the hateful work of war must remember
food and drink, so that afterwards all the more strongly, etc.

Odysseus' point is a common one in Homer: mourning is appropriate only
for a specific amount of time, after which it is necessary to "give up one's
grief" and "return" to the demands of the living. Equally common in Homer
is the use of a communal meal to signify this return to the living. Although
Achilles finally relents and orders the others to eat (275), he refuses to take
part himself, despite the urging of the other leaders. Note once again that the
refusal is linked with a "groan" (T 303-7):

αὐτὸν δ᾽ ἀμφὶ γέροντες Ἀχαιῶν ἠγερέθοντο
λισσόμενοι δειπνῆσαι· ὁ δ᾽ ἠρνεῖτο στεναχίζων·
"λίσσομαι, εἴ τις ἔμοιγε φίλων ἐπιπείθεθ᾽ ἑταίρων,
μή με πρὶν σίτοιο κελεύετε μηδὲ ποτῆτος
ἄσασθαι φίλον ἦτορ, ἐπεί μ᾽ ἄχος αἰνὸν ἱκάνει."

But the Achaean lords were gathered around Achilles
beseeching him to eat, but he with a groan refused:
"I beg of you, if any dear companion will listen
to me, stop urging me to satisfy the heart in me
with food and drink, since this strong sorrow has come upon me."

Instead of eating, he mourns Patroklos, recalling the times when his friend
used to prepare meals for him before battle (T 315-21):

ἦ ῥά νύ μοί ποτε καὶ σύ, δυσάμμορε, φίλταθ᾽ ἑταίρων,
αὐτὸς ἐνὶ κλισίῃ λαρὸν παρὰ δεῖπνον ἔθηκας
αἶψα καὶ ὀτραλέως, ὁπότε σπερχοίατ᾽ Ἀχαιοὶ
Τρωσὶν ἐφ᾽ ἱπποδάμοισι φέρειν πολύδακρυν Ἄρηα.
νῦν δὲ σὺ μὲν κεῖσαι δεδαϊγμένος, αὐτὰρ ἐμὸν κῆρ
ἄκμηνον πόσιος καὶ ἐδητύος, ἔνδον ἐόντων,
σῇ ποθῇ.

There was a time, ill-fated, O dearest of companions,
when you yourself would set the desirable dinner before me
quickly and expertly, whenever the Achaeans were urgent
to carry sorrowful war on the Trojans, breakers of horses.

But now you lie here torn before me, and my heart goes
starved for meat and drink, though they are here beside me,
by reason of your absence.

This passage seems to serve only to underline the alienation of Achilles.
Now that Patroklos is dead, Achilles would appear to have no one to eat
with--no one with whom he cares to establish a communal bond. Finally
Zeus sends Athena to infuse nectar into Achilles, again underlining the fact
that only Achilles has not yet eaten (T 345-48):

οἱ δὲ δὴ ἄλλοι
οἴχονται μετὰ δεῖπνον, ὁ δ' ἄκμηνος καὶ ἄπαστος
ἀλλ' ἴθι οἱ νέκταρ τε καὶ ἀμβροσίην ἐρατεινὴν
στάξον ἐνὶ στήθεσσ', ἵνα μή μιν λιμὸς ἵκηται.

All the others

have gone to take their dinner, but he is fasting and unfed.
Go then to him and distill nectar into his chest, and delicate
ambrosia, so weakness of hunger will not come upon him.

On this last passage Whitman writes, "Achilles refuses mortal food; he has
done with mortality except for dying, and his sustenance comes from the
gods."[17] Sustenance, however, is not the real issue here. What is important
about eating in Homer is the ritual preparing and distributing of food as a
sign of communal solidarity. Any private nibbling by Achilles does not
have the signifying function of a communal meal. Whether one ingests
ambrosia and becomes like a god or whether one eats like a savage is all the
same from the standpoint of culture. So Aristotle says in the *Politics*
(1253a) that "he who is unable to live in society, or has no need for a state
because of his self-sufficiency, must be either a god or a beast." The moment
of Achilles' climactic return is thus dominated by his refusal to share a meal;
and this must be understood in terms of his refusal to be reintegrated into his
culture by "speaking" their communal language.

Nagler's discussion (*Spontaneity*, 140-66) focuses on Achilles' inordi-
nate attachment to the dead Patroklos, characterized by his death wish (Σ 90-
97), his maddened rampage through Books 20-22, attended by a Theomachy
which threatens to confound heaven and earth (Y 54-66), his fruitless attempts to disgrace the body of Hector, and his refusal to wash, sleep and eat.
If Achilles' withdrawal from battle in the beginning of the *Iliad* has resulted

in a disruption of the social order, his return in Book 19 has not achieved a resolution. Achilles' maltreatment of corpses is the dominant indicator of this in his *aristeia*,[18] which is climaxed by his threat to Hector (X 346-47):

αἲ γάρ πως αὐτόν με μένος καὶ θυμὸς ἀνείη
ὤμ' ἀποταμνόμενον κρέα ἔδμεναι, οἷα ἔοργας.

I wish only that my fury and spirit would drive me to hack
your flesh away and to eat it raw for the things you have done.

Even after Hector's death, Achilles refuses to eat and sleep as he wears himself out mourning for Patroklos. When Thetis visits him in Book 24, she chides him for his persistent refusal to perform those actions which would signify his submission to the code of communal behavior (Ω 128-31):

τέκνον ἐμόν, τέο μέχρις ὀδυρόμενος καὶ ἀχεύων
σὴν ἔδεαι κραδίην, μεμνημένος οὔτε τι σίτου
οὔτ' εὐνῆς; ἀγαθὸν δὲ γυναικί περ ἐν φιλότητι
μίσγεθ'.

My child, how long will you go on eating your heart out
in sorrow and lamentation, and remember neither food nor
bed?  It is a good thing even to lie with a woman.

It is only later in Book 24 that Achilles is completely restored, when he shares a meal with Priam, who himself has not eaten or slept since Hector's death (Ω 637-42). Achilles reminds the old man that even Niobe thought of food after losing her twelve children (Ω 601-3, 618-19):

νῦν δὲ μνησώμεθα δόρπου.
καὶ γάρ τ' ἠΰκομος Νιόβη ἐμνήσατο σίτου,
τῇ περ δώδεκα παῖδες ἐνὶ μεγάροισιν ὄλοντο....
ἀλλ' ἄγε δὴ καὶ νῶϊ μεδώμεθα, δῖε γεραιέ,
σίτου.

Now let us be mindful of food;
for even lovely-haired Niobe thought of food
whose twelve children were killed in her palace....
But come glorious old man, let us turn our thoughts to food.

In these passages, the sharing of a meal is explicitly portrayed as the privileged sign of reconciliation.  In Book 24, it is the acknowledged way of "reconciling" oneself to the loss of a loved one, the sign of giving over one's grief. In Book 19 Odysseus insists on a meal as part of a formal reconciliation between Agamemnon and Achilles, including a meal. The sharing of a meal is a ritual act which will bind Achilles once again to Agamemnon and the other Greeks, insuring that Achilles has no lack of δίκη (Τ 180). In both cases sharing a meal reaffirms one's commitment to a community against the claims of some other attachment which conflicts with the best interests of the group (attachment to the dead, Achilles' attachment to his private wrath). It is this step that Achilles refuses to take in Book 19.

In Book 16 Achilles also acts in a way which has often seemed to scholars to be "anti-social."[19] As in Book 9, he refuses to make amends with Agamemnon, despite the fact that the other Greeks clearly feel he no longer has good cause to do so. When Patroklos reproaches Achilles for acting in a way that will benefit no one (Π 29-35), Achilles hyperbolically rejects any interest in the common weal (Π 97-100):

> αἲ γάρ Ζεῦ τε πάτερ καὶ ᾿Αθηναίη καὶ ῎Απολλον,
> μήτε τις οὖν Τρώων θάνατον φύγοι, ὅσσοι ἔασι,
> μήτε τις ᾿Αργείων, νῶϊν δ᾿ ἐκδῦμεν ὄλεθρον,
> ὄφρ᾿ οἶοι Τροίης ἱερὰ κρήδεμνα λύωμεν.

> Father Zeus, Athena and Apollo, would that
> not one of the Trojans or Greeks would escape
> death and that we two alone would survive so
> that we alone could loose Troy's hallowed coronal.

At this point the text switches back to the battle, where Aias gives way and the ships are fired, the condition which Achilles had set for his return. Instead he orders to arms Patroklos, who is conspicuously unable to stand in for Achilles (Π 140-2):[20]

> ἔγχος δ᾿ οὐχ ἕλετ᾿ οἶον ἀμύμονος Αἰακίδαο,
> βριθὺ μέγα στιβαρόν· τὸ μὲν οὐ δύνατ᾿ ἄλλος ᾿Αχαιῶν
> πάλλειν, ἀλλά μιν οἶος ἐπίστατο πῆλαι ᾿Αχιλλεύς.

> Only he did not take the spear of blameless Aiakides
> huge, heavy, thick, which no one else of all the Achaeans
> could handle, but Achilles alone knew how to wield it.

After the catalogue of the Myrmidons, which Nagler notes is "acephalic" and anticlimactic, Achilles gives what is supposed to be an arousal speech to the troops. Instead Achilles reminds them of how they have insulted him in the past (200-9). After they depart, Achilles goes to his tent to prepare a libation to Zeus. This is the only libation in Homer which does not take place in the social context of a meal, and Achilles uses a cup from which *only he* has ever drunk, a detail which seems to be added only to emphasize the anti-social character of Achilles' actions. Achilles' prayer is most significant (Π 236-45):

ἠμὲν δή ποτ' ἐμὸν ἔπος ἔκλυες εὐξαμένοιο,
τίμησας μὲν ἐμέ, μέγα δ' ἴψαο λαὸν Ἀχαιῶν,
ἠδ' ἔτι καὶ νῦν μοι τόδ' ἐπικρήηνον ἐέλδωρ·
αὐτὸς μὲν γὰρ ἐγὼ μενέω νηῶν ἐν ἀγῶνι,
ἀλλ' ἕταρον πέμπω πολέσιν μετὰ Μυρμιδόνεσσι
μάρνασθαι· τῷ κῦδος ἅμα πρόες, εὐρύοπα Ζεῦ,
θάρσυνον δέ οἱ ἦτορ ἐνὶ φρεσίν, ὄφρα καὶ Ἕκτωρ
εἴσεται ἤ ῥα καὶ οἶος ἐπίστηται πολεμίζειν
ἡμέτερος θεράπων, ἦ οἱ τότε χεῖρες ἄαπτοι
μαίνονθ', ὁππότ' ἐγώ περ ἴω μετὰ μῶλον Ἄρηος.

As one time before when I prayed to you, you listened
and did me honor, and smote strongly the host of the Achaeans,
so one more time bring to pass the wish that I pray for.
For see, I myself am staying where the ships are assembled,
but I send out my companion and many Myrmidons with him
to fight. Let glory, Zeus of the wide brows, go forth with him.
Make brave the heart inside his breast, so that even Hector
will find out whether our henchman knows how to fight his battles
by himself, or whether his hands rage invincibly only
those times when I myself go into the grind of the war god.

Hector will indeed find out whether Patroklos' hands are invincible when Achilles does not accompany him: they are not. The whole point of Achilles' withdrawal has been to show the Greeks that they cannot endure without him; Patroklos will also not endure without him, even as it has been prophesied (O 65; cf. Θ 474-76, Π 46-47). There thus seems to be some question about the "intentions" of Achilles.

Achilles' actions in Book 16 are, in fact, quite inexplicable in terms of his stated "intentions." It is difficult to see how sending out Patroklos will profit Achilles at all in reestablishing his lost honor. If Patroklos beats back Hector, how will the Greeks be forced to give Achilles back his due honor? If Achilles now feels that his ends have been accomplished, why does he not return himself? We could state the problem in Riffaterre's terms by saying that in Book 16, the *significance* of the poem, which can be identified thematically with the Διὸς βουλή, the "plan of Zeus" to honor Achilles, begins to contradict the *meaning* of Achilles' actions; that is, the portrayal of Achilles begins to become "ungrammatical." Achilles will achieve his due honor by killing Hector after the death of Patroklos: this has been ordained. Nevertheless, it would be perverse to suggest that this is what Achilles "had in mind" when he made his initial request, or even when he sends out Patroklos in Book 16. It thus seems precipitous to blame or praise Achilles in this book; such claims remain mired in the realm of mimesis. Elsewhere in the poem the Διὸς βουλή is specifically identified as the determinant of the action (O 64-77, O 592-52, Π 249-52, to name only the most salient passages); but in Book 16 the relationship between the Διὸς βουλή and Achilles' actions becomes especially complex. The significance of the contradictions in the behavior of both Achilles and Zeus is a larger issue that we will have to face eventually, but for now it is possible to identify the narrative function of the wolf simile, which is clearly related to this contradiction.

When the Myrmidons prepare to enter the battle, a preparatory meal would be inappropriate, since Achilles' actions are at one level "anti-social." The text thus encounters a crisis. The preparation for battle is an overcoded situation in which, among other things, the cultural unit of a preparatory meal is an established element. The forward movement of the narrative thus dictates an element which is thematically inconsistent with the portrayal of Achilles' actions. The only way to prevent the text from breaking down is to transform the meal element in some way. The text tells us, "they did not eat a preparatory meal, for Achilles' actions run counter to the social cohesion implied by a meal. The kind of eating commensurate with his actions would run something like this: οἱ δὲ λύκοι ὣς κτλ." The traditional dynamics of Homeric narrative thus provide a way to get through the narrative complication. The preparatory meal becomes transformed into a negative meal and is articulated in the text as a savage meal. The wolf simile does for the Myrmidons what Achilles' spear does for Patroklos. The most important thing about Patroklos' arming is what he does *not* do: take the great Pelian ash. The most important thing about the marshaling of the Myrmidons is what they do not do: eat a proper preparatory meal. To return to Riffaterre's terminology, the *matrix* of the simile is "they do not eat a proper meal"; the *model* of the simile, the way the text articulates the matrix, is "they eat a savage meal."

I chose the wolf simile of Book 16 as my first example because of its dramatic "irrelevance" to the narrative event it is ostensibly compared to. This irrelevance makes the simile stick out; it engages the reader and calls out to be integrated into the significance at a deeper level of organization. Many of Homer's similes do not create such a tension with the organization of the text at the level of representation. Hence, they often seem to be simply colorful moments of poetic fantasy. This may indeed be the case with many of Homer's similes, but one need not be content with such a solution. The notion of "organic unity" at the level of the representation became a desideratum of narrative largely as a result of classical philosophy and rhetoric. But this does not mean that archaic poetry had no regard for coherence at that level: indeed, coherence at more than one level of linguistic organization would seem to be characteristic of all literature. It is likely that many of Homer's similes perform narrative functions beyond the usual "decorative" ones. To be thorough, one should investigate all the similes and create a typology of their functions. This, however, is beyond the scope of the present study. I will therefore use a case study approach, choosing some particularly interesting examples.

### Book 11: Simile as Textual Generator

Since in my treatment of the Patrokleia I have assumed that the preparation for battle is an overcoded situation which dictates a preparatory meal, it will be useful to look at the beginning of the great battle in Book 11. No mention is made of a meal, but interestingly enough, the element is once again taken up in the similes. Immediately before Agamemnon's aristeia, we have (Λ 84-90):

"Οφρα μὲν ἠὼς ἦν ἀέξετο ἱερὸν ἦμαρ
τόφρα μάλ' ἀμφοτέρων βέλε' ἥπτετο, πῖπτε δὲ λαός·
ἦμος δὲ δρυτόμος περ ἀνὴρ ὡπλίσσατο δεῖπνον
οὔρεος ἐν βήσσῃσιν, ἐπεί τ' ἐκορέσσατο χεῖρας
τάμνων δένδρεα μάκρα, ἄδος τέ μιν ἵκετο θυμόν,
σίτου τε γλυκεροῖο περὶ φρένας ἵμερος αἱρεῖ,
τῆμος σφῇ ἀρετῇ Δαναοὶ ῥήξαντο φάλαγγας.

So long as it was early morning and the sacred daylight increasing,
so long the thrown weapons of both took hold and the men fell.
But at the time when the woodcutter makes ready his meal
in the wooded glens of the mountains, when he has sated his hands

of cutting down tall trees, and his heart is cloyed with it,
and longing for food and for sweet wine takes hold of his senses;
at that time the Danaans by their manhood broke the battalions.

This simile creates a remarkable foil to the action, and the resulting pathos has often been admired. What is particularly interesting is the play on the notion of appetite in this simile, its use for the woodsman's desire for food as well as for his work. The woodsman turns to prepare his meal because he has "sated" (κορέσσατο) his hands of cutting down trees. A "cloying," ἄδος, overcomes his θυμός. The word ἄδος is a hapax, but its meaning is clearly related to the use of the adverb ἄδην in such phrases as εἰωθότες ἔδμεναι ἄδην (E 203), "accustomed to eating *to repletion*"; οἵ μιν ἄδην ἐλόωσι (N 315), "these can battle him *sufficiently*"; οὐ λήξω πριν Τρῶας ἄδην ἐλάσαι πολέμοιο (T 423), "I will not leave off until the Trojans have their *fill* of fighting"; ἀλλ' ἔτι μέν μίν φημι ἄδην ἐλάαν κακητότος (ε 290), "but still I think I have given him his *fill* of difficulty." The word ἄδος, then, like the verb κορέννυμι, suggests having one's appetite satisfied or oversatisfied.

On the other hand, the verb describing the woodsman's desire for food, αἱρέω, is often used of strong emotions (ἵμερος Ξ 328, δέος Ρ 67, χόλος Σ 322) "overtaking" or "capturing" someone. This sense is connected to the verb's most common use in the "seizing" or "capturing" of someone in battle. At the same time, the verb ὁπλίζω, although commonly used for the preparing of many things, also can mean simply "to arm," to put on one's ὅπλα. Thus the simile contains a mixing of two spheres of activity which should properly be kept separate, not unlike the wolf simile of Book 16. The semantic content of this simile is, indeed, determined by the fact that the Greeks have had no preparatory meal; but the function of the woodsman simile is quite different from that of the wolf simile. It just so happens that the *Zeitangabe* diction which introduces the simile occurs in two other places which illustrate clearly the function the woodsman simile must perform. The first is in Book 8, the beginning of the second day of battle. A general melee is briefly described and then we have (Θ 66-72):

"Οφρα μὲν ἠὼς ἦν καὶ ἀέξετο ἱερὸν ἦμαρ,
τόφρα μάλ' ἀμφοτέρων βέλε' ἥπτετο, πῖπτε δὲ λαός.
ἦμος δ' Ἠέλιος μέσον οὐρανὸν ἀμφιβεβήκει,
καὶ τότε δὴ χρύσεια πατὴρ ἐτίταινε τάλαντα·
ἐν δὲ τίθει δύο κῆρε τανηλεγέος θανάτοιο,

Τρώων θ' ἱπποδάμων καὶ 'Αχαιῶν χαλκοχιτώνων,
ἕλκε δὲ μέσσα λαβών· ῥέπε δ' αἴσιμον ἦμαρ 'Αχαιῶν.

So long as it was early morning and the sacred daylight increasing
so long the thrown weapons of both took hold and men fell.
But when the sun god stood bestriding the middle heaven,
then the father balanced his golden scales, and in them
he set two fateful portions of death, which lays men prostrate,
for Trojans, breakers of horses, and bronze-armored Achaeans,
and balanced in the middle. The Achaeans death-day was heavier.

This is the first time Zeus directly intervenes in the fighting in order to accomplish his promise to Thetis, and Hector's success in this book leads immediately to a crisis for the Greeks and to the embassy. The *Zeitangabe* separates the "other" actions (ὄφρα μὲν) from the crucial turning point in the plot (ἦμος δέ). In fact the whole previous day of battle must be included among these "other" actions which do not get the story any further along. After a substantial retardation, the Διὸς βουλή is finally initiated in Book 8, and the turning point is marked by the same two lines which precede the woodsman simile.

Later, in Book 16, Patroklos' undoing is preceded by the following *Zeitangabe* (Π 777-80):

"Οφρα μὲν 'Ηέλιος μέσον οὐρανὸν ἀμφιβεβήκει,
τόφρα μάλ' ἀμφοτέρων βέλε' ἥπτετο, πῖπτε δὲ λαός·
ἦμος δ' 'Ηέλιος μετενίσετο βουλυτόνδε,
καὶ τότε δή ῥ' ὑπὲρ αἶσαν 'Αχαιοὶ φέρτεροι ἦσαν.

So long as the sun was climbing still to the middle heaven,
so long the thrown weapons of both took hold and men fell.
But when the sun had gone to the time for unyoking cattle,
then beyond destiny the Achaeans were stronger.

The overwhelming success of Patroklos, like the Greek successes of Books 3-7, threaten to take away Achilles' τιμή; the *Zeitangabe* again separates the "other" actions of Book 16 from the divine intervention which will ultimately lead to Achilles' much sought for honor. It marks the return, that is, to the forward movement of the plot after several hundred lines of narrative which retard the crisis created by the firing of the ships.

The *Zeitangabe* of Book 11 serves a similar purpose. It too marks a turning point in the plot, the moment the Διὸς βουλή begins to unfold in the narrative. But instead of direct divine intervention, we have the woodsman simile. This simile, its own semantic content determined by the fact that the Greeks have not taken a preparatory meal, becomes in turn the *model* of the articulation of the Διὸς βουλή. Like the woodsman, the "best of the Achaeans," as Nestor later characterizes them, will fight successfully until a ἆδος overcomes them and they are forced to retire. In a series of parallel episodes, Agamemnon, Diomedes and Odysseus fight and kill only to be wounded themselves. The simile, however, does not merely presage in a general way the imminent setbacks of the Greeks, but determines them in detail. To use Riffaterre's terminology, the *matrix* of the narrative is the Διὸς βουλή (as it was in Books 8 and 16); the *model* of the narrative, the first actualization of the matrix is the woodsman simile.[21]

Note, for example, the use of the ὄφρα μὲν...αὐτὰρ ἐπεὶ diction which describes the action of each hero. First, Zeus sends a messenger to Hector (Λ 186-94):

βάσκ' ἴθι, Ἶρι ταχεῖα, τὸν Ἕκτορι μῦθον ἐνίσπες·
ὄφρ' ἂν μέν κεν ὁρᾷ Ἀγαμέμνονα, ποιμένα λαῶν,
θύνοντ' ἐν προμάχοισιν, ἐναίροντα στίχας ἀνδρῶν,
τόφρ' ἀναχωρείτω, τὸν δ' ἄλλον λαὸν ἀνώχθω
μάρνασθαι δηΐοισι κατὰ κρατερὴν ὑσμίνην.
αὐτὰρ ἐπεί κ' ἢ δουρὶ τυπεὶς ἢ βλήμενος ἰῷ
εἰς ἵππους ἅλεται, τότε οἱ κράτος ἐγγυαλίξω
κτείνειν, εἰς ὅ κε νῆας ἐϋσσέλμους ἀφίκηται
δύῃ τ' ἠέλιος καὶ ἐπὶ κνέφας ἱερὸν ἔλθῃ.

Go on your way, swift Iris, and carry my word to Hector:
*as long as* he beholds Agamemnon, shepherd of the people,
raging among the champions and cutting down the ranged fighters,
*so long* let him hold back and urge on the rest of the people
to fight against the enemy through this long encounter.
*But when*, either struck with a spear or hit by a flying arrow,
he springs back to his horses, *then* I guarantee power to Hector
to kill men, till he makes his way to the strong-benched vessels,
until the sun goes down and the blessed darkness comes over.

These lines are the "second" actualization of the will of Zeus, and they are clearly modeled on the woodsman simile: there will be a spree of success for Agamemnon which will be cut short by a wound. After Agamemnon's withdrawal, Hector kills several Greeks until Diomedes comes up to face him. Diomedes also has an initial success; in fact, he almost kills Hector. Then we have (Λ 357-60):

ὄφρα δὲ Τυδείδης μετὰ δούρατος ᾦχετ' ἐρωὴν
τῆλε διὰ προμάχων, ὅθι οἱ καταείσατο γαίης
τόφρ' Ἕκτωρ ἔμπνυτο, καὶ ἂψ ἐς δίφρον ὀρούσας
ἐξέλασ' ἐς πληθύν, καὶ ἀλεύατο κῆρα μέλαιναν.

*As long as* the son of Tydeus was following his spear's cast
far through the front fighters where it fixed in the earth,
*for so long* Hector caught his breath, and springing back into
his chariot, drove back into the multitude and avoided death.

Shortly after this Paris wounds Diomedes, whose withdrawal brings forth Odysseus, who is taken through a similar sequence. After killing five Trojans and being called "*insatiable* of guile and endeavor" (Λ 430: δόλων ἆτ' ἠδὲ πόνοιο), Odysseus is wounded. When the Trojans see Odysseus' blood, they swarm on him and force him to give way. Aias then comes to his aid and the situation is recapitulated in a simile which again uses the ὄφρα...αὐτὰρ ἐπεὶ diction (473-86):

ἀμφὶ δ' ἄρ' αὐτὸν
Τρῶες ἕπονθ' ὡς εἴ τε δαφοινοὶ θῶες ὄρεσφιν
ἀμφ' ἔλαφον κεραὸν βεβλημένον, ὅν τ' ἔβαλ' ἀνὴρ
ἰῷ ἀπὸ νευρῆς· τὸν μέν τ' ἤλυξε πόδεσσι
φεύγων, ὄφρ' αἷμα λιαρὸν καὶ γούνατ' ὀρώρῃ·
αὐτὰρ ἐπεὶ δὴ τόν γε δαμάσσεται ὠκὺς ὀϊστός,
ὠμοφάγοι μιν θῶες ἐν οὔρεσι δαρδάπτουσιν
ἐν νέμεϊ σκιερῷ· ἐπί τε λῖν ἤγαγε δαίμων
σίντην· θῶες μέν τε διέτρεσαν, αὐτὰρ ὁ δάπτει.
ὣς ῥα τότ' ἀμφ' Ὀδυσῆα δαΐφρονα ποικιλομήτην
Τρῶες ἕπον πολλοί τε καὶ ἄλκιμοι, αὐτὰρ ὅ γ' ἥρως
ἀΐσσων ᾧ ἔγχει ἀμύνετο νηλεὲς ἦμαρ.
Αἴας δ' ἐγγύθεν ἦλθε φέρων σάκος ἠΰτε πύργον
στῆ δὲ παρέξ· Τρῶες δὲ διέτρεσαν ἄλλυδις ἄλλος.

The Trojans crowded around Odysseus, as bloody jackals in
the mountains crowd on a horned stag who is stricken,
one whom a hunter shot with an arrow from the string,
and the stag has escaped him, running with his feet,
*as long as* the blood stayed warm, and his knees were springing
beneath him; *but when* the pain of the flying arrow has
beaten him, then the rending jackals begin to feast on him

in the mountains and the shaded glen. But then some spirit
leads that way a dangerous lion, and the jackals run
in terror, *but* the lion eats it; so *for a while* around wise
much-devising Odysseus the Trojans crowded, valiant and
numerous, *but then* the hero with rapid play of his spear
beat off the pitiless death day. Now Aias came near
him, carrying his shield like a tower, and stood forth
beside him, and the Trojans fled one way and another.

Odysseus then withdraws from battle with the help of Aias. In each of these
three cases, the actions of each hero varies the pattern of action articulated in
the woodsman simile. A closer look at the passages will show that as the
*model* of the action, characteristics of the simile's form and content recur in
the whole passage in significant ways. The simile becomes the *textual generator* of a series of variations of itself. This is especially clear in the
similes.

After he is hurt, Agamemnon remains in the battle until his wound
dries up and the pain becomes unbearable. Note the similarity to Odysseus'
deer simile and the use of ὄφρα and αὐτὰρ ἐπεὶ (264-68):

Αὐτὰρ ὁ τῶν ἄλλων ἐπεπωλεῖτο στίχας ἀνδρῶν
ἔγχεΐ τ' ἄορί τε μεγάλοισί τε χερμαδίοισιν,
ὄφρα οἱ αἷμ' ἔτι θερμὸν ἀνήνοθεν ἐξ ὠτειλῆς.
αὐτὰρ ἐπεὶ τὸ μὲν ἕλκος ἐτέρσετο, παύσατο δ' αἷμα,
ὀξεῖαι δ' ὀδύναι δῦνον μένος Ἀρεΐδαο.

But Agamemnon ranged in the ranks of the other fighters
with spear and sword and with huge stones that he flung,
*as long as* the blood was still running warm from the wound.
*But after* the sore place was dry, and the flow of blood stopped,
the sharp pains began to break in on the strength of Atreides.

Line 268 has a remarkable phonic character: ὀξεῖαι δ' ὀδύναι δῦνον. This
succession of vowels plus δ even seems to generate a simile which continues
the phonic play (269-32):

ὡς δ' ὅτ' ἂν ὠδίνουσαν ἔχῃ βέλος ὀξὺ γυναῖκα,
δριμύ, τό τε προϊεῖσι μογοστόκοι Εἰλείθυιαι,
Ἥρης θυγατέρες πικρὰς ὠδῖνας ἔχουσαι
ὣς ὀξεῖ' ὀδύναι δῦνον μένος Ἀτρεΐδαο.

As the sharp sorrow of pain descends on a woman in labor,

the bitterness that the hard spirits of childbirth bring on,
Hera's daughters, who hold the power of the bitter birthpangs,
so the sharp pains began to break in on the strength of Atreides.

The scholiast complained that such a humble image was unbefitting a man
who had just accomplished such feats as Agamemnon.[22] But the organization of this simile is not primarily mimetic, not even semantic or lexical: it
is phonic. The most important words in this simile are ὠδίνουσαν and
ὠδῖνας. The rest fleshes out this phonic play.[23] And the generative source
for all five lines is none other than the ἄδος of Λ 89, which overtakes the
poor woodsman when he is "sated" of working. In the logic of the structural
parallelism between the woodsman and Agamemnon, the ἄδος and the ὀξεῖ'
ὀδύναι are equivalent: each is the cause of the "retreat" from heroic labor.

The inscription of this equivalence by a phonic echo, itself expanded in
the strongly "ungrammatical" simile of the birthpangs, is a good example of
what Riffaterre calls "overdetermination," a term he borrows from psycho-
analysis. "Poetic" devices such as verbal echo produce connections among
words which are additional to the normal grammatical ones. These "deviant"
connections in turn become symptomatic of the "repressed" matrix. Overdetermination is, according to Riffaterre, the corollary of catachresis ("abusive"
language): the more strange a departure from usage seems to be, the more
strongly motivated it seems to be (*Semiotics of Poetry*, p. 21). The phonic
play between ἄδος and ὀδύνη not only draws attention to the parallelism between the woodsman and Agamemnon, but opens up into other productive
issues of the text: the fact that the woodsman simile itself is determined by
the lack of a preparatory meal by the Greeks, a lack that is a symptom of a
wound in the Greek community because of Achilles' withdrawal; the fact that
Achilles is nursing a wound for which he is demanding satisfaction, a satisfaction which, after the embassy of Book 9, seems to be destined to become
an oversatisfaction. Because we are used to paying attention to more
"grammatical" forms of textual relationships, it is easy for us to underesti-
mate the versatility of texts in drawing propulsive force from any level of
linguistico-textual organization. When the arrow is removed from Diomedes'
foot, there is another proliferation of versions of the ἄδος/ὀδύνη play (Λ
398):

ἐκ ποδὸς ἕλκ', ὀδύνη δὲ διὰ χροὸς ἦλθ' ἀλεγεινή κτλ.

But the phonic play may just as easily have helped determine Odysseus as the next victim of the Διὸς βουλή, as it probably did, albeit on a different level of linguistic organization, in the case of the next Greek to be wounded, Machaon the healer.

The semantic content of the woodsman simile, a conflation of appetite and work (specifically, cutting down trees), recurs in the similes of the narrative. Agamemnon is compared to a forest fire, a common usage; but this fire "fells" shrubbery (Λ 155-58):

ὡς δ' ὅτε πῦρ ἀΐδηλον ἐν ἀξύλῳ ἐμπέσῃ ὕλῃ,
πάντῃ τ' εἰλυφόων ἄνεμος φέρει, οἱ δέ τε θάμνοι
πρόρριζοι πίπτουσιν ἐπειγόμενοι πυρὸς ὁρμῇ·
ὣς ἄρ' ὑπ' 'Ατρείδῃ 'Αγαμέμνονι πῖπτε κάρηνα.

As when obliterating fire comes down on a timbered
forest and the roll of the wind carries it everywhere,
and thickets leaning under the force of the fire's
rush *fall* uprooted, so before Atreus' son Agamemnon
*went down* the high heads [of the fleeing Trojans].

The verb πίπτω is used of warriors falling after being cut down in battle, an event which is often compared to a tree being felled (e.g., Δ 482, E 590). This verb, however, is not particularly appropriate for a "thicket" (θάμνος) which has burnt; but this line is generated by the semic potential of the woodsman simile. Note also the hapax ἀξύλῳ, to describe the forest. The word ξύλα refers specifically to wood which is cut down for lumber. A forest which is ἄξυλος is one which has not yet been thinned by a woodsman. Thus, despite the fact that it is the wind and fire which destroy the forest, the semantic content of the woodsman simile continues to play a text-formative role.

Agamemnon's simile of the lion attacking cattle and eating one of them (172-76) exemplifies the other semic center of the woodsman simile, but lines 175-76 are particularly appropriate:

τῆς δ' ἐξ αὐχέν' ἔαξε λαβὼν κρατεροῖσιν ὀδοῦσι
πρῶτον, ἔπειτα δέ θ' αἷμα καὶ ἔγκατα πάντα λαφύσσει.

First the lion breaks her neck caught fast in the strong teeth,
then gulps down the blood and all the guts that are inward.

The verb ἔαξε (from ἄγνυμι) usually describes the breaking of wooden objects, such as spears and axles. In M 148, it is used of boars rushing through a woods and breaking down trees. The use of ἔαξε, therefore, to describe the "cutting down" of the cow answers to one part of the semantic nucleus of the woodsman simile, the scene as a whole to the other. In Agamemnon's other lion simile (113-20), the deer flees διὰ δρυμὰ πυκνὰ καὶ ὕλην, "through a thick wood and forest," and in Odysseus' boar simile, the boar rushes βαθείης ἐκ ξυλόχοιο (415), "out of a deep copse." Note also that in these similes the teeth of the animals are mentioned: ὀδοῦσιν 114, 175; ὀδόντων 417. The woodsman's work results in a ἄδος for him; the work of the *aristeuontes*, which they perform in the similes with their ὀδοῦσιν, will backfire on them in the form of an ὀδύνη.

The simile of lines 474-81 (quoted above, page 46) is an example of a point-by-point correspondence between narrative situation and simile. Again the labor of war is translated into eating. Odysseus, who manages to kill the man who inflicted the wound on him, corresponds to the deer who is struck by the hunter, whom he eludes despite the wound. The jackals correspond to the Trojans who swarm on the wounded Odysseus until they are in turn chased off by a lion (Aias). This is noteworthy because it shows that in the similes there need not be a tension between mimesis and semiosis, between meaning and significance. There is, however, one minor lapse of correspondence: Aias saves Odysseus from the Trojans; but the lion chases off the jackals only to eat the deer himself. Of the innumerable possibilities for a line ending after the bucolic diaeresis, the textual dynamics generated a phrase determined primarily by its phonic character: αὐτὰρ ὁ δάπτει.

It can thus be seen that the woodsman simile generates not only the general shape of the battle scenes of Agamemnon, Diomedes and Odysseus, but determines details at a number of levels of linguistic organization. Within the scope of the narrative, there are similes generated by the semantic core of the woodsman simile ("woods," "felling of trees," "appetite"),[24] a simile generated by the model of the action (474ff.), and a simile generated by the phonic content of the simile (269-71). The strongest evidence for this view, however, is the exceptional treatment of Aias, to whom we must now turn.

Aias steps forward after the withdrawal of Odysseus and quickly kills five Trojans (489-91). He is then compared to a mountain stream in a simile which continues the semantic expansion of the woodsman simile (Λ 492-5):

ὡς δ' ὁπότε πλήθων ποταμὸς πεδίονδε κάτεισι
χειμάρρους κατ' ὄρεσφιν, ὀπαζόμενος Διὸς ὄμβῳ
πολλὰς δὲ δρῦς ἀζαλέας, πολλὰς δέ τε πεύκας
ἐσφέρεται, πολλὸν δέ τ' ἀφυσγετὸν εἰς ἅλα βάλλει.

As when a swollen river hurls its water, big with rain,
down the mountains to the flat land, pressed on by Zeus' rain,
and sweeps down with it numbers of dry oaks and pine trees,
until it hurls much mud into the salt sea.

Besides the notion of "felling" trees, the Διὸς ὄμβρῳ reintroduces directly the
matrix: Διὸς βουλή. It seems that Aias is about to be taken through the
same sequence as Agamemnon, Diomedes and Odysseus. Now Aias is the
"best of the Achaeans," we have been told, ὄφρ' Ἀχιλεὺς μήνιεν, "as long as
Achilles was angry" (B 769); and if he were to be wounded, that would
quickly bring about the will of Zeus: the rout of the Greeks. That would in
turn pave the way for the return of Achilles. But the text makes an abrupt
*volte face* (497-98):[25]

οὐδέ πω ῞Εκτωρ
πεύθετ', ἐπεί ῥα μάχης ἐπ' ἀριστερὰ μάρνατο πάσης.

nor yet had Hector
heard, since he was fighting at the right of the entire battle.

The sequence will not, it seems, be run for Aias, or at least not yet. Hector's
fighting is briefly described, and then the text makes another switch over to
Paris, who wounds Machaon in a way that recapitulates the pattern of the
other three heroes in brief compass (504-7):

οὐδ' ἄν πω χάζοντο κελεύθου δῖοι Ἀχαιοί,
εἰ μὴ Ἀλέξανδρος, Ἑλένης πόσις ἠϋκόμοιο,
παῦσεν ἀριστεύοντα Μαχάονα, ποιμένα λαῶν,
ἰῷ τριγλώχινι βαλὼν κατὰ δεξιὸν ὦμον.

Even so the Achaeans would not have yielded from his path
had not Alexandros, the lord of lovely-haired Helen,
stopped Machaon, shepherd of the people, *as he was having an aristeia*,
hitting him with a three-barbed arrow in the right shoulder.

After Nestor retreats with Machaon, we return to Hector (521), whose charioteer urges him to face Aias. This they seem to be doing (531ff.) but instead Hector unaccountably steers clear of Aias (542). What does happen is that Zeus mazes Aias and causes him to retreat. The pattern which was begun for Aias at 489 is now taken up again by the direct intervention of Zeus and we have the following simile (548-57):

ὡς δ' αἴθωνα λέοντα βοῶν ἀπὸ μεσσαύλοιο
ἐσσεύαντο κύνες τε καὶ ἀνέρες ἀγροιῶται,
οἵ τέ μιν οὐκ εἰῶσι βοῶν ἐκ πῖαρ ἐλέσθαι
πάννυχοι ἐγρήσσοντες· ὁ δὲ κρειῶν ἐρατίζων
ἰθύει, ἀλλ' οὔ τι πρήσσει· θαμέες γὰρ ἄκοντες
ἀντίον ἀΐσσουσι θρασειάων ἀπὸ χειρῶν,
καιόμεναί τε δεταί, τάς τε τρεῖ ἐσσύμενός περ·
ἠῶθεν δ' ἀπονόσφιν ἔβη τετιηότι θυμῷ·
ὣς Αἴας τότ' ἀπὸ Τρώων τετιημένος ἦτορ.

As when the men who live in the wild and their dogs have driven
a tawny lion away from the mid-fenced ground of their oxen,
and will not let him tear out the fat of the oxen, watching
nightlong against him, and he in his hunger for meat closes in
but can get nothing of what he wants, for the ranging javelins
thrown from the daring hands of the men beat ever against him,
and the flaming torches, and these he balks at for all of his fury
and with the daylight goes away, disappointed of desire;
so Aias, disappointed at heart, drew back from the Trojans.

Again there is an actualization of the semantic nucleus of the woodsman simile, appetite. But here the lion is prevented from eating, despite his great hunger, and he goes away unsatisfied (τετιηότι θυμῷ). This must have seemed unsatisfactory to the poet as well, for he launches into a second simile which "corrects" the first (558-62):

ὡς δ' ὅτ' ὄνος παρ' ἄρουραν ἰὼν ἐβιήσατο παῖδας
νωθής, ᾧ δὴ πολλὰ περὶ ῥόπαλ' ἀμφὶς ἐάγη,
κείρει τ' εἰσελθὼν βαθὺ λήϊον· οἱ δέ τε παῖδες
τύπτουσιν ῥοπάλοισι· βίη δέ τε νηπίη αὐτῶν·
σπουδῇ τ' ἐξήλασσαν, ἐπεί τ' ἐκορέσσατο φορβῆς·
ὣς τότ' ἔπειτ' Αἴαντα μέγαν, Τελαμώνιον υἱόν, κτλ.

As when a donkey, stubborn and hard to move, goes into a field
in despite of boys, and many sticks have been broken upon him,
but he gets in and goes on eating the deep grain, and the children
beat him with sticks, but their strength is infantile; yet at last

by hard work they drive him out when he is glutted with eating;
so around great Aias, the son of Telamon, etc.

This simile is much more closely connected with the woodsman model. The ass retreats only after "sating" himself, in a line which is clearly a variation of line 87 of the woodsman simile:

ἐπεί τ' ἐκορέσσατο χεῖρας (87)
after he had sated his hands

ἐπεί τ' ἐκορέσσατο φορβῆς (562)
after he had sated himself on grain.

The ass even does a little "woodcutting" himself as the children's sticks (πολλὰ ῥόπαλα: cf. Λ 88 δένδρεα μάκρα) are broken on his back (ἐάγη: from ἄγνυμι again). Significantly, the ass has a ἄδος, but no ὀδύνη, a fact underlined by the phrase βίη δέ τε νηπίη αὐτῶν, "but their strength is infantile" (i.e., undamaging). Both similes, in fact, represent a withdrawal unattended by wounds, a contrast to the previous *aristeuontes*, and this is of major interest.

The introduction of Aias in lines 464ff. seems to have created a difficulty. The seriousness of the Greek plight escalates successively from the wounding of Agamemnon to the wounding of Diomedes to the wounding of Odysseus. The series leads the text to Aias, who is "second-best of the Achaeans." Aias' wounding, as I have said, would lead inexorably to the "best of the Achaeans," Achilles. But the Διὸς βουλή, i.e., the plot of the poem, seems hesitant to bring this critical event about at this time. Let us consider again the progression of the action from 489 on.

Aias begins killing Trojans and is compared to a river breaking down trees. The sequence which has been run for the previous three heroes is thus begun for Aias. What is projected by the pattern is for Aias to be wounded and then withdraw. Then the Trojans would advance unchecked to the ships, even as Zeus has promised (Λ 192-93). Instead we are told that Hector, the likeliest candidate to inflict such a wound, is not nearby. This abruptly introduced information short-circuits one possible direction of the narrative flow. Then, just as abruptly, we are told that Paris wounds Machaon, who, surprisingly, was having an *aristeia* (ἀριστεύοντα). Machaon's wounding seems to complete the pattern which was begun for Aias. Hector's charioteer then drives toward Aias, but again the confrontation is avoided (542). Instead Zeus mazes Aias, a much more potent actualization of the will of Zeus. But still Aias is not wounded, and the Trojan spearcasts are in vain, despite their eagerness to *sate* themselves in Aias' flesh: [δούρα] λιλαιόμενα χροὸς ἆσαι (574). The confrontation between Hector and Aias, which will lead to the firing of the ships and pave the way for Achilles' return, is still five books away. As he retreats, Aias prevents the Trojans from making their way to the ships (569): πάντας δὲ προέεργε θοὰς ἐπὶ νῆας ὀδεύειν. The ἆδος of the model does not become translated into an ὀδύνη for Aias, but a retreat in which he wards off the ὀδεύειν of the Trojans, and the text has been laboring for some time to establish this reorientation of the model. Paris then for the third time steps forward and wounds a Greek with an arrow: not Aias, for whom the pattern was begun, but Eurypylos, who then retires to the camp (581ff.). This displacement of Aias by Eurypylos is reflected in the words of Nestor, repeated by both Patroklos and Eurypylos himself, that the "best of the Achaeans," Agamemnon, Diomedes, Odysseus and Eurypylos, have been wounded, ignoring the fact that Aias is still fighting (Λ 658-62, Λ 823-25, Π 23-27).

With Eurypylos, the narrative turns to the Greek camp and the articulation of the will of Zeus grinds to a halt. After an astonishing succession of Greek defeats which climaxes in the slow retreat of Aias, the action reaches a flat spot which will extend all the way through Book 15. In that book, Zeus' intervention will once again bring the Greek plight to a climax with a retreat by Aias; and when Aias can no longer endure against Hector's onslaught (Π 102), the stage will be set for the return of Achilles to battle. Achilles, however, will send out Patroklos; and it will be the death of the latter, and not Aias' wounding, which brings Achilles back into the fighting.

Book 11 of the *Iliad* presents us with an extraordinary example of the workings of a composition technique dominated by the poetics of oral presentation. Let us try to imagine the situation of the poet as he begins line 489. The model of the woodsman simile has already generated three parallel sequences. Homer launches on a fourth with Aias, but suddenly decides that he is not ready for the outcome of the pattern: Aias' wounding. Vergil could have erased these lines and started over; but in an oral performance, once something is said, there is no going back: one can only make an adjustment somewhere along the line. One such adjustment comes at line 497b, when the text switches abruptly to Hector, and stretches to 503. That eliminates Aias' wounding, and the poet then brings the projected pattern to an end with the wounding of Machaon. Next the charioteer of Hector urges him to confront Aias and begins heading to the other side of the battle, but the confrontation of Aias and Hector is again short-circuited, since Hector inexplicably stays clear of Aias (521-42). These lines are yet another example of something begun by the poet, only to be abandoned. Instead of Hector driving Aias out of the field, Zeus mazes him (542) and his retreat proceeds without any further reference to Hector. A simile is generated to handle the development (548-55), but the lion simile gets the appetite seme wrong; Zenodotus athetized the lion simile, and a literate poet could have erased it. Homer instead leaves it and takes another shot, this time focusing on the woodsman simile more sharply and adjusting the transformation of the appetite seme in the lion simile (558-63). As in the previous case, the woodsman model projects another wounding and the poet falls on Eurypylos. Eurypylos' parting remarks emphasize the danger if Aias is wounded (587-91).

Apparently satisfied with this resolution of the textual complexity in which he found himself, the poet turns to Achilles and Patroklos, since it is through the latter that the Διὸς βουλή will make its next major movement (602-4):

αἶψα δ' ἑταῖρον ἑὸν Πατροκλῆα προσέειπε,
φθεγξάμενος παρὰ νηός· ὁ δὲ κλισίηθεν ἀκούσας
ἔκμολεν ἶσος "Αρηϊ, κακοῦ δ' ἄρα οἱ πέλεν ἀρχή.

At once Achilles spoke to his own companion in arms, Patroklos,
calling from the ship, and he heard it from inside the shelter
and came out like Ares, and this was the beginning of his evil.

Achilles sends Patroklos out to discover who has been wounded, for he thinks the time might be right for his return (609-10):

νῦν ὀΐω περὶ γούνατ' ἐμὰ στήσεσθαι 'Αχαιοὺς
λισσομένους· χρειὼ γὰρ ἱκάνεται οὐκέτ' ἀνεκτός.

Now I think the Achaeans will come to my knees and stay there
in supplication, for a need past endurance has come to them.

When Patroklos returns from his mission, he will tell Achilles what has just happened in Book 11 (Π 23-27):

οἱ μὲν γὰρ δὴ πάντες, ὅσοι πάρος ἦσαν ἄριστοι,
ἐν νηυσὶν κέαται βεβλημένοι οὐτάμενοί τε.
βέβληται μὲν ὁ Τυδεΐδης κρατερὸς Διομήδης,
οὔτασται δ' Ὀδυσεὺς δουρικλυτὸς ἠδ' Ἀγαμέμνων,
βέβληται δὲ καὶ Εὐρύπυλος κατὰ μηρὸν ὀϊστῷ.

For all those who were before the best in battle
are lying up among the ships with arrow or spear wounds.
The son of Tydeus, strong Diomedes, was hit by an arrow,
and Odysseus has a pike wound, and Agamemnon the spear-famed,
and Eurypylos has been wounded in the thigh with an arrow.

He will also repeat the request of Nestor (Λ 794-803 = Π 36-43) that Achilles send out the Myrmidons with Patroklos at their head. It seems that it is this escalation of the plot by means of Patroklos' involvement, already formulated by Zeus' prophecy back in Book 8 (475), which had to be set up in the story before Hector could meet Aias. Once this is done, the deferred confrontation between Aias and Hector can be narrated (Π 101-24). But, as Patroklos is returning to the tent of Achilles in Book 11, there is another "fateful" decision: Patroklos is waylaid by Eurypylos (822ff.), and the "main" plot of the poem is waylaid for what turns out to be four books. After the *teichomachia* of Book 12,[26] Poseidon enters the battle unbeknownst to Zeus and begins reversing his βουλή. In Book 14, the "plot" is literally put to sleep with the beguilement of Zeus by Hera. When Zeus awakens in Book 15, he is furious that his plan has been foiled and angrily tells Hera that he and nobody else will decide what the plot of the poem will be (Ο 53-77). He once more initiates his will, this time through the agency of Apollo,[27] and returns the story to the point it had reached at the end of Book 11. The long-awaited confrontation between Hector and Aias finally occurs; and after Hector shears the spear of Aias (Π 114ff.) and fires the ships, the stage is set for the "best of the Achaeans" to enter the battle. It is, of course, Patroklos and not Achilles who enters the battle, but this is not the only instance in the *Iliad* of a narrative trajectory which is truncated or modified, a process often flagged by the use of similes.

The woodsman simile with which we began provides the model of the articulation of the Διὸς βουλή in Book 11. The heroes will labor until they are overcome by a ἄδος/ὀδύνη, and retire to camp. The semantic content of this simile is determined by the absence of a preparatory meal: not, of course, that the Greeks will become hungry for food in the battle, but that the social cohesion that a communal meal signifies is lacking, and it is this which will cause them harm. The form and content of the following narrative is generated by the form and content of the woodsman simile. Several of the larger similes, in particular, are generated by the semantic content; one is generated by a phonic play which has its origin in the woodsman simile. With the introduction of Aias, there is a textual complication necessitating some substantial readjustment. Within the scope of this readjustment, the model of the woodsman simile asserts itself twice with the wounding of Machaon and the wounding of Eurypylos. There is also an example of a simile which restates and "corrects" a preceding simile to conform better with the pattern of the woodsman simile.

This last phenomenon is of great importance for Homer and deserves further comment. Berkeley Peabody has argued that the pattern of statement--retrogression--restatement, or statement--amplification--restatement, is a fundamental characteristic of oral poetry.[28] This basic pattern is responsible for a large part of the ubiquitous "ring composition" that so many scholars have identified in Homer. Peabody suggests, however, that there is a fundamental difference between ring composition in Homer, where it is basically a "correction" device, and ring composition in Pindar or Horace. In the latter, ring composition is cultivated as a rhetorical device, since it is no longer needed as a correction device. This is, in fact, the fate of many characteristics of Homeric narrative. When their functions in the textual dynamics became outmoded or were no longer understood, such features as ring composition, anaphora, etc., were perceived as rhetorical flowers and cultivated by later authors *qua* rhetorical devices. This, I shall argue, is the fate of that touchstone of the Homeric style, the epic simile.

Another example of this correction procedure occurs in the beginning of Book 11, just before the woodsman simile; and since it is connected with the cultural unit of a preparatory meal, it will be useful to consider it. As the Trojans are preparing for battle, Hector's armor flashes like the lightning of Zeus (66). This line introduces the Διὸς βουλή in connection with Hector and his imminent success; that is, it is a statement of the matrix of the narrative. It is followed by a reapers simile (Λ 67-69):

Οἱ δ', ὥς τ' ἀμητῆρες ἐναντίοι ἀλλήλοισιν

ὄγμον ἐλαύνωσιν ἀνδρὸς μάκαρος κατ' ἄρουραν
πυρῶν ἢ κριθῶν· τὰ δὲ δράγματα ταρφέα πίπτει.

And the men, like two lines of reapers who, facing each other,
drive their course all down the field of wheat or of barley
for a man blessed in substance, and the cut swathes drop thickly.

Krischer assigns this simile to the motif of the *unentscheidner Kampf,* often
a moment of pause before some turn in the battle.[29]  The simile is followed
by two and a half lines which amplify the notion of an "equal battle" (70-
72a),[30] and the text seems poised for the plunge into the narrative of the
battle.  The end of line 72 is οἱ δὲ λύκοι ὥς, the same words which intro-
duce the wolf simile in Book 16.  But this simile is left undeveloped; instead,
the poet restates the overwhelming presence of Zeus (75-83).  Then we seem
to have a new beginning with the *Zeitangabe* and the woodsman simile.  But
why this retrogression?

The reapers simile is related to the cultural unit of a preparatory meal,
a connection that would be by no means obvious did not Odysseus use a
similar comparison when he chides Achilles in Book 19 for refusing to eat
before fighting (T 221-25):

αἶψά τε φυλόπιδις πέλεται κόρος ἀνθρώποισιν
ἧς τε πλείστην μὲν καλάμην χθονὶ χαλκὸς ἔχευεν,
ἄμητος δ' ὀλίγιστος, ἐπὴν κλίνῃσι τάλαντα
Ζεύς, ὅς τ' ἀνθρώπων ταμίης πολέμοιο τέτυκται,
γαστέρι δ' οὔ πως ἔστι νέκυν πενθῆσαι Ἀχαιούς.

When there is a battle men suddenly have their fill of it
when the bronze scatters on the ground the straw in the most
numbers and the harvest is most thin, when Zeus has poised
his balance, Zeus, who is steward of men's battles.
There is no way the Achaeans can mourn a dead man by
denying the belly.

Odysseus' comparison is obscurely related to his point; but it is just this
obscurity (this "ungrammaticality") and the fact that the passage has a strong
gnomic character which suggests that there must be some traditional association of reaping with a preparatory meal.[31]  In Λ 67ff. the poet is fishing
about for just the right way to begin the battle.  The cultural unit of a
preparatory meal suggests itself as the semantic focus of the model of the

action by its absence in the preparation of the Greeks. The text generates the reapers simile, but it is not developed into a model for the succeeding narrative. Wolves come to mind, but this is not developed either. By this time the poet has wandered away from his matrix to the point of bringing in Eris, which apparently creates a problem, for the text immediately works itself back to the overwhelming presence of Zeus. Eris is εἰσορόωσα (73), "looking things over," but that is not important. What is important is that Zeus, who wishes to give glory to the Trojans (79) is looking things over: εἰσορόων (82). Now that he is back to Zeus, the poet tries again, this time successfully, to articulate a model for the action.

But why was Eris introduced here at all? Nothing in Homer is completely fortuitous: that is by theoretical fiat. If Eris is inappropriate at one level of the discourse, she must be appropriate at another level; for something generated her appearance in the text. In fact, Eris also has an important place in the semantic field of the communal meal. The basic meaning of ἔρις is, according to Trumpy, "das Bedurfnis sich zu messen,"[32] precisely that which can disturb the δαίς ἐΐση. In Book 1 of the *Iliad*, Hephaistos intervenes in the quarrel of Zeus and Hera, calling on them not to contend (ἐριδαίνετον) over mortals, for it will spoil the feast of the gods (οὐδέ τι δαιτὸς/ ἐσθλῆς ἔσσεται ἦδος, Α 575-76). Eris is also traditionally the one who spoiled the wedding feast of Peleus and Thetis in the *Cypria* (Allen V, p. 102). In the *Theogony* one of Eris' children is Λίμος, "Hunger," the result of an "unequal division." While on the battlefield in Book 4, finally, Eris distributes "equal portions of strife" to both sides, a travesty of the fair portions allotted to the heroes in communal meals (Δ 444-45):

ἥ σφιν καὶ τότε νεῖκος ὁμοίϊον ἔμβαλλε μέσσῳ
ἐρχομένη καθ᾽ ὅμιλον, ὀφέλλουσα στόνον ἀνδρῶν.

She then hurled down *bitterness equally* between both sides,
as she walked through the crowd, augmenting the groaning of men.

The result of her apportioning of νεῖκος is the "groaning of men," recalling the groaning which concludes the wolves' meal in Book 16.

So also, in the passage in Book 11, Eris is πολύστονος, "causing much groaning," reinforcing her connection with the lack of a communal meal in the preparation for battle. If the fair division of a meal signifies communal harmony and singlemindedness, the presence of Eris suggests the breakdown of that harmony. The lack of a preparatory meal at the beginning of Book 11 is a void marked by the presence of Eris, who is sent down to rouse the Greeks (Λ 22ff.). She it is who, screaming with her shrill voice puts σθένος into the heart of each man and makes war seem sweeter than going home.[33] In respect to the cultural unit of a communal meal, therefore, ἔρις πολύστονος has a significance similar to the reapers and the wolves of Λ 67-72. It is this semantic heritage which brings Eris into the text, an introduction which creates an anomaly an another level of textual organization, necessitating the retrogression and restatement of lines 74-84.

The picture of Homeric composition which emerges from this analysis of Book 11 runs counter to the one underlying most essentialist interpretive strategies. The tendency of such critics has been to analyze Homer's epics along the same lines as one would analyze, say, a Pindaric ode or a Vergilian eclogue. In these latter texts, elements of structure are foremost: balance, symmetry, parallelism, etc. Such traits make the linear unfolding of the text secondary to the text's wholeness, its closure, its existence as a single object able to be seen "all at once." At one level, one can say that for such characteristics to be primary requires what an oral poet does not really have and does not really have a need for: the opportunity to consider the poem's whole existence before beginning, or having completed a "first draft," to review it in detail and revise it into an "organically" unified whole. My discussion has emphasized the *forward propulsion* of Homeric narrative, a characteristic likely to be more legible in a text dominated by an oral poetics. The similes of Book 11 are means for propelling the narrative forward, for getting and keeping the text underway, and ring composition is a propulsive version of revision.

It is not that the poet has no idea where the text is going at the beginning; rather, there are innumerable ways of getting there, and as the text rolls forward, the factors which will determine its route are many. Other songs heard or sung, lexical and semantic associations, meter, mimetic considerations, even phonic similarities may lead the text this way or that. If one imagines, for example, the semantic field of Homer's language system as a vast network of connections implied by various coding correlations, each phrase or word of the text suggests many possible directions for development. This "embarass de richesses," as Nagler calls it, is perhaps the major difficulty of continuing an oral performance: not an *aporia*, but a *polyporia*. There are perhaps times when the poet launches on a certain track out of desperation, but this could be the exceptional case. It is more likely that the direction of the continuation will be "overdetermined" by its appropriateness on a number of levels of linguistic organization. All of these levels can be generative, or, when the poet is faced with a plenitude of possibilities from which one must be chosen, determinative.

To these linguistic factors must be added a host of non-linguistic ones: the audience's response, the nature of the occasion for the performance, the poet's physical condition, etc. The many gaps in our knowledge about the particulars of these factors makes it difficult to identify fully the textual dynamics operative at any particular moment. There is, however, one implication of the theory of codes which should be noted. There is no one level of linguistic organization which can be cited as primary; for they all interact simultaneously within the scope of the signifying system whose tendency toward internal coherence gives significance to all of its elements. Thus Eco replaces the notion of a hierarchy of textual "levels" with a scheme of metatextual "boxes" which

> are interconnected in a continuous coming and going. The cooperation of the interpreter at the lower levels can succeed only because some hypotheses which concern upper levels (and vice versa) are hazarded. The same happens also for a generative process: frequently an author makes decisions concerning the deep semantic structure of his story only at the moment in which he chooses at the lexical level, for merely stylistic reasons, a given expression.[34]

The Διὸς βουλή, for example, does seem to be the overall plot of the *Iliad*, but most of the poem can be related to that notion only in a very general way, for as the narrative is propelled forward, local issues of organization often override the larger movement of the plot. Thus, Cedric Whitman's attempt to discover the "geometric" structure of the *Iliad* seems most arbitrary when he deals with the broader correspondences.[35] It is dubious whether ring composition as a structural device could be a primary organizing force on the scale Whitman suggests.

It is a significant fact in itself that the ending of the *Iliad* (and for that matter, the endings of the *Odyssey*, the *Theogony, Beowulf, The Song of Roland*, etc.) have always seemed problematic, if not downright clumsy. The forward propulsion of these texts does not become finally used up or exhausted at the end of these works: it simply stops. The generative potential at the end of these works is just as full as it is anywhere else, and the text could literally have kept on going forever. Closure is anathema to a propulsive poetics, whose entire mechanism is geared to continuation, to preventing the breakdown of the performance. I do not mean to say that the endings of these works are completely fortuitous or that they do not achieve a resolution of sorts. Rather, the point is that the overall plot and its resolution is only one of the many concerns of the poet. The bulk of the *Iliad* and *Odyssey*, as the analysts never tired of pointing out, is devoted to all sorts of things which do not directly move the plot forward. If the *Iliad* and *Odyssey* are at all representative, it seems that Homer and his audience cared less about "getting the story told" (which was, for the most part, traditional and well known) than about all sorts of other things which are brought in along the way. Thus, although we can delineate with Whitman and others the overall plot of the poem, this plot will be a loose "skeleton," not the "soul" of the work, as Aristotle thought. And although it will be a determinative and generative force in the narrative, it will not be so uniformly, nor will it necessarily be the primary generator of text.

On the other end of the spectrum, Berkeley Peabody's assumption that the primary generative force in Greek epic is phonic seems equally imbalanced.[36] The phonic level of linguistic organization has always been deemed important in poetry, but like metrical or mimetic considerations, the phonic level cannot be analyzed apart from the other potentials of language. Homeric narrative, above all, keeps on going, and the way that one thing leads to the next may result from any one or any combination of different levels of linguistic potential. A narrative situation may generate a simile; but a simile may also generate a whole narrative sequence. The critic of Homer will be on safest ground when a swathe of text can be shown to be overdetermined on a number of levels.

More generally, it can be seen that the notion that a text--any text--is "unified" and is an internally coherent system, even in Riffaterre's sense as a "sustained relationship to one structure" (*Semiotics of Poetry*, 6), falls into the trap of seeing literature as mere *repetition*, however innovative. Such a view inevitably minimizes the degree to which texts such as the *Iliad* are examples of social practice, of someone trying to *do* something at a certain moment in a certain social context. Riffaterre identifies the function of poetry in general as aesthetic play, a game with words whose consequences are only aesthetic. This, however, is merely a modernist version of the traditional notion of the poet as "genius" who transmits to his/her audience essential and enduring truths to which the poet has some privileged access.

To replace this romantic notion with a picture of Homer struggling along, becoming confused, changing his mind in midstream, may seem more scandalous than Parry's oral-formulaic theory, but it is a necessary consequence of a perspective which takes seriously the critique of essentialist theories of meaning. If the poet is not merely repeating the words of the gods, but is engaged in some form of social practice, it is not unlikely that he will occasionally stumble; and such human frailty in Homer is not, *pace* Horace, a disgrace.

More importantly, we can add to Riffaterre's thesis that poetry is a transformation or repetition of some *textual* structure the thesis that poetry is also an attempt to transform or preserve a *social* structure, an attempt to raise and resolve the problems and thoughts of a community in which the poet also acts and thinks. This means that the poet is also caught up in the contradictions and problems that the text articulates, and that the poet also has some effect on those problems and contradictions. It is, in fact, the dialectical relationship between code and message, between text and reader, between addressee and addresser, which necessitates this view of the poet. If Riffaterre's "intertextual" analysis is incomplete, he nevertheless is the one who foregrounds for us this dialectic and puts in our hands the very tools with which we can go beyond his more strictly aesthetic concerns; for the social aspect of a literary work is not a *representation* of a social structure which preexists that work, even if a significant part of the labor of textual production is designed to give that impression. The relationship between social structure and text is, rather, one of indirection, distortion and transformation. The relationship between text and society is not *mimetic* (a reflection of social reality), but *semiotic* (a dialectical distortion or transformation of social reality). The social problem or contradiction to which the text tries to articulate a solution can thus be thought of as a sort of hypogram, a system which emerges as the focus of a text in part by its structured *absence*.[37]

This notion is quite different from the various "functionalist" versions of the cultural effects and uses of literature, in which literature merely confirms already existing social relations. It has often been asserted, for example, that Homer's language is a homogeneous and internally coherent system which reflects and confirms a homogeneous and cohesive social order.[38] The function of texts and other cultural practices thus becomes the reinforcement of that cohesiveness and homogeneity. Our focus on the cultural unit of a communal meal as an instance of such cultural reinforcement should allow us to draw the difference between such a "mimetic" view of the *Iliad* and a more properly semiotic one.

### The Meal as Cultural Unit: Conclusion

Let us begin by considering the various examples of the preparatory meals of the *Iliad* as a series. The first day of battle is preceded and closed off by fully described meals (B 410ff. and H 314ff.). On that day, Zeus is not particularly active in advancing his plan to honor Achilles, a fact which led many "old analysts" to hypothesize that the first part of the *Ur-Ilias* consisted of Books 1-2, 8 and 11.[39] It is on the second day of battle that Zeus earnestly begins giving glory to the Trojans and trouble to the Greeks. Before this battle there is only a brief summary of the Greeks' preparation (Θ 53-54) and they eat "hastily" (ῥίμφα). In Book 11, the beginning of the day which will be by far the most disastrous for the Greeks, there is no preparatory meal, and the omission determines in part the character of the subsequent narrative. This disappearing act of the preparatory meal can be taken as an index of the advancing dissolution of the Greek situation due to Achilles' absence. Later that same day, when the Myrmidons go forth without Achilles, there is a conversion of the preparatory meal in the wolf simile (Π 157ff.). On the final day of battle beginning in Book 19, there is Achilles' outright refusal to participate in the preparatory meal advocated by Odysseus, who defends the significance of the cultural unit. At the height of Achilles' mad rampage in Book 22, he threatens to eat Hector raw. Then in Book 23 Achilles diffidently becomes reconciled with the Greeks (see esp. ψ 156-60), and the final resolution comes in Book 24, when Achilles shares a meal with Priam.

The nature of this resolution Nagler treats in terms of Achilles' reconciliation with his own mortality, his "creaturality," a reconciliation by which Achilles achieves a "generic status" and becomes a "counterpoint of the gods" (*Spontaneity*, 197-98). But one can go beyond this view of the poem. Eating is indeed a sign of one's creaturality; but within the scope of any particular culture, the necessity of eating becomes the *occasion* for the ritual affirmation of communal bonds. The simple fact of consuming food is a sufficient indication of one's creaturality; but the ritual preparation, distribution and apportioning of food have a more specific communicative function, a function which is at stake in the *Iliad* in a significant way. Readings like Nagler's see the poem as the unfolding of a predetermined content, culminating in an epiphany in the final scene with Priam and Achilles. A more semiotic reading would show how the text tries to *construct* a certain content which exists only as a series of textualized "versions" which are transformations of each other. But as Riffaterre notes, a rigorous "mimetic" reading is often the precondition for a "semiotic" reading. Thus, we can proceed by following more orthodox interpretations of the poem, concentrating our attention on the communicative aspects, and this will allow us to rethink the significance of the resolution of the poem.

A ritual such as a communal meal is the most predetermined and explicitly coded form of language. As such, it does not admit of much discursive variety: the participation in a communal meal simply signifies one's identification within some social system; and one is, so to speak, either in or out. Achilles rejects his identity within the Greek "culture" by, among other things, refusing to perform the ritual action of sharing a meal. He repudiates the role assigned to him and at the same time tries to assert new grounds for his identity; and this entails asserting his own individual language against the predetermined communal language of the Greeks. When the emissaries come to Achilles in Book 9, they find him and Patroklos sitting together singing in alternation the κλέα ἀνδρῶν, "the glories of men" (I 189). The κλέα ἀνδρῶν (from κλύω, "to hear") comprise the collective cultural history transmitted by the oral tradition. A man's κλέος is his identity as established within the scope of culture.[40] Achilles has rejected the identity assigned to him; and although his "new" identity is largely negative (a "Not-Achilles"), here he and Patroklos seem to be "re-writing" a culture of their own, a situation Achilles expressly wishes for in Book 16 (Π 97-100, quoted above, p. 39):

Father Zeus, Athena, and Apollo, would that
not one of all the Trojans would escape destruction,
nor one of the Argives, but only you [Patroklos] and I
would emerge from the slaughter so that we alone could
break Troy's hallowed coronal.

The first thing Odysseus suggests to Achilles in the embassy is that he is welcome to come and eat with Agamemnon (I 225-8):

χαῖρ' Ἀχιλεῦ· δαιτὸς μὲν ἐΐσης οὐκ ἐπιδευεῖς
ἠμὲν ἐνὶ κλισίῃ Ἀγαμέμνονος Ἀτρεΐδαο
ἠδὲ καὶ ἐνθάδε νῦν· πάρα γὰρ μενοεικέα πολλὰ
δαίνυνθ'.

Your health, Achilles. You have no lack of an *equal portion*
either within the shelter of Atreus' son Agamemnon
nor here in your own. You have good things in abundance
to feast on.

In response to Odysseus' plea that he return to his former role as champion of
the Greeks, Achilles states that he will "speak out his meaning *without consideration of his audience*," τὸν μῦθον ἀπηλεγέως ἀποειπεῖν (I 309).[41]
Achilles' answer strikes the other Greeks as nonsense, for he does not respond
in a way determined by the heroic "code," but in a private language which,
since it is being articulated for the first time, has no appropriate interpretants.
When Achilles sends out Patroklos with the Myrmidons in Book 16, this too
is condemned within the scope of culture by (among other things) the wolf
simile, which assigns a negative value to the actions of Achilles. When
Patroklos is killed, Achilles refuses to eat at all, for now he has no one to eat
*with* (T 315-21, cited above, p. 36):

There was a time, ill-fated, o dearest of my companions,
when you would set the desirable dinner before me
quickly and expertly, at the time the Achaeans were urgent
to carry the sorrowful war on the Trojans, breakers of horses.
But now you lie here torn before me, and my heart goes starved
for meat and drink, though they are here beside me,
for want of you. There is nothing worse than this that I could suffer.

There is no such thing as a culture of just one person. Achilles' attempt to
articulate an alternative "code" results in his total isolation, first from the
other Greeks, then from Patroklos (who does not "observe the word of
Achilles," Π 686). That Achilles has no one to eat with means that he has
no one to "understand" him. He has said in Book 9 that if Zeus honors him,
that will be enough and he does not require τιμή from the Greeks (I 607-10).
But after the death of Patroklos, he finds no joy in the τιμή of Zeus (Σ 72-
81):

καὶ ῥ' ὀλοφυρομένη ἔπεα πτερόεντα προσηύδα·
"τέκνον, τί κλαίεις; τί δέ σε φρένας ἵκετο πένθος;
ἐξαύδα, μὴ κεῦθε· τὰ μὲν δή τοι τετέλεσται
ἐκ Διός, ὡς ἄρα δὴ πρίν γ' εὔχεο χεῖρας ἀνασχών,
πάντας ἐπὶ πρύμνῃσιν ἀλήμεναι υἷας Ἀχαιῶν
σεῦ ἐπιδευομένους, παθέειν τ' ἀεκήλια ἔργα."

τὴν δὲ βαρὺ στενάχων προσέφη πόδας ὠκὺς Ἀχιλλεὺς·
"μῆτερ ἐμή, τὰ μὲν ἄρ μοι Ὀλύμπιος ἐξετέλεσσεν·
ἀλλὰ τι μοι τῶν ἦδος, ἐπεὶ φίλος ὤλεθ' ἑταῖρος,
Πάτροκλος, τὸν ἐγὼ περὶ πάντων τῖον ἑταίρων."

Sorrowing for him, Thetis spoke in winged words,
"Why then, child, do you lament? what sorrow has come upon you?
Speak out, do not hide it. These things are accomplished
through Zeus in the way that you lifted your hands and prayed for,
that all the sons of the Achaeans be pinned on their grounded
vessels for lack of you, and suffer things that are shameful."
Then, groaning heavily, Achilles of the swift feet answered her:
"My mother, all these things the Olympian brought to
accomplishment, but what pleasure is this to me, since my
dear companion has perished, Patroklos, whom I loved
beyond all others."

The words of Thetis in this remarkable passage are as "ungrammatical" as Achilles' actions in Book 16. Does Thetis really think that Achilles has gotten what he wanted? It is possible to explain away the problem by claiming that Thetis is being ironic or simply very insensitive, but such explanations fail to recognize the truly contradictory nature of Achilles' position. Achilles wants to stay, but he wants to leave; he does not want to be "in," but he does not want to be "left out." When he tries to explain this to others, it keeps coming out as a groan. The response of Thetis here, like the response of Patroklos and the other Greeks, foregrounds this inability of Achilles to make himself understood.[42]

After Achilles kills Hector, he seems to come to terms with the other Greeks in Book 23; but his negative actions at the beginning of Book 24 show that things have still not been set right (Ω 1-6):

λῦτο δ' ἀγών, λαοὶ δὲ θοὰς ἐπὶ νῆας ἕκαστοι
ἐσκίδναντ' ἰέναι. τοὶ μὲν δόρποιο μέδοντο
ὕπνου τε γλυκεροῦ ταρπήμεναι· αὐτὰρ Ἀχιλλεὺς
κλαῖε φίλου ἑτάρου μεμνημένος, οὐδέ μιν ὕπνος
ἥρει πανδαμάτωρ, ἀλλ' ἐστρέφετ' ἔνθα καὶ ἔνθα,
Πατρόκλου ποθέων ἀνδροτῆτά τε καὶ μένος ἠΰ.

The games broke up, and the people scattered to go, each
to his fast ship, *and the rest of them took thought of dinner*
and of sweet sleep and its enjoyment; *only Achilles*
wept still as he remembered his beloved companion, nor did

sleep who subdues all overcome him, but he tossed here and there, wanting Patroklos, his manhood and his great strength.

There is a pointed contrast here between the rest of the Greeks, who take dinner and then go to sleep, and Achilles, who neither eats nor sleeps. But in the final scenes of this last book, Achilles achieves a resolution which moves beyond both the predetermined language of the communal meal and idiosyncratic language. This resolution is precipitated by a whole range of structural and thematic issues, that have been noted by many readers of Homer. What follows is a rehearsal of these issues with an attempt to rethink them vis-à-vis the communicative aspects of the situation.

Throughout Book 24, the similarity of situation between Achilles and Priam is pointedly made. Since Hector's death, as he tells Achilles after their meal, Priam too has "groaned" instead of participating in communal activities (Ω 637-42):[43]

οὐ γάρ πω μύσαν ὄσσε ὑπὸ βλεφάροισιν ἐμοῖσιν
ἐξ οὗ σῆς ὑπὸ χερσὶν ἐμὸς πάϊς ὤλεσε θυμόν,
ἀλλ᾽ αἰεὶ στενάχω καὶ κήδεα μυρία πέσσω,
αὐλῆς ἐν χόρτοισι κυλινδόμενος κατὰ κόπρον.
νῦν δὴ καὶ σίτου πασάμην καὶ αἴθοπα οἶνον
λαυκανίης καθέηκα· πάρος γε μὲν οὔ τι πεπάσμην.

For my eyes have not closed underneath my lids since that time
when my son lost his life beneath your hands,
but *always I have been groaning* and swallowing my numberless sorrows,
wallowing in the dung about my courtyard's enclosure.
Now I have tasted food again and have let the gleaming wine
down my throat. *Before I had tasted nothing.*

Like Achilles, Priam has suffered the worst thing possible (compare T 231 with Ω 393-94) and has endured what no other man has endured (Ω 505-6):

ἔτλην δ᾽ οἷ᾽ οὔ πώ τις ἐπιχθόνιος βροτὸς ἄλλος,
ἀνδρὸς παιδοφόνοιο ποτὶ στόμα χεῖρ᾽ ὀρέγεσθαι.

I have endured what no other mortal on earth has gone through,
I put my hands to the lips of the man who has killed my children.

This unique gesture, like Achilles' own attempts to say something "new" and uncoded, is incomprehensible to the other Trojans. Hecuba assumes that Priam has gone mad when he states his intention to go to Achilles (Ω 200-5). Priam, meanwhile, reviles the other Trojans and especially his surviving sons, who he wishes had all died instead of Hector, even as Achilles had wished all but he and Patroklos would survive (Ω 253-54; cf. Π 97-100). All these associations and identifications serve to emphasize that Priam is an appropriate "audience" for the unique and innovative language of Achilles.

The isolation of Achilles and Priam is emphasized throughout the scene.[44] The Trojans weep as Priam leaves the city, "as though he were going to his death" (328). When he enters Achilles' tent, Priam initially escapes the notice of all but Achilles (477), who is himself sitting apart from his companions (473). When Achilles notices Priam, he wonders at him as a man would wonder at the sight of a suppliant who has been banished from his own land, in Greek culture the most alienated situation possible (Ω 480-3). After the plea of Priam, Achilles and he together fill the house with their mutual and reciprocal "groaning" (Ω 509-12):

τὼ δὲ μνησαμένω, ὁ μὲν ῞Εκτορος ἀνδροφόνοιο
κλαῖ᾽ ἀδινὰ προπάροιθε ποδῶν Ἀχιλῆος ἐλυσθείς,
αὐτὰρ Ἀχιλλεὺς κλαῖεν ἑὸν πατέρ᾽, ἄλλοτε δ᾽ αὖτε
Πάτροκλον· τῶν δὲ στοναχὴ κατὰ δώματ᾽ ὀρώρει.

And the two remembered, as Priam sat huddled at the feet
of Achilles and wept for manslaughtering Hector
and Achilles wept now for his own father, now again
for Patroklos. The *sound of groaning* moved in the house.

The groan is, as I have said, an undifferentiated expression, not as yet corre-lated with a differentiated content. It is an expression which is not yet coded, which is not yet language. The wolves, for this reason, groan in the simile of Book 16, for their meal negates the signifying function of a heroic meal. Elsewhere, Achilles opposes groaning to culturally coded behavior, specifi-cally eating a communal meal. Angered as he is about Patroklos' death, for example, Achilles desires not food, but the στόνος ἀνδρῶν, the "groaning of men" (Τ 214). When the heroes gather around him to urge him to eat, he "refuses with a groan" (Τ 304: ὁ δ᾽ ἠρνεῖτο στεναχίζων). When the other

Greeks eat in Book 23, Achilles instead "lies on the beach groaning deeply" (Ψ 60: κεῖτο βαρὺ στενάχων). All the negative, anti-social behavior of Achilles is summarized in this unarticulated groan, perceived by others as nonsense, for it is correlated to a content which is as yet "ineffable" within the scope of culture, and as such is not yet language.[45]

But when Achilles and Priam "groan" together, it seems to be a sort of communicative exchange, a sort of "phatic" address by these two alienated individuals who have so much in common. The lines following this groaning echo the endings of meals as though something comparable to a communal meal had just ended (Ω 513-15):

αὐτὰρ ἐπεί ῥα γόοιο τετάρπετο δῖος Ἀχιλλεύς,
καί οἱ ἀπὸ πραπίδων ἦλθ' ἵμερος ἠδ' ἀπὸ γυίων,
αὐτίκ' ἀπὸ θρόνου ὦρτο, γέροντα δὲ χειρὸς ἀνίστη.

When great Achilles had taken his full satisfaction of *groaning*
and the passion for it had gone from his mind and body,
immediately he rose from his seat and took the old man by the hand.

This initial exchange is then followed by the meal which they share, itself the framework for the articulation of a new language. Here is the end of the meal (Ω 628-34):

αὐτὰρ ἐπεὶ πόσιος καὶ ἐδητύος ἐξ ἔρον ἔντο,
ἤτοι Δαρδανίδης Πρίαμος θαύμαζ' Ἀχιλῆα,
ὅσσος ἔην οἷός τε· θεοῖσι γὰρ ἄντα ἐῴκει·
αὐτὰρ ὁ Δαρδανίδην Πρίαμον θαύμαζεν Ἀχιλλεύς,
εἰσορόων ὄψίν τ' ἀγαθὴν καὶ μῦθον ἀκούων,
αὐτὰρ ἐπεὶ τάρπησαν ἐς ἀλλήλους ὁρόωντες,
τὸν *πρότερος προσέειπε* γέρων Πρίαμος θεοειδής.

But when they had set aside their desire for eating and drinking,
Priam, son of Dardanos, gazed on Achilles, wondering
at his size and beauty, for he seemed like one of the gods.
But Achilles in turn gazed on Dardanian Priam
and wondered, as he saw his brave looks and *listened to him talking*.
But when they had taken their fill of gazing on one another,
*first of the two to speak* was the aged man, Priam the godlike.

This is the acknowledged climax of the poem and it is strikingly "epiphanic" sounding. Nagler sees in these lines a resolution in four dimensions (*Spontaneity*, 197):

> Achilles and Priam are reconciled, they participate together in well-earned creatural enjoyments, they honor one another, and finally, in the act of visual admiration, they realize for one another the all-important element of *charis*.

To these we must add the communicative dimension, for the silent exchange of Priam and Achilles is also the climax of Achilles' attempt to articulate an alternative code. Between the ritual meal, which is predetermined language, and the first words of Priam, the mutual and reciprocal "gazing" constitutes another language act, a reciprocal "defining" of each other. I have emphasized two phrases in the passage above which make up what appears to be a minor "nod" on Homer's part. But μῦθον ἀκούων in line 632 should perhaps be translated "understanding his meaning,"[46] for the entire context seems to imply that the gazing is a form of communication. The position of the gazing, for example, immediately after the formulaic closing of the meal (628), is where one expects someone to get up and speak.[47] Moreover, lines 633-34 themselves resemble such formulaic endings of meals, as though the gazing itself has a social and communicative function similar to a communal meal. The gazing is thus positioned in such a way as to implicitly compare it to both the predetermined language of a meal and verbal language. Achilles and Priam become, as it were, "interpretants" of each other, imitating by this mutual gazing the mirroring effect of language which is its fundamental mechanism: the bouncing back and forth from one sign to another, establishing thereby the sequence of interpretants which circumscribes a content unit. The private language of Achilles is no longer nonsense, for he has found someone to understand it (him). This intense exchange establishes the self-identity aside from the one assigned him by culture that Achilles has sought all along. It is Priam, not Patroklos, not Agamemnon, not even Zeus, from whom Achilles receives his long-sought-for τιμή.

The importance of the communicative aspect of the resolution is that it allows us to frame the poem's various thematic preoccupations within the context of a discursive crisis. That is, the *Iliad* can be seen as an articulation of a crisis, a moment of transformation, in the very *form* of culture: its discursive organization. It is beyond the scope of this study to analyze the precise terms of the social, political and economic turbulence which produced this crisis, but it is possible to sketch out briefly the implications of our view of the poem for certain key conflicts. This should not be taken as a definitive historical account, but rather as an attempt to suggest the kind of cultural "problematic" of which the *Iliad* could be a discursive transformation.

Politically, the *Iliad* brings into full view the arbitrariness of Agamemnon's "hereditary" authority, reflected in the arbitrariness of Zeus himself; for the ideology of "inherited excellence," which justifies hereditary authority is propped up mainly by reference to divine favor. The very fact that the validity of Agamemnon's preeminence becomes a subject for discussion and is no longer "taken for granted," indicates that this piece of aristocratic ideology is already in jeopardy.[48]

Economically, at the same time, the *Iliad* exposes the objective reality of the distribution of prizes: namely, that it is a form of payment for services rendered. For the "misrecognition" of the fact that the *dasmos* is a form of payment is effected by treating the distribution of prizes as an act of generosity independent of the fighting of the heroes, who fight not for prizes but out of a "sense of honor."[49] When Achilles is provoked by Agamemnon's arbitrary seizure of his prize to connect explicitly the value of one's prize with the value of one's labor, he calls into question the entire economic apparatus which supports Agamemnon's authority: his right to give out prizes as he sees fit. Once Achilles has unmasked the *dasmos* for what it is and has refused to submit anymore to the authority of Agamemnon, it becomes impossible for him to be persuaded to return by means of prizes, since that would make him a mere mercenary. Achilles has, so to speak, burned all his bridges back into the Greek community, and hence his wish in Book 16 that all the Greeks and Trojans would die so that he and Patroklos could start over. Patroklos' death provides Achilles with an "honorable" way out of this dilemma, but despite his subsequent deference to Agamemnon in Book 23, Achilles never really "returns."

In terms of social relations, the *Iliad* can be seen to be poised between the breakdown of a social organization based on a shared communality, implicitly acknowledged in rituals such as the communal meal (a *Gemeinschaft*), and a new social organization in which the individual will be constituted as such, and his relationship to society will become more explicitly formalized (a *Gesellschaft*). Such a transition inevitably entails the breakdown of the ties binding together the old *Gemeinschaft*, a process perceived by members of that society as alienation. Achilles and Priam in Book 24 of the *Iliad*, wrenched from their previous communal contexts, bereft of their most precious loved ones and establishing an extraordinary relationship with each other, are, at some level, figures of the kind of individual who will make up this new kind of community; and the little community which Priam and Achilles wordlessly establish is itself a forerunner of this new social organization; but it is a community whose discourse is, in the *Iliad*, still unformulated. The *Iliad* is thus a meditation on a profound cultural dilemma specific to the poet's historical moment. Nevertheless, the historical specificity of that dilemma is masked in part as a representation of an eternal and transcendental crisis faced by "Mankind" in general. To see the poem as an embodiment of some such eternal Truth, however, is to take at face value the claim that the text is a divinely inspired *mimesis*. It is to fall into a trap which is set, so to speak, by the text itself.

## Similes as Textual Interpretants

At the end of Book 2 of the *Iliad*, the setting out of the Greeks is graced with the following simile (B 780-84):

Οἱ δ' ἄρ' ἴσαν ὡς εἴ τε πυρὶ χθὼν πᾶσα νέμοιτο·
γαῖα δ' ὑπεστενάχιζε Διὶ ὣς τερπικεραύνῳ
χωομένῳ, ὅτε τ' ἀμφὶ Τυφωέϊ γαῖαν ἱμάσσῃ
εἰν Ἀρίμοις, ὅθι φασὶ Τυφωέος ἔμμεναι εὐνάς·
ὣς ἄρα τῶν ὑπὸ ποσσὶ μέγα στεναχίζετο γαῖα.

But the rest went forward, as if all the earth with flame were
eaten, and the ground groaned under them, as if Zeus who delights
in the thunder were angry, as when he batters the earth about Typhoeus
in the land of the Arimoi, where they say Typhoeus lies prostrate.
Beneath their feet the ground groaned heavily.

This remarkable simile is the only one in Homer which explicitly alludes to another song, the Typhonomachy. By coincidence, there is an account of the Typhonomachy extant in Hesiod's *Theogony*, so that here is a rare opportunity for an intertextual study in the narrow sense. That is, this simile allows us to look at a simile generated at the most complex level of linguistic organization: another song. In our discussion, however, we will not be concerned with the historical relationship between Homer and Hesiod, although the following analyses will seem to assume that Homer knew Hesiod's text in detail. Meaning is produced by difference. By invoking Hesiod's text as an interpretant of Homer, meaning will be produced in this intertext. This would be true regardless of the precise historical circumstances surrounding the composition of these works, regardless of the conscious or unconscious intentions of Homer.

A message does not have a meaning because someone intended that meaning; it has meaning because it exists in a system. There are many potential interpretants which can produce meaning in a message. Of particular interest among these possibilities is a contemporary text like Hesiod's. Despite gaps in our knowledge about the history of Greek epic, it is clear that Hesiod and Homer are nearly contemporary and are products of related traditions. This means that the signification system of Homer is closer to the signification system of Hesiod than anything else. Hence, meaning produced by the collocation of these texts will be privileged historically, particularly in view of the absence of alternatives of equal status. Thus, the question of Hesiod's influence or Homer's direct knowledge of Hesiod can be laid aside as a matter beyond substantiation. Instead we can assume that Hesiod and Homer both vary some prior "text" of the Typhonomachy, and that however numerous the mediations, Hesiod's text can give privileged information about the coding correlations which are an explanatory condition for Homer's text.

An example will perhaps clarify the issue. In B 87ff., the Greek host is compared to a swarm of bees. What sort of implications could such a comparison have? What in the configuration of the sememe of bees in Homeric culture could have made the production of this particular simile at this particular place appropriate at some level? For a modern reader, reared on the pastoral tradition, bees may suggest an ideally harmonious society; but this is not necessarily a Homeric notion. In Hesiod there are two bee similes (*Theogony* 594-600; *Erga* 304-7), both times as examples of social inequity: the bees work hard; the lazy drones do nothing but consume honey. Now Achilles accuses Agamemnon of being a δημοβόρος βασιλεύς (A 231; cf. I 330-33), a king who "consumes the people" and does nothing himself. The comparison of the Greeks to bees perhaps suggests the fruitlessness of their labors when they have a drone for a king.[50] The Hesiodic loci are not necessarily the source for the Homeric simile, but they do imply information about the sememe of bees in archaic epic, information which is more relevant to Homer than, say, Semonides' comparison of the model wife to a bee. What then does Hesiod's account of the story of Typhoeus imply about Homer's Typhoeus simile? The Typhonomachy is part of the succession myth of Zeus. Whatever else one may want to say about this story, it is clear that Typhoeus challenges the preeminence of Zeus; or in Homeric terms, he challenges the τιμή of Zeus as king of the gods. The plot of the *Iliad*, the Διὸς βουλή, is to establish Achilles' injured τιμή. When Thetis intercedes for Achilles, she reminds Zeus that she herself had previously acted to guarantee his preeminence (A 396-406). The identification of the τιμή of Achilles and the τιμή of Zeus is immediately made by Hera's challenge (A 552-59) and Zeus' response (A 564-67; cf. also Hephaistos' warning to Hera in A 580-81). Elsewhere when someone intervenes to help the Greeks, Zeus again treats this contravention of the plot as a threat to his τιμή (Θ 5-27, O 14-33). In short, the simile of Typhoeus is one of a series of identifications made between the establishment of Zeus' honor and the establishment of Achilles' honor. The Greeks' attempt to sack Troy without Achilles is like Typhoeus' attempt to overthrow Zeus.

These preliminary remarks could have been made on the basis of a summary knowledge of the Typhonomachy, but the text of Hesiod allows us to analyze in a detailed way how the Typhoeus story plays a text-constitutive role in Book 2 of the *Iliad*. We will not be so interested in how the general framework of a succession myth is "realized" in the *Iliad*; nor will we be interested in showing how both texts are "multiforms" of some underlying plot pattern. Rather, we will be trying to reconstruct the traditional network of correlations associated with Typhoeus and investigate the text-formative role they play in the *Iliad*.

To begin with, the Typhoeus simile is itself an expansion of the initial comparison of a vast fire, an image which is also found before the catalogue:

Οἱ δ' ἄρ ἴσαν ὡς εἴ τε πυρὶ χθὼν πᾶσα νέμοιτο (B 780)

But the rest went forward, as if all the earth with flames were eaten.

ἠΰτε πῦρ ἀΐδηλον ἐπιφλέγει ἄσπετον ὕλην (B 455)

As obliterating fire consumes a boundless forest.

The scorching of the earth makes up a large part of the description of the Typhonomachy. Here are some of the relevant passages (*Theogony* 844-47, 859-61):

καῦμα δ' ὑπ' ἀμφοτέρων κάτεχεν ἰοειδέα πόντον
βροντῆς τε στεροπῆς τε πυρὸς τ' ἀπὸ τοῖο πελώρου
πρηστήρων ἀνέμων τε κεραυνοῦ τε φλεγέθοντος,
ἔζεε δὲ χθὼν πᾶσα καὶ οὐρανὸς ἠδὲ θάλασσα....
φλὸξ δὲ κεραυνωθέντος ἀπέσσυτο τοῖο ἄνακτος
οὔρεος ἐν βήσσῃσιν ἀϊδνῆς παιπαλοέσσης
πληγέντος· πολλὴ δὲ πελώρη καίετο γαῖα.

The purple sea was seized by heat from both,
from the thunder and lightning, and from the fire the
monster bore: the burning hurricane and blazing thunderbolt.
The whole earth boiled and the heaven and the sea....
A flame leaped from the lightning-blasted lord,
when he was struck, on the jagged mountainside.
Great earth was widely scorched by the awful blast.

Similar details describe the battle with the Titans (*Theogony* 693-97):[51]

ἀμφὶ δὲ γαῖα φερέσβιος ἐσμαράγιζε
καιομένη, λάκε δ' ἀμφὶ πυρὶ μεγάλ' ἄσπετος ὕλη·
ἔζεε δὲ χθὼν πᾶσα καὶ Ὠκεανοῖο ῥέεθρα
πόντος τ' ἀτρύγετος· τοὺς δ' ἄμφεπε θερμὸς ἀϋτμὴ
Τιτῆνας χθονίους, φλὸξ δ' ἠέρα δῖαν ἵκανεν
ἄσπετος.

The fertile earth being burnt, roared out,
the voiceless forest cried and crackled with fire;
the whole earth boiled and Ocean's streams, and the
unfruitful sea. The hot blast reached the earthborn
Titans; flames unspeakable rose to the upper air.

The fire which overtakes the earth during these battles threatens the "cosmic balance" at the mythological level; earth, heaven and sea are confounded and the result is chaos. One of the peculiar manifestations of this chaos is the "groaning" of the earth (*Theogony* 843, 858):[52]

ἐπεστενάχιζε δὲ γαῖα

στενάχιζε δὲ γαῖα πελώρη

The heavens also "groan" in the Titanomachy (*Theo.* 679):

ἐπέστενε δ' οὐρανὸς εὐρὺς.

This detail is not only repeated in the Typhoeus simile (B 781, 784), but also occurs in the initial mustering of the troops (B 95):

τετρήχει δ' ἀγορή, ὑπὸ δὲ στεναχίζετο γαῖα.

And their meeting place was shaken, and the earth groaned.

The gathering of the troops to set out without Achilles is thus framed by these two references to the earth's groaning, and nowhere else in Homer does the earth groan. She does, however, make other similar noises. In the midst of the sequence of similes preceding the catalog, the earth "thunders" under the feet of the Achaeans (B 465-66):

αὐτὰρ ὑπὸ χθὼν
σμερδαλέον κονάβιζε ποδῶν αὐτῶν τε καὶ ἵππων.

But the earth below
the feet of the men and horses thundered terribly.

The earth also "thunders" in the Typhonomachy (*Theo.* 839-40):

σκληρὸν δ' ἐβρόντησε καὶ ὄβριμον, ἀμφὶ δὲ γαῖα
σμερδαλέον κονάβησε καὶ οὐρανὸς εὐρὺς ὕπερθεν.

But Zeus thundered mightily and fiercely, and the
earth thundered terribly, and also the heavens above.

These are the only two occurrences of the earth's "thundering" in either text and like the other inarticulate sounds that the earth, sea and heavens make, it seems to signify a moment of undecidability, of unintelligibility, such as accompanies a challenge to a principle of order.

Another unusual word which seems to have a similar function is the verb σμαραγέω/ σμαραγίζω. Three forms of this rare word appear in Hesiod only in reference to the Titanomachy (*Theo.* 678-79, 693-94):

δεινὸν δὲ περίαχε πόντος ἀπείρων,

γῆ δὲ μέγ' ἐσμαράγησεν, ἐπέστενε δ' οὐρανὸς εὐρύς.

The boundless sea roared terribly around;
The great earth *rumbled* (?), and the broad heaven groaned.

ἀμφὶ δὲ γαῖα φερέσβιος ἐσμαράγιζε
καιομένη, λάκε δ' ἀμφὶ πυρὶ μεγάλ' ἄσπετος ὕλη.

The fertile earth being burnt *roared out* (?)
the voiceless forest cried out from the great fire.

After the defeat of the Titans, they are sent to Tartarus, which is described at length. Then we have (*Theo.* 813-16):

πρόσθεν δὲ θεῶν ἔκτοσθεν ἀπάντων
Τιτῆνες ναίουσι, πέρην χάεος ζοφεροῖο.
αὐτὰρ ἐρισμαράγοιο Διὸς κλειτοὶ ἐπίκουροι
δώματα ναιετάουσιν ἐπ' Ὠκεανοῖο θεμέθλοις.

And further on, apart from all the gods
the Titans live, out beyond Chaos' gloom.
But the allies of *wide-thundering* (?) Zeus
inhabit homes on the ocean floor.

Aside from these, there are only three other occurrences of this rare word in archaic literature;[53] and two of them are in similes describing the host in Book 2 (B 208-10, B 459-63):

αὖτις ἐπεσσεύοντο νεῶν ἄπο καὶ κλισιάων
ἠχῇ, ὡς ὅτε κῦμα πολυφλοίσβοιο θαλάσσης
αἰγιαλῷ μεγάλῳ βρέμεται, σμαραγεῖ δέ τε πόντος.

But they rushed back from the ships and the tents
with a roar, as when a wave of the much echoing sea
crashes on a great beach, and the sea *roars* (?).

τῶν δ' ὥς τ' ὀρνίθων πετεηνῶν ἔθνεα πολλά,
χηνῶν ἢ γεράνων ἢ κύκνων δουλιχοδείρων,
Ἀσίῳ ἐν λειμῶνι, Καϋστρίου ἀμφὶ ῥέεθρα,
ἔνθα καὶ ἔνθα ποτῶνται ἀγαλλόμενα πτερύγεσσι,
κλαγγηδὸν προκαθιζόντων, σμαραγεῖ δέ τε λειμών.

These, as the many nations of winged birds

of geese, and of cranes, and of long-necked swans,
in the Asian meadows beside the Kaystrian waters
this way and that make their flights in the pride of their wings,
then settle in clashing swarms and the whole meadow *echoes* (?).

It is interesting that the exact meaning of σμαραγέω is dubious and that the various passages from Homer and Hesiod leave its meaning vague. In fact, "mimetic" considerations play a minimal role in determining the use of this verb in the two passages from Homer. Like the scorching and groaning of the earth, the "smaraging" sound of the sea and meadow is a poetic sign pointing to the interpretant of the actions of the Greek host: the earthborns' uprising against Zeus. And once again it is the peculiarity of these expressions which gives them the effect of "poeticity," which suggests that they are related to each other in sharing some semiotic pertinence.

The other occurrence of σμαραγέω is in an equally pertinent context. After Achilles kills Asteropaios in Book 21, he vaunts over the dying man by claiming that the children of Zeus are more powerful than the offspring of rivers (Φ 184-85). Achilles then boasts of his own descent ἐκ Διός, ending by saying that even Ocean, the origin of all waters, fears Zeus' powers (Φ 198-99):

ἀλλὰ καὶ ὃς δείδοικε Διὸς μεγάλοιο κεραυνὸν
δεινήν τε βροντήν, ὅτ' ἀπ' οὐρανόθεν σμαραγήσῃ.

But even Okeanos is afraid of the bolt of great Zeus
and the terrible thunder, when it *crashes* (?) from the sky.

The occurrence of this rare word here in a speech contrasting those who are ἐκ Διός and those who were born of the prior generation of the gods can be no coincidence.[54] What follows is, in fact, Achilles' battle with the river Skamander, which turns out to be a "cosmic" struggle, complete with "scorching of the earth" (342ff.) and a theomachy (358ff.). As the gods crash together, the earth "echoes" (Φ 387: βράχε) and the heavens "blast out like a trumpet" (388: σάλπιγξεν).

The extraordinary sequence of events which makes up Achilles' *aristeia* in Book 21 is a gold mine of mythological motifs. Nagler discusses this section of the poem in connection with the archetype of the deluge-creation story. Skamander, he maintains, resonates with the figures of the chthonian monster, the death god, and the chaos demon who must be overcome by the sky god, who is in turn the guarantor of cosmic order. The paradigm of culture hero vs. chaos demon does, in fact, clarify a number of issues in this very strange episode of the *Iliad*. But a mythic paradigm, although a convenient descriptive device, is not a text-constitutive force as such, unless one takes such a paradigm to belong to a universal constituent of human thinking (a *sphota*).

The Near Eastern sources which Nagler takes into account are by no means fortuitous interpretants, for it is generally recognized that Near Eastern civilizations influenced Greek culture. This same material is also cited by West and others as sources for Hesiod's *Theogony*.[55] Thus despite the interest of more ancient accounts, Hesiod's text reflects the *reception* of Near Eastern myths better than any other extant text. It is Zeus' battles with the earthborn monsters which provide the most suitable clues for the background (the sememe) of a battle between a chaos demon and a culture hero. The highly mythologized narrative of Books 20-21 of the *Iliad* bears a fruitful comparison with the Hesiodic battles of Zeus. But the one nature simile in the episode with the river is particularly noteworthy, since it takes up another aspect of the sememe of Typhoeus, an aspect also important for the narrative of Book 2.

Hephaistos dries up the plain with his fire like Boreas (Φ 346-8):

ὡς δ' ὅτ' ὀπωρινὸς Βορέης νεοαρδέ' ἀλωὴν
αἶψ' ἀγξηράνῃ, χαίρει δέ μιν ὅς τις ἐθείρῃ
ὣς ἐξηράνθη πεδίον πᾶν.

As when the north wind of Autumn suddenly makes dry
a garden freshly watered and makes glad the man tending it,
so the entire plain was parched.

The background of this simile is the association of the evil winds with Typhoeus, no doubt by a folk etymology,[56] but made explicit in a passage of the *Theogony* (869-80):

ἐκ δὲ Τυφωέος ἔστ' ἀνέμων μένος ὑγρὸν ἀέντων,
νόσφι Νότου Βορέω τε καὶ Ἀργέστεω Ζεφύρου τε·
οἵ γε μὲν ἐκ θεόφιν γενεή, θνητοῖς μέγ' ὄνειαρ,
αἱ δ' ἄλλαι μὰψ αὖραι ἐπιπνείουσι θάλασσαν·
αἳ δή τοι πίπτουσαι ἐς ἠεροειδέα πόντον,
πῆμα μέγα θνητοῖσι, κακῇ θυίουσιν ἀέλλῃ.
ἄλλοτε δ' ἄλλῃ ἄεισι διασκιδνᾶσί τε νῆας

ναύτας τε φθείρουσι· κακοῦ δ' οὐ γίνεται ἀλκὴ
ἀνδράσιν οἳ κείνῃσι συνάντωνται κατὰ πόντον·
αἳ δ' αὖ καὶ κατὰ γαῖαν ἀπείριτον ἀνθεμόεσσαν
ἔργ' ἐρατὰ φθείρουσι χαμαιγενέων ἀνθρώπων,
πιμπλεῖσαι κόνιός τε καὶ ἀργαλέου κολοσυρτοῦ.

And from Typhoeus comes the fierce, rain-blowing winds--
not Boreas or Notos or bright Zephyros, for
these come from the gods, and they refresh mankind--
but others, reckless gusts, blow on the sea;
some fall on the misty sea and bring calamity
to men; as evil storms they rage;
each blows in season, scattering ships and
killing sailors. Men who meet them
have no defense against their power.
And sometimes over the vast and blooming earth
they blast the lovely fields of earthborn men
and fill the land with dust and dreadful noise.

The first few lines of this passage exhibit some minor ring composition,
which seems to be motivated by the conflict of line 869 and an earlier passage (Theo. 378-80) where the winds are said to be born of Eos and Astraios.
This conflict is immediately amended by the poet in lines 870-71, and these
lines are a classic case of retrogression and restatement as a correction device.
The evil winds, however, have no names and the distinction Hesiod makes
here is not observed elsewhere in Hesiod or in Homer: the winds who are
"born of the gods" are the only winds there are, and they are sometimes a
bane and sometimes a boon.[57] Nevertheless, the division of the good and bad
aspects of the winds, and the assignment of the latter to Typhoeus must have
traditional roots, and the division is pertinent to the wind similes of Book 21
and of Book 2.

In Book 21, Boreas is clearly a θνητοῖς μέγ' ὄνειαρ, for the farmer
rejoices at its effects on his field. In addition, the ameliorative action of the
wind in this simile is its "drying" function, whereas in the Hesiod passage,
the evil winds are specifically wet (μένος ὑγρόν). In Book 2, on the other
hand, there are two wind similes describing the host of the Achaeans which
suggest connections with the evil winds of Typhoeus. After Agamemnon
orders the Greeks to eat, we have (B 394-97):

ὣς ἔφατ', 'Αργεῖοι δὲ μέγ' ἴαχον, ὡς ὅτε κῦμα
ἀκτῇ ἐφ' ὑψηλῇ, ὅτε κινήσῃ Νότος ἐλθών,

προβλῆτι σκοπέλῳ· τὸν δ' οὔ ποτε κύματα λείπει
παντοίων ἀνέμων, ὅτ' ἂν ἔνθ' ἢ ἔνθα γένωνται.

So he spoke, and the Argives shouted aloud, as surf crashing
against a sheerness, driven by Notos descending,
some cliff out-jutting, left never alone by the waves from
all the winds that blow, as they rise now here, now there.

Despite the fact that Notos is specifically named, this wind is clearly one of
the wet, nasty ones which falls on the sea and is a πῆμα μέγα θνητοῖσι.[58]
Here is the other wind simile of Book 2 (B 144-49):

κινήθη δ' ἀγορὴ φὴ κύματα μακρὰ θαλάσσης,
πόντου Ἰκαρίοιο, τὰ μέν τ' Εὖρός τε Νότος τε
ὤρορ' ἐπαΐξας πατρὸς Διὸς ἐκ νεφελάων.
ὡς δ' ὅτε κινήσῃ Ζέφυρος βαθὺ λήϊον ἐλθών,
λάβρος ἐπαιγίζων, ἐπί τ' ἠμύει ἀσταχύεσσιν.

And the assembly was shaken as on the sea the big waves
in the main by Ikaria, when Eurus and Notos
driving down from the clouds of Zeus the father whip them.
as when Zephyr moves across the grain deep-standing,
boisterously, and shakes and sweeps it till the tassels lean.

This is actually a double simile, and the second one again seems to have a
corrective function. The first three lines bring in the wind whipping up the
sea, not unlike the scene in B 394. The picture ends, however, with the
phrase Διὸς ἐκ νεφελάων, and this introduces an anomaly: for these winds
are ἐκ Τυφωέος. The poet thus launches into another simile of the winds
blowing ashore on the works of the field, a πῆμα also attributed to the winds
of Typhoeus by Hesiod (*Theo.* 879-80, cited above, p. 80). Thus, whereas
the wind simile of Book 21 relates to the "fair" winds which are ἐκ θεόφιν
γενεή (*Theo.* 871), the wind similes of Book 2 relate to the "foul" winds
which are ἐκ Τυφωέος. In both passages the similes are generated by the
sememe of the Typhonomachy, which thus functions as an interpretant both
for the behavior of Agamemnon and the other Greeks toward Achilles and for
Skamander's attack on Achilles in Book 21, an attack that the river god
himself boasts will thwart Zeus' plan to give honor to Achilles (Φ 316-23).[59]
    The various elements of the Typhonomachy which appear in the *Iliad*
are what Riffaterre calls *textual interpretants*, fragments of a text quoted in the
text that they serve to interpret. One of the characteristics of such textual

interpretants, according to Riffaterre, is that they explicitly focus attention on intertextuality, "especially on how the poem exemplifies the type of intertextual conflict where two conflicting codes are present within its boundaries" (*Semiotics of Poetry*, 109-10). This characteristic has special appropriateness for the *Iliad*'s allusion to the battles of Zeus against the Titans and Typhoeus, for the *Iliad* is very much about the conflict of codes, and Zeus is in a most ambiguous position vis-à-vis "cultural order" in the *Iliad*. If Agamemnon's attempt to take Troy without Achilles is an affront which causes the earth to "groan," Achilles' actions throughout the poem are also affronts to principles of cultural order; and in fact it is Achilles who is the premier "groaner" in the *Iliad*. If Zeus is the guarantor of cosmic order, he has in this instance taken the side of the figure in the poem whose behavior is most frequently portrayed as negative and "anti-social." But the *Iliad* is not simply a representation of the consequences of anti-social behavior, but an articulation of a new "code" against the background of an old one. Zeus embodies the contradictory claims to which this situation gives rise, indicated, at the least, by his rather twisted plan to give glory to Achilles. The "double" wind simile of B 144-49 shows this contradictory portrayal at work in a small scale. The ambiguity about whether the destructive winds mentioned there are from Zeus or not, which triggers the second "corrective" simile, is based on the ambiguous position of Zeus himself: are his actions here for or against culture? Thus when we call Zeus the "guarantor of cosmic order," we should qualify this by saying "guarantor of cultural order *such as it is*"; and in the *Iliad* it is rather messy and self-contradictory, a consequence of its being at stake in the poem itself.

The story of Zeus' clash with the earthborn is a particularly apt interpretant for the Διὸς βουλή of the *Iliad* and references which can be related to it crop up all over the *Iliad*. Details which describe some sort of cosmic chaos occur in so many similes describing the onslaught of Greeks and Trojans that they are considered to be typical details of battle scenes.[60] But this is an argument *ex silentio*; is it not also possible that these details are not typical of Homeric narrative in general, but of this particular poem, which derives so much generative energy from the conflicts of Zeus against the earthborn?[61] Nearly any battle scene would be an appropriate place to allude to the Typhonomachy, since Achilles' τιμή is always at stake in a general way, along with the Διὸς βουλή. Nevertheless, the Typhonomachy is only one text-constitutive force in the *Iliad*. To say this or that simile is a textual interpretant pointing to the Typhonomachy does not give a full account of their functioning in the poem. If "ungrammaticality" is a key characteristic of poetic discourse, so is appropriateness at a number of levels of organization.

Thus, for example, Agamemnon's *aristeia* contains the following simile (Λ 155-58, cited above, p. 49):

> As when obliterating fire comes down on the timbered forest
> and the roll of the wind carries it everywhere, and thickets
> leaning under the force of the fire's rush fall uprooted,
> so before Atreus' son Agamemnon went down the high heads.

This simile suggests the association of the scorching of the earth (cf. *Theo.* 694 and B 455). Now Agamemnon's *aristeia* is an appropriate enough place for this element to be generated, but I have said above that this simile is determined in part by the model of the woodsman simile. Hence the whole picture, with wind and fire and thickets "felled" by the blast of fire is overdetermined in the simile by its connection to both the Typhonomachy and the woodsman simile. But Tilmann Krischer has shown that in the narrative subcode of the *aristeia*, a series of *Einzelkämpfe* is regularly followed by an *Ansturm auf die Phalangen*, and that this stage of the action is regularly accompanied by a simile of a "Naturgewalt der nichts standzuhalten vermag" (*Formale Konventionen*, 49). All these factors, and no doubt others as well, came together at this point in the narrative to determine the precise character of the simile.

### Conclusion: Propulsion and the Epic Simile

It has been my object in the preceding pages to investigate the functions of the similes in the poetics of Homer; that is, to identify their text-constitutive functions, their roles in the dynamics of the narrative. It is now possible to generalize about the various roles played by the similes and construct a picture of Homeric "narratology."

All narratives recount a series of events; that is, things which "happen" in a "world" constructed in the text. A simple chronicle links a series of punctual events to a series of verbal units. Since the description of action (*praxis*) always implies a "logic of action" as part of the interpretive apparatus by which it is to be understood, we call this one-to-one correlation of a series of verbal units to a series of actions the *proairesis*. No narrative,[62] however, consists entirely of a chronicle of events; sooner or later, proairesis becomes inadequate for one reason or another. Narrators have a variety of devices to call upon at such moments. Homer, for example, can leap into the narrative *in propria persona* and call someone a fool for doing something or other. This is an explicit act of overcoding, gathering together a series of events and assigning additional meaning to them as a unit: "he did such and such, *and these actions show him to be a fool.*" Such interjections and various other devices occur at moments when it is no longer possible to "let the actions speak for themselves." Such moments in the narrative are marked by a *shift in discursive mode:* from proairesis to some other mode. Similes are examples of such shifts, and in the preceding analyses I have tried to establish the mechanism which determined the shift in each case. These mechanisms can be thought of as three narrative roles.

"Preparation for battle" is an overcoded sequence of events resulting in a narrative subcode. One of the punctual events in that series is a communal meal. In Book 16, where the value of the preparation scene is negated, the element of a communal meal presents an obstacle to the text's unfolding. A meal is called for by the narrative subcode, but is thematically inconsistent with Achilles' "negative" portrayal. This motivates a shift in discursive mode and the cultural unit of a meal is handled in the wolf simile. The meal thus fills the gap left by the omission of a narrated meal; and although from an interpretive standpoint, one can certainly say that the wolf simile does more than get the text from point A to point C, in terms of the poetics of the narrative, this is precisely its role. If one were to represent the text of Homer graphically, the proairesis could be thought of as a straight line, suggesting a succession of punctual events, whose arrangement is determined by some (overcoded) logic of action. In such a graph, the wolf simile is actually a substitution for a point on the line corresponding to the narration of a preparatory meal.

The woodsman simile of Book 11 has a text-generative function; it articulates in brief compass a narrative sequence: working, satiety, retirement. This little sequence articulates the Διὸς βουλή and subsequently generates a series of variations of itself in the narrative. The action of the *aristeuontes* "rearticulates" the sequence: fighting, ὀδύνη, retirement. In our graphic representation of the narrative, these rearticulations can be thought of as "loops" which retrace the same narrative ground in a succession of variations. This looping characteristic is common in all narratives and can occur in numerous forms. It corresponds loosely to the rhetorical figure of *amplification* in the sense that it gives a more articulated view of the action, much like the instant replay of sports telecasting, which reviews a play in slow motion, "stopping" the action at various crucial places to clarify the narrative development.[63]

In Book 11 we have a simile establishing the narrative sequence and subsequently being rearticulated by the narrative. More commonly something will be narrated proairetically and then renarrated in a simile. The simile of the jackals and the deer in Λ 474-82 exemplifies this "looping" role, renarrating not only what has just happened to Odysseus, but also varying the woodsman model. This looping role, or "replay" role, is a text-constitutive force. It is a way of continuing the narrative, although it is not, in terms of our graphic representation of the narrative, *linear*. It is, however, propulsive; that is, it keeps the narrative going. One use of the looping role has already been discussed above: the correction or restatement feature of "ring composition." The ass simile of Λ 558-63 is a loop which restates the situation of the preceding lion simile, a restatement necessitated by the modeling function of the woodsman simile.

Another function of this looping role is suggested by several of the similes of Book 11 discussed above. The woodsman simile functions primarily as a textual generator for a rather large swathe of narrative. The similes which expand the semantic content of the woodsman simile in the subsequent narrative can be thought of as moments where the text "pauses" and "refocuses" attention on the semantic nucleus of the woodsman model. This can be seen as a propulsive version of the use of structural symmetries and isotopies; or even as a propulsive version of a literate poet's outline. It is a way the oral poet can exercise control "on the fly," so to speak, over the development of the poem as a whole. Since the oral poet is mainly preoccupied with what is immediately at hand (with "propelling" the narrative forward), he maintains his orientation by periodically shifting discursive modes (which "stops" the proairesis) and reestablishing his bearings. The ass simile of Λ 558-63 not only reestablishes the textual model of the woodsman simile, but sets up the special variation applied to Aias.

The looping role is basically intratextual. It consists of a textual variation of something which has already been produced within the scope of the narrative. Often, however, a text will connect the narrative at hand with a variety of "extra-textual" issues. Nestor is the preeminent example of this type of narrative digression (from the proairesis, that is), fond as he is of launching off on a tale of his youthful exploits in order to exhibit some pattern of behavior which is somehow relevant to the situation of his auditors.

If the proairesis is thought of as a horizontal line, this third general role could be represented as a vertical line perpendicular to the proairesis, pointing outside the narrative to some other text, or to some other textually established code. Many similes in Homer perform this role, and the Typhoeus similes discussed above have been dealt with in these terms: the groaning of the earth, the "smaraging" sound of sea and meadow, the chaotic effects of wind and fire, and the mention of Typhoeus himself all couch the narrative at hand within a larger cultural context and provide interpretants to the action.

These three narrative roles are often not easily separable. The wolf simile of Book 16 performs a role in the proairesis of the narrative subcode of preparation; but it also constitutes an important thematic comment on the narrative by its relationship to the cultural unit of a communal meal. So also, the forest fire simile for Agamemnon (Λ 155-7) "loops" back to the woodsman simile, is part of the narrative subcode of the *aristeia*, and evokes the cosmic chaos of the Typhonomachy. The similes of Homer can perform any or all of these three main narrative roles and thereby function in an important way in the textual dynamics of the narrative, as well as in the interpretive apparatus provided by the textual strategy. Moreover, the similes can assume these roles at any level of linguistico-textual organization. I have purposely stressed this diversity in order to avoid the oft-made assumption that the function of Homer's similes is determined primarily by their rhetorical form. Rather, the similes are shifts in discursive mode, and their functions are determined by their relationship to the forward movement of the poem.

A final example from Book 16 of the *Iliad* will clarify the notion of a shift in discursive mode along with a number of other issues of both theory and interpretation. Patroklos' entry into battle in Book 16 causes a turning of the tide, but the poet works up to this shift in stages. Initially, when the Trojans see Patroklos, "each man looks for his escape" (284). Patroklos kills Pyraechmes, whose followers flee (292), and then all the Trojans flee (294). There is then a simile of Zeus moving a cloud from a mountaintop (296-301). Then we are told that the Trojan flight is not headlong (303-5), but that they only yielded from the ships. There is then a series of *androktasiai* (306-51), after which there is a wolf simile describing the headlong flight of the Trojans (352-57). Hector and Aias are still engaged with each other, but Hector does *not* retreat (358-63). There is then an obscure simile in which Zeus moves a cloud into the heavens and creates a hurricane (364-65). The Trojans flee "in no good order" (οὐδὲ κατὰ μοῖραν: 367), along with Hector himself (368). There then follows a chaotic scene in which Patroklos sets upon Hector, followed by a remarkable storm simile (384-93). After this simile Patroklos continues his *aristeia* by killing a number of Trojans, climaxed by the slaying of Sarpedon.

The turning of the tide (ἑτεραλκέα νίκην: Π 362) of this passage clearly manifests a series of textual complexities, and the similes are the key indicators of the difficulties encountered and resolved by the forward movement of the narrative. Here is a scheme of the text:

278-83: Patroklos appears and the Trojans look to flight.

284-90: Patroklos kills Pyraechmes.

290-96: the Paeones and then all the Trojans flee.

297-300: Cloud simile.

303-5: The Trojans stand their ground again.

351-57: Wolf simile--headlong flight of the Trojans.

358-63: Hector and Aias: Hector stands firm to save his people.

364-65: Cloud simile.

366-83: Hector and the Trojans flee.

384-93: Storm simile.

394ff.: Patroklos continues killing Trojans and is in complete control of the situation.

The crucial points in the text are the shifts of mode which mark out lines 352-93. Before and after this passage are *androktasiai*; but the significance of the second of these two series is quite different from the significance of the first, a difference which is established by the intervening shifts in discursive mode.

The *androktasiai* of 306-51 are a good example of Homeric scene composition. The section begins and ends with the statement that "each of the Greek leaders killed a man" (306, 351). The scene thus begins and ends with a statement of the single proairetic event which is amplified in lines 307-50. This amplification, however, does not serve to correct or rearticulate the proairesis with significant variation: it is just fight, fight, fight. To judge from the *Iliad*, such detailed sequences of battle scenes were part of what the audience had paid to hear, comparable, perhaps, to the violence and special effects which are at present a great attraction in film. If we think of our sports telecasting analogy, such a scene could be compared to the case when a particularly elegant moment is replayed numerous times: not so the action will become more clear, but just so the viewers can savour the delicious moment again and again.

Nearly all the Trojans killed in this scene are mentioned here for the first and only time. Of the nine, only Akamas and Erymas are mentioned elsewhere, the latter only here and in Π 415, where he is killed for a second time. These characters are thus the kind of secondary figures who are introduced only to be killed off. Patroklos' kills immediately after the storm simile of 384-93 have a similar character, but occur in the context of a new orientation to the narrative.

The passage from 352-93 articulates a hypogram of the breakdown of order. The verb διέτμαγεν, "becomes scattered," of the wolf simile (354) is picked up by τμάγεν (374) and ἀποτμήγουσι (390) in the storm simile. The "folly" (ἀφραδίηισι 354) of the shepherd in the wolf simile is reflected in the crooked judgments of the men in the storm simile which makes Zeus angry (387-88). The λαιλάψ of Zeus in 365 is picked up by the ἀέλλη of 374 and the λαιλάψ of 384. Significantly, the earth is "weighed down" (βέβριθε χθών: 384), the rivers overflow their banks with a groan (στενάχουσι: 391), "rushing headlong and diminishing the ἔργα of men" (392); the Trojan horses also groan as they run (στενάχοντο θέουσαι: 393). These two singular uses of στεν- words can be connected with the groaning of the earth in the Typhonomachy and Book 2 of the *Iliad*. The matrix of the entire passage is, in fact, explicitly rendered in the words describing the flight in line 367: οὐδὲ κατὰ μοῖραν, "not according to *moira*." The word μοῖρα, literally, a portion, is directly opposite to διέτμαγεν, "divided up without order"; but more important, this word, in a passage filled with images of disorder at every level, leads us to Zeus, the allotter of portions, the one who establishes *fate* (μοῖρα). Zeus' conspicuous presence in the similes of this passage reminds us that his involvement in the plot of the poem is the source of both thematic and textual order, that the plot of the poem is the Διὸς βουλή.

The problem is this. Achilles has prayed for victory for the Trojans in order to have his honor restored. In Book 16, however, he prays for Patroklos' victory, thus making two contradictory requests. Moreover, Zeus has agreed to honor these contradictory requests, making his own position ambiguous. But the Διὸς βουλή is the plot of the poem, and thus Zeus' vacillation becomes immediately translated into a textual crisis. How can Zeus will both a Trojan and a Greek victory? How can he honor both of Achilles' requests?

The first cloud simile of Π 297 is the first modal shift resulting from the textual complication. The Trojans turn and run: but a Trojan retreat is against the old βουλή. A simile is generated in which Zeus moves a cloud away from a mountain so that everything becomes clear (297-300):

ὡς δ' ὅτ' ἀφ' ὑψηλῆς κορυφῆς ὄρεος μεγάλοιο
κινήσῃ πυκινὴν νεφέλην στεροπηγερέτα Ζεύς,
ἔκ τ' ἔφανεν πᾶσαι σκοπιαὶ καὶ πρώονες ἄκροι
καὶ νάπαι, οὐρανόθεν δ' ἄρ' ὑπερράγη ἄσπετος αἰθήρ.

As when Zeus the thunder-gatherer moves a dark cloud
from the lofty summit of a great mountain; and all
the lookouts and the high peaks and glens become
visible, and the boundless aether bursts heavenward.

This "clarifying" act of Zeus is immediately followed by the statement that the Trojans' regrouped and stood their ground. The Greeks, it is also said, get a breather (302); the poet too takes a breather by killing off a number of Trojans until he establishes a way to circumvent the textual problem.

The passage beginning with the wolf simile and ending with the storm simile articulates the textual and thematic chaos which is the result of the prevarication of Zeus. As the Trojans make their "ill-sounding" (δυσκελάδος) retreat, a retreat which contradicts the old βουλή, the text comes backs to Aias and Hector. Earlier (Π 114-15) Hector had rendered Aias defenseless, paving the way for the return of the "best of the Achaeans." Instead, Patroklos enters the battle according to the new βουλή. Now the climactic duel of Hector and Aias is broken off. Hector, however, "stands his ground" (363). This is an action commensurate with the old βουλή, and another shift of mode is generated (Π 364-67):

ὡς δ' ὅτ' ἀπ' Οὐλύμπου νέφος ἔρχεται οὐρανὸν εἴσω
αἰθέρος ἐκ δίης, ὅτε τε Ζεὺς λαίλαπα τείνῃ,
ὣς τῶν ἐκ νηῶν γένετο ἰαχή τε φόβος τε,
οὐδὲ κατὰ μοῖραν πέραον πάλιν.

As when the cloud comes into the heavens from Olympus
out of the brilliant aether, when Zeus stretches forth a
hurricane; so there was a cry and flight from the ships
as they made their way back in no good order.

Before, Zeus "cleared" the sky when the Trojans stood their ground, mediating the shift from the new βουλή to the old. Now, he darkens the sky when Hector and the Trojans flee οὐδὲ κατὰ μοῖραν, mediating the shift from the old βουλή (Hector's stand in 363) to the new (Hector's retreat in 367-68). Aias had been "trying to strike" Hector (ἵετ' ἀκοντίσσαι: 359). He now drops out of the picture for several hundred lines, and in his place Patroklos "tries to strike" Hector (ἵετο γὰρ βαλλέειν: 383); for it is the confrontation between Patroklos and Hector, and not that of Hector and Aias, which will bring Achilles back into battle.

Then, after a most vexing passage (366-83), full of ring composition, in which chariots are driverless, foot soldiers are trapped in a ditch which is apparently no obstacle to the chariots of Hector and Patroklos,[64] we have the great storm simile, filled with images of overwhelming chaos (Π 384-93):

ὡς δ' ὑπὸ λαίλαπι πᾶσα κελαινὴ βέβριθε χθὼν
ἤματ' ὀπωρινῷ, ὅτε λαβρότατον χέει ὕδωρ
Ζεύς, ὅτε δή ῥ' ἄνδρεσσι κοτεσσάμενος χαλεπήνῃ,
οἳ βίῃ εἰν ἀγορῇ σκολιὰς κρίνωσι θέμιστας,
ἐκ δὲ δίκην ἐλάσωσι, θεῶν ὄπιν οὐκ ἀλέγοντες·
τῶν δέ τε πάντες μὲν ποταμοὶ πλήθουσι ῥέοντες,
πολλὰς δὲ κλιτῦς τότ' ἀποτμήγουσι χαράδραι,
ἐς δ' ἅλα πορφυρέην μεγάλα στενάχουσι ῥέουσαι
ἐξ ὀρέων ἐπικάρ, μινύθει δέ τε ἔργ' ἀνθρώπων·
ὣς ἵπποι Τρῳαὶ μεγάλα στενάχοντο θέουσαι.

As when the whole earth is weighed down under a hurricane,
and becomes black, on a late summer day, when Zeus pours
down the rain most heavily, when he is very angry at men

who make crooked judgments in the courts by force,
and drive out justice, caring not that the gods watch them.
All their flowing rivers become swollen
and the mountain torrents cut away all the banks,
and they groan, flowing to the purple sea from the
mountains, headlong, and they diminish the works of men.
So the Trojan mares groaned greatly, running.

Most prominent is the breakdown of the relationships between Zeus, the guarantor of cosmic order, men and nature. In the narrative to follow, the initial request of Achilles and Zeus' promise to Hector that he would fight successfully the rest of the day after Agamemnon is wounded (Λ 186-94) are laid aside for a contradictory claim. When the narrative picks up Patroklos' *aristeia* in 394, approximately where it left off in Π 300, the poem has entered a new dispensation, one which extends all the way to Π 777, where a *Zeitangabe* ushers back in the old Διὸς βουλή. Apollo there comes to confront Patroklos in order to prevent a ὑπὲρ αἶσαν (777-87; see above, p. 44).

In the Sarpedon episode which begins in line 419, the ambiguous position of Zeus becomes explicit. As he see Patroklos about to engage Sarpedon, Zeus vacillates about whether he should save his son. Hera's response is a famous theological crux (Π 440-47):

αἰνότατε Κρονίδη, ποῖον τὸν μῦθον ἔειπες.
ἄνδρα θνητὸν ἐόντα, πάλαι πεπρωμένον αἴσῃ,
ἂψ ἐθέλεις θανάτοιο δυσηχέος ἐξαναλῦσαι;
ἔρδ᾽· ἀτὰρ οὔ τοι πάντες ἐπαινέομεν θεοὶ ἄλλοι.
ἄλλο δέ τοι ἐρέω, σὺ δ᾽ ἐνὶ φρεσὶ βάλλεο σῇσιν·
αἴ κε ζὼν πέμψῃς Σαρπηδόνα ὄνδε δόμονδε,
φράζεο μή τις ἔπειτα θεῶν ἐθέλῃσι καὶ ἄλλος
πέμπειν ὃν φίλον υἱὸν ἀπὸ κρατερῆς ὑσμίνης.

Most lordly son of Kronos, what word have you spoken?
Do you wish to save from dire death a man whose
death was long ago established by fate?
Do it then, but the other gods will not praise you.
And put away in your thoughts this other thing I tell you;
If you bring Sarpedon back to his home, still living,
think how then some other one of the gods might also
wish to carry his own son out of the strong encounter.

This is one of two places in Homer where there seems to be a "fate" or some ordering principle independent of Zeus' will to which Zeus must accommo-

date himself (cf. X 178-81). Hera's words imply that if Zeus intervenes in
this instance, the other gods will feel free to do so also, resulting in chaos.
This is indeed odd and inconsistent with the actions of Zeus and the other
gods elsewhere in the *Iliad*. But what we have here is not a theological crux,
but a textual one. Zeus' will is the plot of the poem, and it is as a textual
function that his words and actions are contradictory in this passage.[65]

The similes of the Trojan retreat show clearly the propulsive character
of Homeric narrative. When the proairesis encounters an obstacle, the text
effects a shift in discursive mode which allows the continuation of text and
meaning production in an appropriate way. It has often been noted that Book
16 has the densest accumulation of similes in the poem; it is also the book
with by far the most poetic intrusions *in propria persona*. These and other
shifts of mode testify to the textual and thematic complexity of this book.
When Patroklos finally falls, Hector addresses him in the following words (Π
837-42):

ἆ δείλ', οὐδέ τοι ἐσθλὸς ἐὼν χραίσμησεν 'Αχιλλεύς,
ὅς πού τοι μάλα πολλὰ μένων ἐπετέλλετ' ἰόντι·
"μή μοι πρὶν ἰέναι, Πατρόκλεες ἱπποκέλευθε,
νῆας ἔπι γλαφυράς, πρὶν 'Έκτορος ἀνδροφόνοιο
αἱματόεντα χιτῶνα περὶ στήθεσσι δαΐξαι."
ὣς πού σε προσέφη, σοὶ δὲ φρένας ἄφρονι πεῖθε.

Ah wretch, Achilles, although excellent, was no use to you;
he remained behind, telling you many things as you went forth:
"Do not return, horseman Patroklos, to the balanced ships,
until you have split the tunic of man-killing Hector
about the breast and made it bloody."
So he must have spoken to you, and you, fool, were persuaded.

Hector's reconstruction of the proairesis is, of course, false. Achilles said no
such thing to Patroklos. But his hypothesis is one which is, from the way
things fell out, quite sensible. As it is, neither Hector nor anyone else in the
poem can figure out the "real" logic of Achilles' actions; in this book, more
than in any other, the contradictions constitutive of the poem's unfolding
keep rendering the representation problematic, making it inscrutable from the
standpoint of "mimesis," and necessitating again and again the abandonment
of proairesis for other modes.

In a literary tradition which has emphasized structure and organic
unity, the propulsive character of Homeric narrative has been obscured in a

number of ways. Ironically, the Parry-Lord theory of oral composition has in its own way obscured this point as well. The conception of formula systems and typical scenes as "building blocks" implies the preeminence of structure, of a form into which these prefabricated units can be fitted. But it is precisely this notion of organizational structure, of architectonics, which becomes more important *after* Homer. A crucial ingredient for a poetics based on structure is *revision*, the self-conscious evaluation of the work of art in terms of some preconceived *form*. In this later development, the propulsive functions of similes, ecphrasis, ring composition, etc., become the relics of an outdated poetics. Their text-constitutive and propulsive functions become taken over by elements of structure; while they themselves survive as exteriorities, formal devices employed for numerous other uses.

The later development is, of course, related to the introduction of writing, and studies of the cognitive implications of changes in the means and modes of communication have emphasized that the introduction of writing results in the acceleration of skills relating to formalization and classification.[66] Indeed, one cannot imagine the compilation of tables of formulas such as those made by Parry without the use of writing. The recognition and analysis of formula systems requires a "decontextualization" of utterance and a reorganization of it according to some formal principle (e.g., meter). But such tables of metrically similar phrases produce collocations of utterance which could never have occurred or been recognized as such in a strictly oral culture, where all utterance is contextual. Formula systems like those drawn up by Parry and Lord cannot be the "real mental furniture" of the oral poet, any more than tables of declensions of nouns and verbs are the mental furniture of speakers in general. Such tables, however useful and illuminating in certain respects, must be recognized for what they are: formalist fictions valuable only heuristically.[67]

The circumstances of the composition of the *Iliad* are beyond certainty. The predominance of a propulsive poetics seems best explained as rooted in continuous oral performance, a predominance which can be seen in things like the revision-which-leaves-a-trace phenomenon. In such a poetics, structural and formal considerations will be likely to play a minimal role. In general, this seems to be the case with Homer; and his similes exemplify this fact. The whole notion of similitude with point-for-point correspondence requires a sort of tabular thinking which is characteristic of the written register; it requires that the qualities of two objects or actions be reduced to a series of spatially conceived "boxes," which can then be manipulated into alignment. This is not impossible in a continuous oral performance, simply less likely.

Homer is the beginning (for us anyway) of a tradition. The other authors whom we will consider either directly or indirectly imitate him, which is to say that they evoke Homer as an interpretant of their own texts. The use of an epic simile always says, at the least, "this text is serious, like Homer was serious." The use of such similes became so closely associated with the epic tradition that it is possible to see them as symptomatic of the "epic" aspirations of a text. These aspirations will be articulated by a certain signifying practice which posits (or "stitches together") a certain kind of "epic totality." We have already seen that similes are an important part of the "stitching" that holds together Homer's epic poetry. If Homer's successors transform the epic simile, put it to new uses, the problem of stitching still remains. We shall thus keep an eye on what the similes do in the texts of Homer's successors, what they no longer do, and what replaces the functions similes used to do.

# APOLLONIUS

## Culture and Non-Culture

The *Argonautica* of Apollonius of Rhodes is a work of the third century B.C., and the leap from the archaic period to the Hellenistic age is a vast one. At the same time, there are strong links of cultural heritage between the two periods. Thus, the *Argonautica* takes its subject matter from archaic Greek mythology and patently harks back to the style and language of Homer, even as it articulates preoccupations quite foreign to archaic literature. As we turn to the *Argonautica*, it will be useful to keep in mind the picture of the signifying practice of Homer which emerged from our analysis of the *Iliad*, since we will want to pay attention to the way Apollonius interprets and redeploys elements of that signifying practice. The wolf simile with which we began turned out to be an anti-meal, an isomorphically constructed negative image of a proper Homeric meal. The opposition which underlies the relationship of this simile to the descriptive system of a heroic meal is basically "correct" vs. "incorrect," and the problem of Achilles is that in Homeric culture there is little middle ground between this opposition. Having rejected his role in his culture, Achilles can only act as a non-Achilles, or more precisely, as an anti-Achilles. For whatever is not defined within the scope of culture is anti-culture; and "anti-culture" does not have a mechanism or internal coherence of its own except as a negative reflection of culture.[1] Thus, when Homer compares the Myrmidons to wolves, he is not suggesting that there is an "analogy" between the way the Myrmidons act and the way wolves act. The description of the wolves is entirely dependent on the description of heroic meals, and the "natural history" of wolves is entirely secondary to this consideration.

Another example of this negative portrayal is the description of Thersites, who is everything a βασιλεύς is *not* (B 212-20):

Θερσίτης δ' ἔτι μοῦνος ἀμετροεπὴς ἐκολῴα,
ὃς ἔπεα φρεσὶ ᾗσιν ἄκοσμά τε πολλά τε ᾔδη,
μάψ, ἀτὰρ οὐ κατὰ κόσμον, ἐριζέμεναι βασιλεῦσιν,
ἀλλ' ὅ τι οἱ εἴσαιτο γελοίϊον 'Αργείοισιν
ἔμμεναι· αἴσχιστος δὲ ἀνὴρ ὑπὸ "Ιλιον ἦλθε·
φολκὸς ἔην, χωλὸς δ' ἕτερον πόδα· τὼ δέ οἱ ὤμω
κυρτώ, ἐπὶ στῆθος συνοχωκότε· αὐτὰρ ὕπερθε
φοξὸς ἔην κεφαλήν, ψεδνὴ δ' ἐπενήνοθε λάχνη.
ἔχθιστος δ' 'Αχιλῆϊ μάλιστ' ἦν ἠδ' 'Οδυσῆϊ.

Only Thersites of the *unmeasured speech* still scolded,
who knew in his head many words, but *with no order* to them;
*vain* and *without decency* he would quarrel with the princes
with any word he thought would amuse the Greeks.
This was the *ugliest* man who came beneath Ilion.
He was *bandy-legged* and *lame* of one foot, with shoulders
*stooped* and *drawn* over his chest, and above this his
skull *went up to a point* with the wool grown *sparsely* over it.
He was especially hateful to Achilles and Odysseus.

Poor Thersites apparently has no socially redeeming characteristics. It would be easy to show that this passage, like the wolf simile of Book 16, is a full-scale conversion of the descriptive system of Homeric heroes. Within the scope of Homeric culture, a βασιλεύς is contrasted with a δήμου ἄνδρα, "a common man" (compare B 188 and B 198), but Thersites is neither of these. He is an anti-βασιλεύς, and the fact that he takes the side of Achilles in this particular instance, contrary to his usual practice, is a significant index of Achilles' situation.[2]

The *Iliad*, however, is not a simple rehearsal of what is and is not "correct" within the scope of culture. The fact is that Achilles does achieve in a small way an identity outside of his culturally determined role, an identity which is not simply a negation of that role. The establishment of this "other" culture with Priam intimates the possibility that non-culture need not be anti-culture, an intimation which gains momentum in the period after Homer. When Archilochus says that he left his shield by a bush (West, fr. 5), he is not simply portraying himself as the negation of a warlike person;

he is implying that there are other cultural values besides those of the epic hero which are more suitable to him. So also, when the Delphic oracle states that the gods prefer to be worshipped νόμῳ πολέως (Xenophon, *Memorabilia*, IV, 3, 16), this is a recognition that religious ritual is only "relatively" correct, not absolutely right or wrong. Finally, when Protagoras asserts that "whatever seems right and admirable to a particular city is truly right and admirable during the period of time in which the opinion continues to be held" (*Theatetus* 167c), he is expressing in the most general terms the relativity of human values and institutions.

In the period after Homer, in fact, the Greeks find themselves involved to a great degree in "international relations." Instead of the relatively under-girded, univocal culture of Homer, the Greek world becomes a more interactive culture. Non-culture is no longer viewed as something necessarily antinomous and inherently dangerous, but as "other" culture: other systems of values which have their own internal coherence and with which there can be intercourse and exchange. Herodotus reports with amusement the mutual repulsion of the Greeks and Indians at each other's practice of disposing of the dead. From this he concludes that Pindar was correct in calling νόμος the king of all things.[3] A culture's νόμοι are the means by which that culture defines itself; and Herodotus' point that customs and laws have only a relative value is the precondition for international relations.

For a culture to recognize the validity of another culture's values, it is necessary to become conscious of itself in new ways; specifically, it is necessary to be able to to view one's culture as a model, a *form* for behavior. That Greek philosophy from Thales on was preoccupied with form is a well-known fact--a preoccupation which was to lead to the apotheosis of form in the philosophy of Plato. It is in this period that thinkers begin to intellectualize about forms of government, forms of religion, etc. When the form of a cultural institution is abstracted into a model, it is then possible to establish comparisons with other models. In fact, comparison with other institutions is itself a privileged means by which an institution can be thought of *formally*.

The cognitive implications of such a formalization process is, as Goody notes,[4] twofold: it is *reductive*, in the sense that any decontextualization is a simplification which results in distortion; and it is *generative*, in the sense that it creates new ways of looking at things, a greater consciousness of things previously "taken for granted." This in turn can lead to the "corruption of the youth," of which the sophists were so frequently accused.

In the *Phaedrus*, Socrates asks his interlocutor if he should present, as he often does, the opposing argument. When Phaedrus agrees, Socrates cites a proverb to justify his procedure (272c):

λέγεται γοῦν, ὦ Φαῖδρε, δίκαιον εἶναι καὶ τὸ τοῦ λύκου εἰπεῖν.

Thus it is said, Phaedrus, that it is just for the wolf also to have his say.

In the *Iliad* the wolf, as the figure of the *Other*, never "gets his say," for he has no words of his own. Since the wolf is there defined as "anti-culture," he has no signifying system of his own. He can only groan inarticulately to indicate the absence of signification. In Plato, the wolf has his own signifying system, whose structuredness allows him to enter into a dialogue with other systems and work out a dialectical solution.

These brief remarks are not meant to take the place of a cultural or intellectual history. The purpose is simply to call attention to the increased tendency towards formalization in Greek thought concomitant with the shift from the more univocal cultural perspective of Homer to the more relativistic perspective of the subsequent period. The point is not that Homeric man was more narrow-minded than his classical counterpoint, but that the question of cultural value was posed in a new way and under different circumstances; and, I might add, Goody might be closest to the mark when he connects this shift in the semiotics of culture to changes in the means and modes of communication.[5] At any rate, in the new intellectual climate of Greece, the function and understanding of the simile is also reoriented significantly, a fact illustrated in a striking way by the discussions of Homer's similes in the rhetorical tradition and in the Homeric scholia. A brief consideration of the key texts in Aristotle and the scholia will serve us as a transition to Apollonius of Rhodes in the third century.

### The Simile as Reciprocal Exchange

Aristotle does not discuss similes in his *Poetics*, but his treatment of the use of example (παράδειγμα) in the *Rhetoric* deals with similes. Marsh McCall has shown that in Aristotle, as in antiquity in general, there were several terms used for what we have come to think of as a simile. Aristotle, however, consistently uses the term παραβολή for a comparison used as an element of proof, and εἰκών for a simile used as a feature of style.[6] Although Aristotle indicates various ways in which the εἰκῶν can add to the persuasiveness of an argument, we have here already an example of the division between function and ornament so prominent in formalist discussions of figures of speech. The εἰκών is discussed in the third book of the *Rhetoric*, chapters 4, 10 and 11.

From his fourth century perspective Aristotle does not recognize the generative function of Homer's similes, but he makes provision for it. In discussing the means to attain an urbane style (τὸ ἀστεῖον), Aristotle observes that metaphor and simile are especially helpful, since they allow us to "get hold of fresh ideas easily" (*Rhetoric* 3, 10, 1410b 2-3):

ἀρχὴ δ᾽ ἔστω ἡμῖν αὕτη· τὸ γὰρ μανθάνειν ῥᾳδίως ἡδὺ φύσει πᾶσιν ἐστί, τὰ δὲ ὀνόματα σημαίνει τι, ὥστε ὅσα τῶν ὀνομάτων ποιεῖ ἡμῖν μάθησιν, ἥδιστα. αἱ μὲν οὖν γλῶτται ἀγνῶτες, τὰ δὲ κύρια ἴσμεν. ἡ δὲ μεταφορὰ ποιεῖ τοῦτο μάλιστα· ὅταν γὰρ εἴπῃ τὸ γῆρας καλάμην, ἐποίησε μάθησιν καὶ γνῶσιν διὰ τοῦ γένους· ἄμφω γὰρ ἀπηνθηκότα, ποιοῦσι μὲν οὖν καὶ αἱ τῶν ποιητῶν εἰκόνες τὸ αὐτό· διόπερ ἂν εὖ, ἀστεῖον φαίνεται. ἔστι γὰρ ἡ εἰκών καθάπερ    εἴρηται    πρότερον,    μεταφορὰ    διαφέρουσα προσθέσει.

Let us begin by saying that getting hold of new ideas easily is naturally pleasing; all words mean something, so that words which make us learn something are most pleasant. Strange words we do not understand, and common words we know already. It is metaphor that creates this effect best; for when the poet calls old age "a withered stalk," he conveys a new idea, a new fact to us by means of what is common to both: both have lost their bloom. The similes of the poets do the same thing; and therefore if they are good ones, they give the effect of urbanity. The simile, as I have said before, is a metaphor, differing only by the addition of a particle.

Aristotle is here concerned with the cognitive implications of metaphor and simile, particularly their ability to *generate* new ideas. But the generative function ascribed to simile and metaphor by Aristotle is quite different from those we noted in Homer's similes. The Aristotelian εἰκών allows one to "get hold of new ideas easily" by positing a relationship between two sememes based on some sort of commonality (διὰ τοῦ γένους). This is, for reasons which would be worthy of investigation of themselves, our most commonsense idea of how figures like simile and metaphor work: some sort of commonality between two things makes it possible to posit an analogy based on that commonality, so that it is possible to say "they are alike in this way." This notion is thought of by Aristotle as an *exchange* between models, a semiotic mechanism which presumes a process of formalization.

The notion of exchange and reciprocity in similes is made explicit by Aristotle in several key passages. In the first one he states that reciprocity and exchange are the very characteristics which distinguish successful similes from failures (*Rhet.* 3, 11, 1413a 13):

ἐν οἷς μάλιστα ἐκπίπτουσιν οἱ ποιηταὶ ἐὰν μὴ εὖ, καὶ ἐὰν
εὖ εὐδοκιμοῦσιν· λέγω δ' ὅταν ἀποδιδῶσιν.

It is in these respects that poets fail worst when they fail and succeed best when they succeed; I mean *when they set up an exchange.*

The verb ἀποδίδωμι means literally "to give back" or "to give in return." In Homer it means simply "to make atonement for something." Later, as in Herodotus, it can refer specifically to commercial exchange, to "take something somewhere for the purpose of selling" (e.g., *Histories* 2, 5). With a genitive of price, it can mean simply "to sell." The extension of this term to mean "to interpret one word by another" (*LSJ* s.v. 11) suggests the establishment of a structure of exchange between signs, or better, between *codes*. The structure of exchange which underlies Aristotle's treatment of simile is truly the structure of "international relations"--relations between different cultures, economies, etc.

The verb ἀποδίδωμι occurs again in Aristotle's discussion of the "analogical metaphor" (ἡ μεταφορὰ κατ' ἀναλογίαν), the type of metaphor to which, in his view, the simile is closest. That Aristotle chooses to make simile a subordinate part of metaphor creates certain difficulties which need not detain us here; but it is clear that what makes simile and the analogical metaphor akin to each other for Aristotle is that they share the structure of exchange (*Rhet.* 3, 4, 1407a 4):[7]

ἀεὶ δὲ δεῖ τὴν μεταφορὰν τὴν ἐκ τοῦ ἀνάλογον
ἀνταποδιδόναι καὶ ἐπὶ θάτερα τῶν ὁμογενῶν· οἷον εἰ ἡ

φιάλη ἀσπὶς Διονύσου, καὶ τὴν ἀσπίδα ἁρμόττει λέγεσθαι
φιάλην "Αρεος.

The analogical metaphor should always set up a reciprocal
exchange between the two things of the same genus; for instance,
if the goblet is the shield of Dionysus, then the shield may
properly be called the goblet of Ares.

In this, the best type of metaphor for Aristotle, there is an exchange ἀνὰ
λόγον, "according to a *logos*"; that is, according to a formalized proportion
able to be thought of as a code establishing correlations between the
*comparata*. This point is made again in Aristotle's discussion of the analogical metaphor in the *Poetics*, where the same example of the goblet and the
shield is used (*AP* 1457b):

τὸ δὲ ἀνάλογον λέγω, ὅταν ὁμοίως ἔχῃ τὸ δεύτερον πρὸς τὸ
πρῶτον καὶ τὸ τέταρτον πρὸς τὸ τρίτον· ἐρεῖ γὰρ ἀντὶ τοῦ
δευτέρου τὸ τέταρτον ἢ ἀντὶ τοῦ τετάρτου τὸ δεύτερον. καὶ
ἐνίοτε προστιθέασιν ἀνθ' οὗ λέγει πρὸς ὅ ἐστι. λέγω δὲ
οἷον ὁμοίως ἔχει φιάλη πρὸς Διόνυσου καὶ ἀσπίς πρὸς "Αρη·
ἐρεῖ τοίνυν τὴν φιάλην ἀσπίδα φιάλην "Αρεως.

By analogical metaphor I mean this: when a first is related to a
second in the same way that a third is to a fourth, then a poet
will say the fourth instead of the second and the second instead of
the fourth. And sometimes the transferred term of the metaphor
is used together with what is relative to the supplanted term. For
instance, a cup is to Dionysus what a shield is to Ares; so that
the poet will call the cup "the shield of Dionysus" and the shield
the "cup of Ares."

Here the structure of exchange is schematically laid out in its most general
form: 1 is to 2 just as 3 is to 4. Although Aristotle takes for granted that
the two *comparata* are already alike to begin with, thus somewhat begging
the question, it is clear that the process of replacing terms is a kind of exchange based on the *value* of the terms. The full-blown analogy is the most
explicit form of this process of exchange. Both the εἰκών and the analogical
metaphor are less explicit about the relationship of the terms, but are most
successful for Aristotle when they are based on an underlying analogy.[8]
     The functioning of the εἰκών is thus based on a structural similarity
in two models; or to use our semiotic terms, a similarity in the structure of

the codes which constitute the *comparata* into sememes. For an εἰκών is basically a matter of *code-switching:* speaking of Ares in the drinking code or of Dionysus in the fighting code. The point of entry from one code to another is determined by a structural similarity in the configuration of the code; or at least this is the way it is seen by Aristotle. The structures of codes are, it should be remembered, established on the basis of a *message*: when a given text postulates them as an explanatory condition. In a given discourse, the factors which determine code-switching may be any number of things, but the message will always *imply* a certain configuration of codes for its own interpretation. In this way a text always gives the impression that the codes existed prior to itself, although this is not always the case. Indeed, the "fresh ways of looking at things" proceed in part from the way innovative texts can restructure the configuration of codes. Thus whereas Aristotle speaks of an exchange between the terms of already constituted models, we can specify more accurately that the process is one of an exchange of the *models themselves*, thus emphasizing the *constitutive* function of comparison. For such a process is not necessarily *based on* values, but often can be that which *produces* values.

The semiotics of many of Homer's similes, it should be clear, is not that described by Aristotle. The point of entry for the wolf simile of Book 16 of the *Iliad*, for example, is not a structural similarity between a formal model of the Myrmidons' behavior and a formal model of the wolves' behavior. The point of entry is a textual complication which necessitates a shift in discursive mode, a shift which generates text at a point where the proairetic mode had become blocked. The simile is not a shift from the code of the heroes to the code of the wolves, but a shift from one narrative *mode* to another. The code which determines the description of the wolves is still that of the heroes. The wolf simile is generative in the sense that it is propulsive: it allows text-production to continue.

This function, along with the others described above, are rather "conservative" in nature: they are not designed to seek out "fresh ways of looking at things," but rather to keep the text from going awry. Whether a simile manages the circumvention of an obstacle to the proairesis, as in Π 155ff., whether it establishes a generative model for the articulation of major developments in the plot, as in Λ 84ff., whether it "corrects" a local muff in the flow of the story, as in Λ 558ff., or whether it performs the role of textual interpretant, as in B 780ff., in each case it could be argued that the simile is a device for containing textual deviation rather than for setting off on a semantic adventure of some sort. There is always the possibility, however, that such textual devices will themselves generate "new ways of seeing things," that they will produce readings which will enrich a code; the difference with Homer is that the *semiotic mechanism* for this process is not fully developed. The tendency to divide everything up into culture and anti-culture, between what belongs to us and what does not belong to us, is not peculiar to traditional societies like that of Homer; nor did it suddenly disappear in the fifth century, as a glance at the use of the word *barbaros* will show (= both "non-Greek" and "repulsive"). But the increasing tendency toward formalization which marks the post-Homeric world put at the disposal of the Greeks of that period a tool for exchanging models; and Aristotle's perception of the simile and his prescriptions for its use are a function of this development.

### Apollonius and the Structure of Exchange

Despite the fact that Aristotle's view of the simile is inappropriate to Homer's poetics, the scholiast tradition on Homer shows the direct influence of the conception of the simile as having the structure of exchange. The most prominent readerly expectation evident in the Hellenistic commentaries on Homer's similes is *parallelism*. Thus, the sememe of "wolf," for example, is a sign system whose structuredness can be abstracted into a model and then exchanged with the model of the sememe of "warrior." If a warrior is compared to a wolf, the simile should, it seemed to Hellenistic critics, establish an exchange between elements of the sememe of "warrior" and elements of the sememe of "wolf." This expectation, Adolf Clausing notes, is often completely frustrated in Homer's similes:[9]

> Wenn man sich auf den Standpunkt stellte, dass auch bei Homer eine genauere Parallelisierung zwischen den beiden Teilen des Vergleichs möglich ist, und wenn man zu den weiteren Ausmalungen Beziehungen konstruieren wollte, musste man auf die allerbedenklichsten Abwege geraten und zu geradezu lächerlichen Interpretationen verführt werden.

With Apollonius the situation is different. As Clausing shows in a number of examples, Apollonius' imitations of Homeric similes conform more closely to the current literary and rhetorical theories. Specifically,

1. Apollonius is more careful to make analogical correspondence.

2. He usually keeps the number of things equal in the two parts of the simile.

3. He carefully correlates the *wie* and *so* particles, a matter Homer is often careless about.

4. He occasionally adds an explanatory antapodosis to the simile which precisely identifies the relationships of the things compared.

5. He is most careful that the ethos of the things compared be akin, another failing for which Homer was often criticized.[10]

All of these characteristics indicate a textual strategy which presupposes a reading based on the structure of exchange; it is a textual strategy which reflects, as Clausing points out, the influence of the Hellenistic criticism of Homer's similes.

One should hasten to point out that the "failings" of Homer's similes are, of course, failings from the standpoint of the rhetorical tradition, not from the standpoint of Homer's own poetics; and this fact leads to a number of ironies. Carspecken, for example, notes that in contrast to Homer, Apollonius' similes reflect the tendency "to make poetic ornamentation be, or, possibly more often and more accurately, seem to be, functional or structural."[11] Homer's similes, however, are indeed functional in his propulsive (but not particularly structural) poetics. At the same time, it is just because Apollonius' similes are used "as part of a pre-conceived design" (Carspecken, 67) that they become more ornamental than Homer's. Clausing notes that Apollonius' similes are often simply *"indirekt Darstellung,"* taking up something which *could have been represented directly* (*Kritik* 46); but this is the very formula for an ornament. Apollonius' similes are not text-building strategies generated by the needs of a propulsive textual dynamics, but rhetorical devices introduced *qua* device to adorn the narrative, to make it "urbane."

Thus, for example, the woodsman simile of Λ 86ff., is imitated in *Argonautica* 1, 1172-77. After rowing prodigiously, the heroes reach the land of the Mysians:

ἦμος δ' ἀγρόθεν εἶσι φυτοσκάφος ἤ τις ἀροτρεύς
ἀσπασίως εἰς αὖλιν ἑήν, δόρποιο χατίζων,
αὐτοῦ δ' ἐν προμολῇ τετρυμένα γούνατ' ἔκαμψεν
αὐσταλέος κονίῃσι, περιτριβέας δέ τε χεῖρας
εἰσορόων κακὰ πολλὰ ἑῇ ἠρήσατο γαστρί --
τῆμος ἄρ' οἵγ' ἀφίκοντο Κιανίδος ἤθεα γαίης.

At the time when the vinedresser or the plowman goes eagerly
from the field homeward, thinking of dinner; in the vestibule
he bends his worn-out knees, shriveled by the dust, he
looks at at his worn-out hands and curses the belly which commands
such toil; at that time they landed on the Cianian coast.

The weary vinedresser, after wearing out his hands by working all day long, heading home for dinner, parallels the heroes, who row until they are exhausted and then arrive among the Mysians where they have a feast. Like the woodsman simile in *Iliad* 11, the Apollonian imitation is a *Zeitangabe*; but the Iliadic simile did not so much mark *mimetic* time as it marked the introduction of Zeus' influence. It was a transition from one *type* of narrative to another; and it was, moreover, the textual generator of the subsequent narrative. The Apollonian simile is a transition from one punctual event (the rowing) to the next proairetically determined punctual event (the landing). It is, in short, a *Zeitangabe* and that is all.

The difference can be looked at another way. Space and time can be thought of as formal parameters for organizing narrative action. Clearly a logic of action (proairesis) is based on a spatial-temporal logic: sequentiality and contiguity. In Homer, however, the use of explicit references to time and space rarely play a significant role in organizing the *mimesis* (in Riffaterre's sense). *Orts-* and *Zeitangaben* are generative elements which can play any number of roles in the propulsive poetics of Homer. Any role in organizing the narrated events is likely to be secondary to their function in text and meaning production. Hence Homer's use of spatial-temporal relationships is generally rather foggy, and occasionally downright "ungrammatical."[12] In Apollonius spatial-temporal organization is quite prominent.[13] Carspecken, for example, notes that in his similes Apollonius seeks "to convey directly to the reader a total impression of a scene, a sense of its logical and emotional meaning" (89). He compares *Odyssey* 6, 102-8 with *Argonautica* 3, 875-84 and concludes (79):

> Homer's simile is not really organized as a scene. In contrast, Apollonius has created a formal, systematic grouping of the figures.... It has as a scene the close spatial organization expected in representational art designed to attract attention within a restricted area of vision.

Carspecken's remark points out the difference between a poetics in which the simile is primarily a *semiotic* device for performing various textual functions and one in which the simile has become a kind of decorative device whose main function lies in clarifying the relationships among things at the level of the *mimesis*.

The distinction between Homer and Apollonius is, of course, a relative one. Homer's narrative is not amorphous with respect to space and time, but the minimal role they play in explicitly organizing the narrative action points to the overall lack of structure at that level in Homer. The increased use of spatial-temporal organization in Apollonius is an index of the increased formalization and schematization of phenomena which distinguishes the Hellenistic world from that of Homer. In the *Republic* Plato describes at length the structure of an ideal state, but the purpose of the discussion is to provide an extended analogy for the structure of the soul. Such an extended analogy is unthinkable in Homer, for this kind of formal analysis relies on a mechanism for exchanging models.[14] Such a notion is the basis of Aristotle's conception of the simile; it is also the precondition of *"indirekt Darstellung."*

## Generative Functions in Apollonius' Similes

Clausing gives as an example of "indirekt Darstellung" the similes which describe the battle with the Bebrukes in Book 2 of the *Argonautica*. The battle consists of a series of individual encounters in the Homeric manner followed by a double simile. Here is the passage (*Argo.* 2, 123-35):

ὡς δ' ὅτ' ἐνὶ σταθμοῖσιν ἀπείρονα μῆλ' ἐφόβησαν
ἤματι χειμερίῳ πολιοὶ λύκοι, ὁρμηθέντες
λάθρῃ ἐυρρίνων τε κυνῶν αὐτῶν τε νομήων,
μαίονται δ' ὅ τι πρῶτον ἐπαίξαντες ἕλωσι,
πόλλ' ἐπιπαμφαλόωντες ὁμοῦ, τὰ δὲ πάντοθεν αὔτως

στείνονται πίπτοντα περὶ σφίσιν--ὥς ἄρα τοίγε
λευγαλέως Βέβρυκας ὑπερφιάλους ἐφόβησαν.
ὡς δὲ μελισσάων σμῆνος μέγα μηλοβοτῆρες
ἠὲ μελισσοκόμοι πέτρῃ ἔνι καπνιόωσιν,
αἱ δ᾿ ἤτοι τείως μὲν ἀολλέες ᾧ ἐνὶ σίμβλῳ
βομβηδὸν κλονέονται, ἐπιπρὸ δὲ λιγνυόεντι
καπνῷ τυφόμεναι πέτρης ἑκὰς ἀΐσσουσαν--
ὣς οἵγ᾿ οὐκέτι δὴν μένον ἔμπεδον ἀλλὰ κέδασθεν.

As when grey wolves terrify a great flock of sheep on a
winter's day, falling on them unnoticed by the shepherds
and the keen-scented dogs; they look to see which they
should pounce on and carry off first, inspecting them all
together. The sheep crowd into a mass and trample on each
other. Just so the Argonauts terrified the haughty Bebrukes
in their plight. As shepherds or beekeepers smoke a great
swarm of bees in a rock; for a while there is a tumult in
the hive and an angry buzzing from the crowded bees; then
blinded by the thick smoke they dart out of the rock.
Just so the Bebrukes could no longer hold their ground, but fled.

The wolf simile and the bee simile indirectly represent two punctual events:
the fear which overtakes the Bebrukes when they realize they are lost and then
the flight. Each of the similes expands a single simple notion: ἐφόβησαν
and οὐκέτι δὴν μένον, and the details of the scene are relegated to the similes. But more importantly, these similes reveal a peculiarly Apollonian (in
contrast to Homer, that is) preoccupation.

To begin with, the verb φοβέω has a different meaning in Homer than
it does in Apollonius, a change which reflects an important shift in perspective in the Greek language. In Homer, φοβέω means not "to terrify," but "to
set to flight"; it does not describe in Homer an internal emotion, but an
action determined by other actions. This shift in meaning and a number of
other similar shifts from "concrete to abstract" have often been commented
on.[15] But it is particularly interesting in the present example, since the wolf
simile, in effect, interjects into the logic of the action (the proairesis) a
punctual event which does not even exist in Homer. The bee simile describes
the actual flight of the Bebrukes; the wolf simile describes the emotions they
feel at the moment between fighting and fleeing. The implication is that
before one flees, something else happens, another "event" occurs, which
determines the fleeing; and this event is an *internal* one that can be depicted as
a specific event quite apart from fleeing. The articulation of the action here

to include a slot for a psychological event is of great importance for Apollonius' epic technique. Whatever faults critics have found in the *Argonautica*, everyone is in agreement that Apollonius excelled in psychological portrayal, in giving depth to his characters--even that he was preoccupied with this matter to a fault.[16] The epic simile provided Apollonius with a medium for giving concrete expression to a host of internal, private realities whose existence the Greek language had come to recognize.

The bee simile which immediately follows shows similar concerns. Fraenkel has suggested that this simile is a Stoic conceit. Both Epictetus and Marcus Aurelius use a comparison of a smoke-filled room whose door is always open to illustrate that man is always free to commit suicide when his inner peace is threatened by external pressures.[17] A reference to a Stoic notion about the maintenance of inner peace shows again Apollonius' preference to represent the internal implications of narrative actions. Many of Homer's heroes "give way" in various situations without necessarily implying anything about their character. Usually, in fact, retreat is represented by Homer as the direct influence of divine agency. In Apollonius, however, men retreat because they are cowards, and the logic of these inner events is more interesting to him. At the same time, if the simile is a reference to Stoicism, it is a textual interpretant, an invocation of an extra-textual "code of behavior" to interpret the actions of the characters in the story. But the flight of the Bebrukes is not ethically comparable to Stoic suicide--the latter is supposed to be heroic, not cowardly. The passage thus exemplifies a type of "intertextual conflict" between two codes, such as we noted in the Iliadic references to the Typhonomachy (pp. 82-83, above). Do we have here in the *Argonautica* a thematization of some fundamental social conflict? Is the text groping to formulate an imaginative solution to some real social contradiction? Hardly. It is much more likely that Apollonius is being *ironic*, that he is simply poking fun at the Stoics by implying that suicide is really the coward's way out.

Now irony is something which is unlikely in Homer--although not theoretically impossible--for irony presumes a certain relationship of mastery toward conflicts raised in a text, an ability to stand above them, to be able to laugh at them. This kind of ironic distance seems to be more frequent in Apollonius; and often Homeric conventions are themselves the object of such irony. Clausing and others, in fact, have noted numerous examples of similes which seem to be criticisms of Homer's epic technique.[18] That similes should themselves be pretexts for irony of this sort in Apollonius is a particularly pertinent point: Homer's similes are often attempts to exercise control over the course of the narrative; for this reason, they are at one level symptomatic of a certain *lack of mastery*. In fact, a dense accumulation of similes in Homer often signifies textual complexities. If Homer's similes are places where the narrative needed to "catch its breath" for one reason or another, the similes of the *Argonautica* often seem to be places where Apollonius flaunts his mastery over the narrative flow. The issue here is not that Apollonius is so much more in control of his narrative than Homer--although certainly literacy had specific advantages in this regard--it is that Apollonius' similes are no longer devices for exercising control; they no longer function to propel the narrative forward.

Thus, for example, a survey of the content of Apollonius' similes shows that he introduces a much broader and more exotic range of material into his similes. Like other Alexandrian poets, Apollonius prefers unusual and often obscure versions of myths as well as arcane geographical references. Also noteworthy are the numerous astral comparisons which make it possible for Apollonius to display his considerable astronomical learning.[19] Another contrast between Apollonius and Homer can be seen in the use of double similes and alternatives within a single simile. In Homer, we saw examples of double similes having a "corrective" function.[20] Double similes in the *Argonautica*, however, provide some of the most extraordinary examples of rhetorical flourish in the entire poem. Commenting on two magnificent double similes falling between lines 1280-1302 of Book 4, Carspecken writes (82):

> The poet is not offering true alternatives. Although each part could, conceivably, stand by itself, it is in the combination of parts that the effect of the simile lies, in the relation of each part to that preceding and that following, in the accumulation of incident and detail according to a predetermined pattern of increasing emotional tension.

Once again, what is a propulsive device in Homer becomes significantly redeployed in Apollonius. A double simile in Homer often suggests that a first simile did not resolve a textual complexity adequately; and such "correction" devices are necessary in Homer just because "predetermined patterns" are such weak text-constitutive forces in Homer's propulsive poetics. Although Apollonius has no need of such correction devices, he imitates the *form* of Homer's double similes while at the same time producing new and sophisticated rhetorical effects. Again this redeployment of a Homeric device often involves the articulation of the emotional world of figures in the epic.

The reference to Stoicism in the bee simile cited above is also pertinent because of what such a philosophy reflects about Hellenistic culture. The Stoics viewed man as a microcosm; not so much as an element in a larger system, but as an internally coherent system himself. The cosmos was studied not so much to find one's place in it, but as a model for man's inner *logos*.[21] Hence Zeno's famous dictum, ὁμολογουμένως ζῆν, "life according to a *logos*." The possibility of a "homologous" life presumes the structure of exchange to predicate a "little world" within man. The autonomization at the heart of the Hellenistic philosophies has as its corollary (perhaps its cause) a lesser interest in man as a cultural entity. The early Stoa was thus apolitical, particularly in contrast to Panaetius and the middle Stoa; the Cynics and the Epicureans were notoriously doctrinaire in this regard.[22]

The differences between Homer and Apollonius exemplify these changes. Homeric narrative is populated by generative elements, interacting at various levels of linguistico-textual organization, whose propulsive dynamics set up relationships among basically static and role-determined characters. Character in Homer is determined by one's status, one's relationship with others, not by the λόγος of one's ψυχή. Many critics have noted the typical nature of Homeric characters, that there is generally no conception of an "inner life" of the mind or soul and that the origin of action is represented as coming from outside of the heroes.[23] Homeric characters do different things and enter into new and shifting relationships with each other, but there is very little in the *Iliad* to encourage the view that any of the heroes actually undergoes a metamorphosis or grows inwardly. The *Iliad* is interested in individuals as cultural entities.

In Apollonius, the individual as the sum of a series of cultural relations is no longer the focus of interest. Instead, the individual as such has become interesting in a new way. The rise of the new Hellenistic philosophies testifies to this focus on individuals apart from culturally defined roles. So also, the new realism in art, the move toward depicting the peculiar and even grotesque indicates a fascination with the particular.[24] This is, to be sure, not something which suddenly appears in the Hellenistic period; for the "rise of the individual" is something already heralded in the *Iliad*; but in Apollonius the influence of this development is pervasive. For example, Carspecken notes that certain groups of similes describing particular figures in the poem seem to form a series which together articulate a "developing symbolism." Thus Jason is compared to a star on several occasions, but with different aspects foregrounded so that a sort of psychological evolution is delineated (Carspecken, 97-98). Much more famous, and very distinctive of the difference between Homer and Apollonius, is the set of extraordinary similes which describe the inner turmoil of Medea as she begins to fall in love with Jason.[25] Thus, if Apollonius' similes are less functional with respect to narrative propulsion than those of Homer, being often merely an alternative way of representing proairesis, they are nevertheless productive. Specifically (but by no means exclusively), the Apollonian simile predicates models for the inner world of humans and establishes equivalences between this unseen world and the seen world. In this way his similes create *character* as a *logos*, a structured entity produced by exchange with other structures. The constitution of character is one important way that the generative potential of the εἰκών becomes realized in the *Argonautica*. Apollonius uses the structure of exchange to articulate the "human cosmos," thereby delineating a new "psychology."

A related observation can be made about the quest structure of the *Argonautica*. The quest is a narrative form in which the questing subject can be transformed by exchange with his environment. As the quester moves from one place to another, from one situation to another, he becomes the locus of predication. In a quest there is the potential for an endless consecution of situations related to each other only by the presence of the questing subject. The *Argonautica* is thus episodic in a way that the *Iliad* is not. In Homer, the characters are the *data*, the backdrop for the narrative process. In Apollonius, the propulsive, generative functions of language are relegated to the inner world of the individual; the drama of internal processes is played out against the narrative backdrop of the quest. Apollonius' handling of the quest form makes its role as a backdrop conspicuous. Arthur Heiserman has called attention to the fundamental shift in interest suggested by a comparison of the *Argonautica* and Pindar's fourth Pythian ode, which has a long digression on the Argonauts. This ode, with its patent political overtones, is focused on the conflict between Pelias and Jason, allowing Pindar to insert *gnomae* about justice and right rule.[26] However, the conflicting claims of Pelias and Jason are not even mentioned in the *Argonautica*. We are not told why Jason accepts the quest; the fleece, once taken, is soon forgotten. The *Argonautica*, in fact, ends with the abrupt declaration that the heroes made it home safely without further mishap. Nothing is said of Jason's winning of the throne from Pelias. Whatever purpose the voyage had is left in silence. This is because its main purpose was to provide a narrative scheme which would allow Apollonius to articulate character.

To say that the *Argonautica*'s lack of interest in the constitution and organization of culture differentiates him from Homer is, however, not enough. For the difference between the two texts is not simply thematic (as though Apollonius more or less arbitrarily chose to do something new); the difference lies in the very character of discourse itself. There is a vast difference between the relatively homogeneous community of the *Iliad* and the far-flung Hellenistic empires. The latter consist of a loose articulation among individual city-states already constituted as such. The relationship among the heterogeneous sectors of Alexander's empire do not make up a unity based on a shared commonality, but a loose "association" based on more abstract relationships such as economic reciprocity. If comparison of the *Argonautica* to Homer's epics has led critics to view Jason as "alienated" or as an "anti-hero,"[27] that is because Hellenistic culture as a whole looks fragmented and alienated from the standpoint of Homeric culture. After all, social transformation is thematized in the *Iliad* as the disintegration of "community" (*Gemeinschaft*), as alienation and anti-heroism (see above, p. 72).

When Apollonius sets out to imitate Homer, to "interpret" him, he continues a movement already incipiently at work in the *Iliad*. Given the constitution of the individual as such, the *Argonautica* documents his lateral movement among other individuals with whom an explicit exchange (a "contract") can be established. If the Homeric simile can be seen as attempts to "homogenize" heterogeneities which the narrative flow encounters for one reason or another, the Apollonian simile can be seen as attempts to set up diplomatic relations with various heterogeneities the narrative has set out to discover. Returning to the economic parallel underlying Aristotle's discussion of metaphor and simile, we can characterize Apollonius' use of the simile as "laissez-faire" meaning production. Given this difference from Homer, it is easy to see why the *Argonautica* has suffered by comparison with the "classic line," despite the fact that it was immensely popular in antiquity. The centrifugal impulse, the resistance to closure and containment of meaning, has led critics to claim that the *Argonautica* is less unified than its Homeric counterparts; that it is "anti-heroic," and a "failed epic"; that it is "merely romantic," and "escapist"; or that it is "decadent" and "novelistic."[28] But unlike Homer, Apollonius would have been able to recognize these value judgments as grounded in aesthetic suppositions which are only relative.

# VERGIL

## Republic vs. Empire

Apollonius of Rhodes can be said to represent a certain moment in the "history" of the simile. He is neither the first nor the last representative of this moment; he is not even necessarily its best representative. But one could hardly find a more poignant contrast to Homer. As such, Apollonius is an important alternative precedent for Vergil's *Aeneid*, for the Roman epic will take up both the question of the heroic individual as he is constituted by the various institutions of culture, and also heroic "character" as something more personal and apart from the institutions of culture. Indeed, the relationship of private and public realms is a key issue raised in the *Aeneid*, and criticism of the poem is divided as to the intentions of Vergil on this point: whether he was trying to promote the subjection of the private to the public, or trying to critique this "imperial subjectivity."[1] In either case (and these two readings do not exhaust the possibilities), Vergil was involved in an explicit political practice, and the dynamics of his poetics are profoundly influenced by this fact. This practice took the form of an overt celebration of Augustus and of the empire that he had established. Moreover, this celebration has a specifically historical character to it, so that the empire is shown to be superior to its predecessors. Vergil is thus implicitly occupied with the relative value of political institutions, a matter in which Apollonius apparently had little interest, and a question which Homer did not have the tools to formulate explicitly. There was, however, an important traditional debate about which was the best form of government, a debate which compared various models of rule in order to weigh the advantages and disadvantages of each. This discussion did not take the form of an epic poem, but the histories of Herodotus and Polybius and the philosophical dialogues of Plato and Cicero, to name some of the more salient examples, are texts which raised issues of "epic" scope and which perceived themselves as doing so. Before turning to Vergil, therefore, it will be necessary to consider briefly the terms of this discussion. Cicero's *Republic* will serve as our example, since it will provide the closest contrast with Vergil.

The republic is described by Cicero as a form of government which is "mixed," having elements from monarchy, democracy and aristocracy:[2] it is a form which arises from the dialectic of these three simple forms. Here is the passage from the *Republic* (I, xlv, 69):

> regio autem ipsi praestabit id quod erit aequatum et temperatum ex tribus primis rerum publicarum modis. placet enim esse quidam in re publica praestans et regale, esse aliud auctoritati principum inpartitum ac tributum, esse quasdam res servatas iudicio voluntatique multitudinis. haec constitutio primum habet aequabilitatem quandam magnam, qua carere diutius vix possunt liberi, deinde firmitudinem, quod et illa prima facile in contraria vitia convertuntur, ut exsistat ex rege dominus, ex optimatibus factio, ex populo turba et confusio; quodque ipsa genera generibus saepe conmutantur novis, hoc in hac iuncta moderateque permixta constitutione rei publicae non ferme sine magnis principum vitiis evenit. non est enim causa conversionis, ubi in suo quisque est gradu firmiter collocatus, et non subest quo praecipitet ac decidat.

> Better even than monarchy, however, is that constitution which is a balanced and tempered compromise among the three primary forms of government. For it is fitting for a government to have a royal aspect, the first citizens have some claim to power, and certain things are reserved for the judgment and will of the people. Such a constitution has in the first place a sort of balance, without which freedom is scarcely possible for long, and then a stability: for those primary forms of government are easily inverted into their perverse forms, so that from monarchy arises tyranny, from aristocracy, oligarchy and from democracy, anarchy; and furthermore, these types often are changed into others. But in the mixed and moderate constitution, this does not happen without grave faults of the leaders; for there is no cause for a change where each is firmly established in his proper place, and there is no underlying perverted form into which this type of constitution can degenerate.

Cicero recognizes that monarchy, aristocracy and democracy are three internally coherent systems, each with its own advantages and disadvantages. The republic, on the other hand, is a sort of modulation among these three simple forms. The republic sets up a *ratio*, a *logos*, among the three primary forms, a system of exchange and reciprocity. Roman history, as Scipio presents it in the second book of the *Republic*, exemplifies this process of dialectical exchange among the three types of rule. Each of the three classes of people (royal, aristocratic, popular) gives and takes, makes "trade-offs," in order to achieve a balance of power.[3]

One could hardly find a more succinct statement of the two different structures of culture's relationship to non-culture discussed above. The three simple forms of government are each paired with an isomorphically constructed negative image: tyranny, oligarchy and anarchy. The relationship between the members of each of these pairs is that of culture to anti-culture. The inherent weakness of these simple forms is that they will degenerate into their anti-types (*Rep.* I, xxviii, 44):

nam illi regi, ut eum potissimum nominem, tolerabili aut si voltis etiam amabili Cyro subest ad inmutandi animi licentiam crudelissimus ille Pharlaris, cuius in similitudinem dominatus unius proclivi cursu et facile delabitur. illi autem Massiliensium paucorum et principum administrationi civitatis finitimus est qui fuit quodam tempore apud Athenienses triginta virorum illorum consensus et factio. iam Atheniensium populi potestatem omnium rerum ipsi, ne alios requiramus, ad furorem multitudinis licentiamque conversam pesti....

For underneath the tolerable, or, perhaps even, the loveable King Cyrus lies the utterly cruel Pharlaris, impelling him to an arbitrary change of character; for the absolute rule of one man will easily and quickly degenerate into a tyranny like his. And a close neighbor to the excellent Massilian government, conducted by a few leading citizens, is such a partisan combination of thirty men as once ruled Athens. And as for the absolute power of the Athenian people--not to seek other examples of popular government--when it changed into the fury and license of the mob....

One is reminded of the *Iliad* where the question is posed: what can Achilles become, after rejecting his cultural role, besides an anti-Achilles?

What the republic offers instead is a mutual reciprocity among the three forms of government--a reciprocity which achieves a balance of power. A monarchy is faced with two possibilities, a good king or a bad one. But the republic has no underlying perverted form into which it can plunge and sink (*non subest, quo praecipitet ac decidat*). It has, like the Aristotelian εἰκών, the structure of exchange and peaceful coexistence among internally coherent systems. With this give and take structure, it can withstand internal and external shocks without resulting in a *conversio*, because it has a mechanism for adjusting and tuning itself:   a mechanism whose process is exemplified by Roman history.

The republic is, to modify Zeno's dictum, ὁμολογομένως κρατεύειν, "government according to a *logos*." And as in the case of the Stoic ideal of life, this does not mean government according to any *logos*, but according to the one, all-encompassing *Logos*. For Cicero, nature provides certain impulses and tendencies, such as the need for *virtus* and the desire to defend the common safety (*Rep.* I, i, 1), which a government must express in its form. This immanent *Logos* is, for both Plato and Cicero, justice. It is manifested in government by reciprocal exchange:   everyone getting his due.[4] The republic is for Cicero the best form of government because it has the *ratio* of nature built into it.[5] What is significant about Cicero's argument is the way in which the structure of reciprocity and exchange becomes centralized in the form and content of that argument. There is an opposition established between governments which are composed of type and anti-type (monarchy/ tyranny, aristocracy/ oligarchy, democracy/ anarchy) and a government which is based on exchange. The dynamics of the former is one of *conversio*:[6] conversion of a system. The dynamics of the latter is a process of exchange among systems. The former is generative in the sense that one form of government will inevitably produce its anti-type. The latter is generative in the sense that change can produce better equivalences among the systems (as Roman history shows). The dynamics intrinsic to the republic are perceived by Cicero as bringing men ever closer to the ideal state *ubi in suo quisque est gradu firmiter collatus*, in which there is a perfect reciprocity (justice) and hence no cause for further change. But even as a continuing process, it has a certain balance (*aequabilitatem*) and stability (*firmitudinem*: *Rep.* I, xlv, 69).

Cicero's conception of the republic represents a further elaboration of the semiotics of comparison, an elaboration, to be sure, well represented before and after Cicero, but nevertheless one which allows us to speak of a "history" of the exchange process. In Apollonius the simile produces *logoi*. As the Argonauts travel here and there, they are made to encounter various exotica which are rendered intelligible by exchange, an epic version of the mechanism underlying "ethnologies" like those of Herodotus. The Ciceronian elaboration involves taking a series of already constituted *logoi* as manifesting a more general *Logos*, as being species of a genus. Cicero is not so interested in this or that particular stage of the republic's development, but in delineating the immanent *Ratio* which modulates the whole process. When Scipio discusses the ideal nature of Rome's site in Book Two of the *Republic*, Laelius interrupts him to praise his *modus operandi* (*Rep.* II, xi, 5):

> illa de urbis situ *revoces ad rationem*, quae a Romulo casu aut necessitate facta sunt.

> What Romulus did concerning the site of the city by chance or necessity, *you refer back to a definite principle.*

The Apollonian simile constitutes *logoi* by predicating exchange. The function of exchange in Cicero is to effect a *revocatio ad rationem*: the production not of more *logoi*, but of an underlying *Logos*. If Herodotus' ethnologies exemplify the former, the attempt to articulate an "international" body to modulate exchange among various independent politico-economic entities can exemplify the latter. Both functions are based on the structure of exchange, but in each case the basis for comparison (code, *ratio, logos*) is thought of differently. We will have more to say about the Ciceronian function below, but we have now laid the groundwork for a consideration of the next "moment" in our history of the simile.

I said initially that Vergil was concerned with the relative value of cultural institutions; but it is clear that he does not pose this question in the same way that Cicero does in the *Republic*. Vergil does not weigh the advantages of an empire against the advantages of a republic or a democracy; he weighs a good emperor against a bad one, a morally fit leader against a morally weak one, a pious hero against a mad and violent one. Provisionally, it can be said that Vergil's encomium of Augustus and the empire is a defense of one of the three simple forms of government discussed by Cicero. Indeed, the *Aeneid* does seem to revert to the view of non-culture as anti-culture. Basic themes of the epic, as numerous scholars have pointed out, involve the opposition of sanity and madness, concord and discord, *pietas* and *furor*, etc.[7] It has often been said that there is a lot of Turnus and Dido in

Aeneas; but Aeneas is not "like" Turnus and Dido in the way that the Bebrukes are like sheep in the *Argonautica*; he is like them more in the way that the Myrmidons are like wolves in Book 16 of the *Iliad*. Dido and Turnus are Aeneases gone awry, representations of what Aeneas is always in danger of degenerating into. But the representation of culture in the *Aeneid* is not identical to that of the *Iliad*; and now we must turn to the text itself.

## Nature and Culture in Vergil

The very first epic simile of the *Aeneid* compares the storm of Book 1 to a political sedition (147-54):

> ac ueluti magno in populo cum saepe coorta est
> seditio saeuitque animis ignobile uulgus
> iamque faces et saxa uolant, furor arma ministrat;
> tum, pietate grauem ac meritis si forte uirum quem
> conspexere, silent arrectisque auribus astant;
> ille regit dictis animos et pectora mulcet;
> sic cunctus pelagi cecidit fragor.

> And as often happens when in a great crowd a sedition
> arises and the ignoble mob rage in their minds
> and soon torches and stones fly, for fury finds weapons;
> then, if by chance they catch sight of a man remarkable
> for service and righteousness, they fall silent and
> give ear to him; and he rules their minds with his words
> and softens their hearts; just so the clamor of the sea subsided.

This simile has no real antecedent in Homer. B 144-48 is often cited as a likely source of inspiration; but there a mob is compared to a storm, the reverse of the Vergilian situation. Here a "natural" disaster is compared to a political event. The raw and untamed fury of the storm is likened to an ungoverned people; the agency of Neptune is likened to the impact of an eminent statesman. The sedition "arises" (*coorta est*) it would seem, by spontaneous generation, the word *coorior* being an example of the middle voice in Latin describing things which arise of themselves.[8] Sedition is here portrayed as a natural condition among people when they are not controlled (n.b., *saepe*), much like the winds of the storm scene narrated earlier (1, 52-61):

hic vasto rex Aeolus antro
luctantis ventos tempestatesque sonoras
*imperio premit* ac vinclis et carcere frenat.
illi indignantes magno cum murmure montis
circum claustra fremunt; celsa sedet Aeolus arce
sceptra tenens *mollitque animos* et temperat iras
*ni faciat, maria ac terras caelumque profundum
quippe ferant rapidi secum uerrantque per auras;*
sed pater omnipotens speluncis abdidit atris
hoc metuens.

In a vast cave King Aeolus
*imposes his power* on the howling winds and the
blustering storms and reins them in with chains and cages.
They all indignant, with a great murmuring, rage
around the enclosure of the mountain; Aeolus sits
in his citadel holding the scepter and *softens their
minds* and their anger; *if he did not, they would surely
carry with them the seas and the earth and the heavens
and sweep through the air.* But the omnipotent father,
fearing this, hid them in these dark caves.

Without the *imperium* imposed by Aeolus, the winds would pursue their natural course of destructiveness. It is this same "ruling" influence which calms the eruption of *furor* in the simile: *ille regit dictis animos et pectora mulcet.* Specifically, it is the political virtue of the great man (*pietate gravem ac meritis*) which calms the people. Cicero, it will be recalled, viewed nature as possessing a *ratio*, which a good government must instantiate: the republic is the best form of government because it has this *ratio* built into its structure. The implication of the first simile of the *Aeneid*, however, is that nature lacks a *ratio* of its own, and that it is culture which must provide one.

This implication is given full expression in the *Georgics*, a poem devoted to man's domination of nature. Men must take up arms against an unwilling and recalcitrant earth in order to conquer her (*Geo.* 1, 160-61), for if nature is left to her own devices, everything will deteriorate (*Geo.* 1, 197-200):

vidi lecta diu et multo spectata labore
degenerare tamen, ni vis humana quotannis

maxima quaeque manu legeret: sic omnia fatis
in peius ruere ac retro sublapsa referri.

Yet even those culled and cared for with great pain
have I seen degenerate, did not human force choose
out the largest by hand year by year: thus all things
by fate impelled hasten to the worse and backward
borne slip away from us.

As Brooks Otis has noted,[9] the entire first book of the *Georgics* sounds this
theme of the raw and hostile nature of the environment. Book Two pictures
the gratifying results obtained by imposing order on nature, the beauty of the
cultivated vines and trees. One striking image here is particularly noteworthy
(*Geo.* 2, 276-87):

sin tumulis accliue solum collisque supinos,
indulge ordinibus; nec setius omnis in unguem
arboribus positis secto via limite quadret:
ut saepe ingenti bello cum longa cohortis
explicuit legio et campo stetit agmen aperto,
derectaeque acies ac late fluctuat omnis
aere renidenti tellus, necdum horrida miscent
proelia, sed dubius mediis Mars errat in armis.
omnia sint paribus numeris dimensa uiarum.

But if you plant on rising ground or sloping hills,
give the rows room; when the trees are set, let
each line be squared to perfection:
just as often in a great war, when the legion's length
deploys its cohorts and the column stands in an open field
and the battle lines are set, the whole earth rippling
with the flashing bronze; nor has the grisly fight yet
begun, but Mars wanders doubtful between the armies,
so let all be drawn up in equal rows.

This passage not only suggests that order must be imposed on nature to improve its performance, but that the order so imposed on nature should be that
of the quintessential institution of the Roman state, a battle line. Nature, it
seems, progresses and improves as it takes on the characteristics of the
Roman state. It is culture that legitimates nature and gives it a viable
form.[10]

    The fourth book of the *Georgics*, devoted to beekeeping, is the climax

of this portrayal. The bees are a fitting climax because they, more than anything else, imitate the model of empire, having (*Geo.* 4, 4-5):

magnanimosque duces totiusque ordine gentis
mores et studia et populos et proelia.

great-souled leaders, a nation's history
its traits, its bent, its clans and its battles.

After an initial section on the establishment of the hive (8-115), Vergil turns
to the special endowments they have received from Jupiter (149-50). The description of the bees' hive and activities which follows is filled with images
of the Roman state. The bees live in a city (*urbis* 154; cf. *sub moenibus
urbis*193 and *aulas et cera regna* 202), and have laws (*legibus* 154), acknowledge a fatherland (*patriam* 155) and household gods (*penatis* 155). They labor
according to a fixed contract (*foedere pacto* 158), build their homes by laying
foundations (*ponunt fundamina* 161). Some educate the youth (*educunt fetus*
163), the *spem gentis* (162); others guard the gates (*ad portas...custodias*
165). When the drones make an uprising, the bees fall into a Roman
military formation (*agmine facto* 167) to drive them out. Finally, they are
entirely devoted to their king (*rege incolumni mens omnibus una est* 212).

The anthropomorphism of the description of the bees can be compared
to Homer's portrayal of the wolves in *Iliad* 16. There we saw that the description of the wolves' meal in the simile was determined by the descriptive
system of a heroic meal. Here too, the bees are a *simulacrum* (although not a
negative one) of the Roman state. They are not an *objet trouvè* which is
discussed according to its own *logos*; the model of the Roman state has been
imposed on them. Jupiter, it is in fact said, has "added" these special characteristics to them as a sign of his gratitude (149-52); they thus share in the
*divina mens* (220). The bees are an ideal society because they are a
thoroughly Romanized society. This is quite different from saying that the
Roman state is natural because it is like a community of bees.[11]

The relationship of culture and nature which emerges from the *Georgics* is the opposition of "organized" versus "disorganized."[12] In such a
framework, culture views itself as possessing a model which is self-sufficient
and prior. Non-culture is not only that which is not organized according to
the model of culture, but that which is not organized at all. In the univocal
culture of Homer, non-culture is organized as a negative image of culture--and
thus was inherently antinomous and dangerous. In the Vergilian perspective,

non-culture is viewed as the raw material for the further expansion of culture. The possibility is recognized that order can be imposed, that non-culture can be "assimilated" and brought within the bounds of culture, that the world can be "civilized."

The view of nature as something which is disorganized and in need of some sort of discipline implies that spontaneity and acquiescence to natural impulses have a negative value. In Book 2 of the *Aeneid*, for example, Aeneas responds to Troy's desperate situation by urging his companions to arms and certain death (355-58):

> sic animis iuuenum furor additus. inde, lupi ceu
> raptores atra in nebula, quos improba ventris
> exegit caecos rabies catulique relicti
> faucibus exspectant siccis, per tela, per hostis
> uadimus.

> In this way fury was added to the minds of the youths,
> and like wolves, plunderers in a black fog, whom the
> shameless frenzy of the stomach drives blindly on, and
> the cubs who are left behind await with dry throats,
> through weapons, through enemies we go.

The wolves of the simile follow a natural appetite (hunger), an appetite which is expressly called *improba*. In so doing, they leave behind their young ones. Now family responsibilities are a key aspect of the virtue of *pietas*; and the wolves' acquiescence to their "natural" hunger has a deleterious consequence. The implication of the simile is that Aeneas has regressed into the realm of nature, that he has allowed a spontaneous impulse to overcome his commitment to culture. When Venus appears to rebuke Aeneas for his folly, she reviles him in just such terms (2, 595-98):

> quid furis? aut quonam nostri tibi cura recessit?
> non prius aspicies ubi fessum aetate parentem
> liqueris Anchisen, superet coniunxne Creusa
> Ascaniusque puer?

> Why are you raging so? where has your care for me gone?
> should you not first look to where you left your
> father Anchises, worn out with old age; see whether

your wife, Creusa, is alive, and your son, Ascanius?

Care for one's young may or may not be instinctive, but consistent devotion to the family is a virtue of culture (*pietas*): an improvement on nature provided by the model of the state.[13] The wolves of the *Aeneid* are different from the wolves of both the *Iliad* and the *Argonautica*. The Iliadic wolves are an isomorphically constructed negative image of culture. In the *Argonautica*, wolves have their own little culture organized according to their own little *logos* (which can thus be exchanged with the *logos* of the Argonauts). In the *Aeneid* wolves are a part of nature: they are thus without any *logos* at all. Theoretically, they could be assimilated, they could take on the model of the state and become domesticated. But if they simply follow their natural propensities, their actions will be random and "uncultivated" (*Geo.* 1, 199-203):

> sic omnia fatis
> in peius ruere ac retro sublapsa referri,
> non aliter quam qui adverso vix flumine lembum
> remigiis subigit, si bracchia forte remisit,
> atque illum in praeceps prono rapit alueus amni.

> Thus all things by fate impelled
> hasten to the worse and backward borne slip away
> from us. Just as a man who drives a boat upstream
> with oars; if he perchance slackens his arms, the
> channel will snatch him also headlong downstream.

The simile of this passage opposes two situations: rowing upstream, which is the role of the cultural hero (in this case the farmer) and not rowing at all, which is to abstain from cultural behavior. But the simile implies a third possibility: rowing downstream, which is to engage in anti-cultural behavior. The immediate context of this passage is walnut trees, so we could pose the three options in this way: rowing upstream is to cultivate the trees; not rowing is to do nothing for the trees, in which case they will degenerate; to row downstream would be like burning down the walnut trees. Culture in Vergil opposes itself to both of these latter alternatives, but the relationship to each is distinct. To clarify the difference, it is necessary to look at the two great adversaries of Aeneas, Dido and Turnus.

Dido: *Carthago Delenda Est*

Our first look at Carthage in book one of the *Aeneid* is of a burgeoning city being built by an industrious people. Several things in the description of the city are clear anachronisms of the Roman polity, particularly the Roman custom of the *sulcus* (425) and the *sanctum senatum* (426). But more important is the bee simile (430-36), which is based on phrases and whole lines used in *Georgics* 4, 162-69. Here is the simile:

> qualis apes aestate noua per florea rura
> exercet sub sole labor, cum gentis adultos
> educunt fetus, aut cum liquentia mella
> stipant et dulci distendunt nectare cellas,
> aut onera accipiunt uenientum, aut agmine facto
> ignauum fucos pecus a praesepibus arcent;
> feruet opus redolentque thymo fraglantia mella.

> Just as in summer bees work through the flowery fields
> under the sun, when some lead out the full-grown young
> of the race, or others pack the flowing honey and
> pack the honeycombs with sweet nectar, or receive
> the burden of those coming in, or forming in columns
> drive out of the hive that worthless pack of drones;
> the work is fervent and the fragrant honey is sweet with thyme.

Here is the passage from the *Georgics*, which was summarized above (4, 162-64, 167-69):

> aliae spem gentis adultos
> educunt fetus; aliae purissima mella
> stipant et liquido distendunt nectare cellas...
> aut onera accipiunt uenientum, aut agmine facto
> ignauum fucos pecus a praesepibus arcent;
> feruet opus, redolentque thymo fraglantia mella.

The anachronistic description of Carthage together with the simile which refers to the ideal polity of the *Georgics* identifies the city as an image of culture: a city which, like the bees, has taken on the model of the Roman state. As in all monarchies, the soundness of the polity arises from the virtue of the leader, in this case Dido. Her entrance is graced by a simile comparing her to the chaste Diana (498-503). Now *amor*, we know from the

*Georgics*, is the nastiest of all the natural impulses which must be disciplined (*Geo*. 3, 209-11):

Sed non ulla magis uiris industria firmat
quam Venerem et caeci stimulos auertere amoris,
siue boum siue est cui gratior usus equorum.

But no other practice firms up the strength more
than the avoidance of Love and the goads of blind passion,
whether one is training bulls or horses.

In fact, the bees of the *Georgics* are especially praiseworthy because they reproduce without *amor* (*Geo*. 4, 197-202). Dido's chastity is the key to her success as a queen, and it is in regard to this virtue that she undergoes a *conversio*.

At the beginning of Book Four, the hapless Dido vacillates about the "old flames" (23) Aeneas has rekindled in her. Her confidante Anna urges her not to fight against a pleasing love (38): *placitone etiam pugnabis amore?* Dido, of course, gives in and "looses her shame" (*soluitque pudorem*, 54); her love is described with a number of stereotypical images from elegiac poetry (a wound, a flame, a sickness), a most "unepic" set of interpretants. Once likened to the huntress Diana, now Dido is compared to a careless doe (*incautam ceruam*) who is wounded by a hunter (69-73). Suddenly, Dido finds that words fail her (76): *incipit effari mediaque in voce resistit*; for *amor* is the epitome of disorganization, and language is of the realm of culture and organization.[14] Dido has stopped rowing; and the result for her city is immediately registered (4, 86-89):

non coeptae adsurgunt turres, non arma iuuentus
exercet portusue aut propugnacula bello
tuta parant; pendent opera interrupta minaeque
murorum ingentes aequataque machina caelo

The towers rise no more; the youth no longer exercise
in arms, nor do they prepare the harbors or the
battlements for war. The works are idle, broken off;
the massive menacing rampart walls, even the crane,
defier of the sky, now lies neglected.

The portrayal of *amor* as a sort of uncultural sloth is given full scope in the fourth book of the *Aeneid*, a matter aptly handled by numerous scholars. But whereas Aeneas is awakened from his folly by divine intervention before he "goes downstream" too far, Dido is portrayed as taking a further step.

As she sees Aeneas leaving, Dido hurls a fearful curse against him and his people (613-29), in which she hopes that Carthage and Rome will always be enemies (*nullus amor populis nec foedera sunto*, 623), that a great avenger will arise from her bones to attack Rome (625-27), and finally (628-29):

> litora litoribus contraria, fluctibus undas
> imprecor, arma armis: pugnent ipsique nepotesque.

> I pray that our shores always war upon theirs, our
> waves against theirs, our arms against theirs: let
> these and their children always be at battle.

What Dido prays for is that Carthage will become an anti-Rome. Carthage thus is represented as that part of non-culture which becomes anti-culture: that irreducible residue resistant to the end to assimilation into the empire.[15] *Carthago delenda est*, the old Cato used to say at the end of every speech; and indeed Carthage was destroyed and its soil sown with salt. The figure of Dido in the *Aeneid* makes this end seem inevitable and necessary, for she herself underwent a *conversio* from rowing upstream to rowing downstream. Her *pudor* made her city rise; her *amor* made it stop; her final madness made it collapse.[16] As she throws herself on the pyre, the city resounds with wails (669-71):

> non aliter quam si immissis ruat hostibus omnis
> Karthago aut antiqua Tyros, flammaeque furentes
> culmina perque hominum uoluantur perque deorum.

> It was just as if all Carthage or ancient Tyre were
> collapsing in ruin, an enemy entering the gates, and
> raging fires were rolling over the homes of gods and men.

Empire must impose itself on whatever is disorganized. The preeminent example of this is the conquest of nature by cultivation. But empire must destroy its enemies, those who insist on rowing downstream. A neutral observer may have looked at the clash of Carthage and Rome as the struggle between two empires, as an encounter between two independent systems each trying to impose itself on the same "third world." But few Romans (and no doubt few Carthaginians) would have perceived it in that way. To them it

was the dark against the light, heaven against hell, culture against anti-
culture.

## Turnus: *Bellum Civile* and the Origin of the State

In Book 12 of the *Aeneid*, as Turnus prepares himself for the upcom-
ing duel with Aeneas, he is compared to a bull (12, 103-6):

> mugitus ueluti cum prima in proelia taurus
> terrificos ciet aut irasci in cornua temptat
> arboris obnixus trunco, uentosque lacessit
> ictibus aut sparsa ad pugnam proludit harena.

> As when a bull preparing to do battle awakes tremendous
> bellows; trying to hurl his rage into his horns,
> he butts up against the trunks of trees and lashes at
> the winds with blows or practices for the battle by
> pawing at the sand.

The simile is strongly reminiscent of *Georgics* 3, 228-36, where a bull driven
by the goads of *amor* prepares himself to fight another bull. Lines 105-6 are
in fact exact repetitions of *Geo*. 3, 223-24. That an intertext of Turnus'
simile is the digression on *amor* of the *Georgics* is not surprising: his
portrayal throughout the latter books of the *Aeneid* is, as Otis has shown,
that of a mad and violent man. As a cultural hero, Turnus is quite clearly a
failure like Dido; and the difference between his *ethos* and that of Aeneas is
immediately registered in the passage at hand (*Aen*. 12, 107-12):

> Nec minus interea maternis saeuus in armis
> Aeneas acuit Martem et se suscitat ira,
> oblato gaudens componi foedere bellum.
> tum socios maestique metum solatur Iuli
> fata docens, regique iubet responsa Latino
> certa referre uiros et pacis dicere leges.

> Meanwhile Aeneas, no less keen for battle and ruthless
> in the arms his mother gave to him, calls up his
> indignation, happy that the war is to be settled by a
> compact. He comforts his companions, stays the fears of
> sad Iulus; he teaches them the ways of fate. Then
> he orders his men to carry back his firm answer to

King Latinus and dictates the terms of peace.

There can be no question that the *ethos* of Aeneas, his portrayal as a hero of culture, is represented as a justification of his ultimate victory in the *Aeneid*. But the intertext from the *Georgics* is not so important in terms of characterizing Turnus as it is for characterizing the nature of the conflict itself. The Latin war is, after all, a *bellum civile*: Italy is not to be destroyed like Carthage; it is destined to become the very seat of the Roman state. The Latin conflict will not decide whether Italy will become Rome or anti-Rome: as in the battle of the bulls in the *Georgics*, the conflict will decide who the leader will be, whether it will be Rome under Aeneas or Rome under Turnus.

The problem can be better focused by considering the simile which describes the final confrontation of Aeneas and Turnus. As they at last come together, the heroes are compared to two bulls (12, 715-24):

ac uelut ingenti Sila summoue Taburno
cum duo conuersis inimica in proelia tauri
frontibus incurrunt, pauidi cessere magistri,
stat pecus omne metu mutum, mussantque iuuencae
quis nemori imperitet, quem tota armenta sequantur;
illi inter sese multa ui uulnera miscent
cornuaque obnixi infigunt et sanguine largo
colla armosque lauant, gemitu nemus omne remugit:
non aliter Tros Aeneas et Daunius heros
concurrunt clipeis, ingens fragor aethera complet.

And just as on huge Sila or on lofty Taburnus, when
two bulls charge together into hostile battle with
butting brows: the trainers shrink back in terror,
the whole herd stands mute with fear, the heifers wonder
who will rule the woods, whom the whole herd will follow;
the bulls with massive force trade wounds, and struggling
gore each other and wash their shoulders and legs with
much blood, and the whole woods bellows with their groans:
Just so Trojan Aeneas and Daunian Turnus crash together
with their shields, and their violence fills the air.

This simile is also strongly reminiscent of the *Georgics* passage on the fighting bulls (*Geo.* 3, 219-23). Although only a single half line of the *Aeneid* simile is an exact repetition of the *Georgics* passage (*Geo.* 3, 220b = *Aen.* 12, 720b), the two scenes have numerous connections: the mention of

Sila (these are the only two Vergilian occurrences), the *iuuencae* standing by, the bodies of the bulls washed with blood, and the forest echoing with the bulls' bellowing. Again, the *Georgics* passage does not provide an insight into the *ethos* of the contestants so much as an insight into the nature of the conflict itself. For the battle of the two bulls is not a battle of culture and anti-culture, or even between culture and nature. It is a struggle which is prior to the establishment of what is and is not culture; or more accurately, it is the struggle which will itself establish culture.

From the battle of the bulls emerges a victor who will have the *imperium* of the herd and will be solely responsible for generating offspring (cf. *Geo.* 3, 224: *nec mos bellantis una stabulare*). So too, in the battle between Turnus and Aeneas, a victor will emerge who will *then* become *ex post facto* the hero of culture; and whatever qualities he had will be "metaleptically" established as the virtues of culture. The victor, in other words, becomes the positive sign of culture; the conquered becomes its negative sign. In the Vergilian perspective, the leader is the generative origin of culture; he is the model which is imposed on everyone else. From the emperor himself comes all good and evil and everyone must conform or become anti-culture. Imperial culture, in short, is defined as that which the emperor does.

The struggle which precipitates this emergence of cultural definition is chronologically prior to culture itself. Significantly, in the two lines preceding the bull simile, the earth "groans" and "chance and virtue are indistinguishable" (713-14):

> dat gemitum tellus, tum crebros ensibus ictus
> congeminant, fors et uirtus miscetur unum.

> The earth gives out a groan, then they redouble the
> heavy blows of their swords: chance and virtue mingle into one.

Chance and *virtus* are mingled into one because this is the primal moment of *undecidability*: it is only *after* a victor emerges that it can be established what *virtus* is. Like the various stages of the succession myth in Hesiod, the struggle of Aeneas and Turnus produces a moment of unintelligibility, the "cosmic chaos" which precedes the establishment of some principle of order. Like similar instances in Hesiod and the *Iliad*, the earth groans (*dat gemitum tellus*), signifying the absence of intelligibility.[17]

Unlike the *iuuencae* of the simile who wait to see who will rule them, we know and have known from the beginning of the epic that Aeneas will win. The fact that he wins allows us to define him as the cultural hero. Once we have such a definition, it is possible to go back and write the prehistory of culture metaleptically. In retrospect, the battle of Turnus and Aeneas was not the primal conflict prior to order, for cultural order, embodied in Aeneas, existed all along. Retrospectively, the victory of Aeneas seems inevitable, because he has always been himself; that is to say, he has always been the cultural hero. The bull simile represents the moment in the *Aeneid* which is prior to the rest of the poem. It is only from the vantage point of the outcome of this conflict that the *Aeneid* can be written (as opposed to a *Turneid*). Aeneas won, just as Augustus won: and it is this historical fact which is the generative starting point of Vergil's epic.

A comparison with Cicero's *Republic* will once more clarify the issues here. Although Cicero clearly implies that the Roman success story is itself an argument for the superiority of the republic as a form of government, this is not the real basis of his exposition. Roman history is for Cicero an *exemplum* of a process of exchange and reciprocity, and it is this process in which he is interested. Rome's history proves his point only insofar as it manifests the operation of the mechanism he is delineating. It is for this reason, perhaps, that Cicero sets his dialogue in the time of Scipio, a time when the republic seemed most healthy: more recent history had abandoned the mechanism of reciprocity and exchange. For Cicero, to repeat what has been said, this mechanism is prior; the *ratio* of the republic is something already immanent in nature before it was ever applied to government.[18]

In Vergil, the opposition of culture and non-culture is portrayed as organization versus disorganization. Since the origin of culture was the moment of organization, there is nothing which precedes culture but non-culture. Nevertheless, the model of culture, once established at a particular point in history, is retrospectively represented as prior, as actually being there all along. Immediately following the bull simile of *Aeneid* 12, 715ff., the representation of this aboriginal moment of undecidability, we read the following lines (725-27):

Iuppiter ipse duas aequato examine lances
sustinet et fata imponit diuersa duorum,
quem damnet labor et quo uergat pondere letum.

Jupiter himself holds up two scales in equal balance
and places the diverse fates of the two on the balance;
the one doomed by this conflict, his weight sinks down.

That this gesture of Homer's Zeus[19] is introduced at this point shows clearly the basic workings of the *Aeneid*. The victory of Aeneas is a historical fact; however, it cannot be represented as a mere contingency; it must be both a discrete historical event and at the same time it must be structurally determined as the only possible result. The notion of fate, something which is "spoken" beforehand but only recognized retrospectively, fulfills this role of simultaneously affirming and denying history. In the context of a historical project such as the *Aeneid*, fate is nothing but the metaleptic representation of history. Things fell out that way: therefore, from the winner's standpoint, they were meant to fall out that way. Cicero identified the *ratio* of the republic with justice: Vergil's Jupiter is identified with the ineluctable reality of history. After the scales are introduced, Turnus is routed and soon killed.[20] The order of the whole passage implies that Jupiter's will was prior to the outcome of the battle, that the model of culture was prior and history only its palpable manifestation.

The *Georgics* relate how nature can be conquered by man, how disorganized nature can be assimilated into organized culture. The Dido episode of the *Aeneid* looks forward to the destruction of anti-culture. The climax of the last half of the *Aeneid* describes how culture is born, how it arises out of and separates itself from nature. It is a fitting sequence of subject matter, since the entire rhetoric of Vergil is a vast *hysteron proteron*, implying that last things are really first and first things really last. The *Aeneid* announces its theme to be the great struggle which *produced* the Roman present (*tantae molis erat Romanum condere gentem*), but the *Aeneid* is really the production of a past which *reflects* the present. The *Aeneid* recounts the contingencies which led to the present at the same time that it tries to dispel the very possibility of contingency with respect to the present.

The *Aeneid* has often been interpreted as a narrative of self-constitution: the development of Aeneas from the old heroic (i.e., Homeric) virtues to civilized (i.e., Augustan) virtues. At the same time, Aeneas' career is seen as a *simulacrum* of the struggle of Rome herself. But the model of signification which emerges from our discussion seems to make Aeneas the kind of fully finished and self-same being typical of Homeric epic. Aeneas won; that fact makes him by definition the hero of culture. Aeneas' character does not change in the *Aeneid*; it unfolds before us. What Aeneas learns he learns by revelation, the unfolding before his own eyes of what he means, what he has meant, and what he always will mean; and when he goes awry, as he does by dallying in Carthage, a divinity must intervene and get him to "come back to himself." By viewing the *Aeneid* as the process by which Aeneas *becomes* the Roman model of a hero, we fall prey to the fiction that culture is somehow prior to itself.

Vergil, of course, tries to have it both ways. Aeneas is not simply represented as a "completely externalized" being, "absolutely equal to himself," and "lacking any ideological initiative."[21] Aeneas does seem at times to be a locus of agency, in possession of something which moves the story along and not someone who who is simply moved along by it. And as in the case of another of his literary ancestors, "resourceless Jason," the fact that Aeneas possesses some ideological initiative is nowhere so strongly marked as in those places where he seems to be temporarily *without it*. Our opening view of Aeneas as frozen with fear and "groaning" (*ingemit*) at his plight in the midst of the storm (*Aen.* 1, 92ff) raises the possibility that Aeneas might fail, that things might turn out differently unless he *acts*. There can only be a limited amount of this potential evoked in the poem, for it runs counter to the main model of signification; and in this first instance in Bock One, as in the Trojan episode in Book Two, as in the Dido episode of Book Four and as in the final battle with Turnus, the possibility of things turning out in an unexpected way is quickly countered by divine agency. The dynamics of the poem treat initiative on the part of individuals in the poem the same as "nature" in general; if there is something valuable there to begin with, what it is can only be said retrospectively, from the standpoint of culture, after it has been acknowledged and named by culture.

Turnus and Dido are indeed Aeneases gone awry, but what can this mean other than that they lost? Put another way, how is Aeneas' independent initiative, his "character," any different from that of Dido and Turnus? There is a difference--one is good, one is bad--but that difference is only established from a perspective which transcends the action: sometimes embodied figuratively in the poem as Jupiter, it is clearly nothing other than the judgment of Rome's imperial present. This judgment is articulated in the poem in many ways: the speeches of Jupiter, the parade of heroes in Book 6, the shield in Book 8--and also in the similes. The similes of Vergil are not propulsive in the way that Homer's were, nor are they productive of "new ideas" like those of Apollonius. The similes of Vergil are preeminently concerned with assigning value, with naming something ambiguous as good or bad from the perspective of its historical outcome. Thus, to return to the storm scene of Book One, the initiatives of Juno and Neptune are equally arbitrary and private until the sedition simile names one as chaotic and the other as disorderly. Elsewhere, Aeneas can have his moments of *furor* and *insania,* just as his opponents can have their moments of *pietas.* Such vacillations provide the story with narrative possibilities and movement; the similes, and numerous other devices, impose on that movement an interpretant outside of discourse. The imperial model of signification is one which imposes a preestablished meaning on that which is ambiguous, a process which would presumably go on until there is *imperium sine fine (Aen.* 1, 279), until all non-culture is assimilated and organized according to the imperial model. Then there would be a golden age in which, to rewrite a line from *Eclogue* 4 (22): *nec magnos metuent armenta lupos,* "nor would the flocks fear the great wolves."

## Apollonius, Cicero, Vergil

Before we turn to Dante, it will be useful to consider schematically what has been said about the "history" of the epic simile. In Homer we noted that the simile was, like other generative elements in the propulsive textual dynamics of Homer, a text building strategy capable of a variety of uses. With the acceleration of the cognitive skills pertaining to formal analysis, the simile becomes a semiotic mechanism for organizing and producing meaning. The characteristic operation by which this mechanism produces meaning is exchange (*apodosis, redditio*). Since exchange is a metaphor derived from commerce, it is tempting to explore this metaphor more fully, mindful of Cicero's dictum, *omne simile claudicat,* but mindful also of Aristotle's claim that this is the best way "to get hold of new ideas."[22]

In the first chapter of *Capital,* Marx discusses the basic workings of the exchange of commodities. He notes that initially objects have a "use-value"; that is, they have value to someone because they are useful to that someone. At some point, however, it becomes necessary or desirable to acquire one object from someone else in exchange for another. In such a situation, it becomes necessary to establish the "exchange-value" of each object in relation to the other, and at that moment each object becomes a *commodity.* Exchange-value in its simplest form will be determined by some formula such as x amount of commodity A = y amount of commodity B. Numerous factors will determine the outcome of such an "equation," but the important thing for our comparison is that exchange-value arises in terms of a predicated exchange and that from it a *code* will emerge establishing equivalences between some pertinent features of each commodity.

The evolution of an object with use-value to a commodity with exchange-value parallels, *mutatis mutandis*, the change of the function of the epic simile from Homer to Apollonius. In the *Argonautica*, the simile is no longer text-constitutive in the way that it was in Homer. Rather, it is, so to speak, *logos*-constitutive. To return to our semiotic terminology, the simile is used for code-making. Apollonius articulates character by predicating a network of formal relationships to man's inner life, constituting it into a microcosm. And although a comparison may be motivated by the desire to render some phenomenon intelligible by setting up equivalences between that phenomenon and some better known one, it is in the predication of the comparison that both phenomena are constituted into models. The two models become *functives* correlated on the basis of a text. The structure of codes is established on the basis of a message, when a text postulates them as an explanatory condition for its interpretation, just as exchange-value arises on the occasion of a specific exchange.

The exchange of commodities achieves a greater degree of sophistication, according to Marx, when some one commodity (namely, gold) becomes privileged as *the* commodity to which everything else is compared. Instead of the evaluation of commodities in terms of *ad hoc* exchanges, gold becomes substituted for the exchange process, becomes the universal standard and authentication for exchange. This structural moment, the production of a transcendental value, is analogous to the Ciceronian function of the simile, when an analyst such as Aristotle takes a number of codes and establishes a *meta-code*, a *Logos* with a capital "L". Thus for Aristotle the interest of the dialectical exchange of models is not so much in producing *logoi* (as it was for Apollonius), but in the ability of the process to refer one back to a more general model (*Rhet.* 3, 10, 1410b 2-3):

ὅταν γὰρ εἴπῃ τὸ γῆρας καλάμην, ἐποίησε μάθησιν καὶ γνῶσιν διὰ τὸ γένους· ἄμφω γὰρ ἀποθνηκότα.

For when the poet calls old age a "withered stalk," he produces learning and knowledge *by means of what is common to both*: both have degenerated.

It is the production of this commonality (*genos*) in which Cicero is interested: in showing that the particular exchanges which characterize the history of the republic are modulated by a transcendent *ratio* (*revocatio ad rationem*). Furthermore, the production of this *ratio* is perceived as the disclosure of im-

plicit meaning, as making manifest a *ratio* which is immanent.   Thus
Aristotle states that the most successful similes and metaphors will be based
on a common formal heritage (*Rhet.* 3, 2, 1405a 12):

> "Ετι δὲ οὐ πόρρωθεν δεῖ, ἀλλ' ἐκ τῶν συγγενῶν καὶ τῶν
> ὁμοειδῶν μεταφέρειν τὰ ἀνώνυμα ὠνομασμένως ὃ λεχθὲν
> δῆλόν ἐστιν ὅτι συγγενές.

> Furthermore, metaphors must not be far-fetched, but must give
> names to things without names by deriving the metaphor from
> what is *akin* and *of the same form,* so that as soon as the
> metaphor is uttered, the kinship is clearly seen.

The words συγγενῶν and ὁμοειδῶν in this passage remind us that Aristotle
defines the four types of metaphor in the *Poetics* in terms of the species-
genus relationship (εἶδος-γένος).  The knowledge that metaphor produces is
thus the recognition of the true "genealogy" (kinship) among superficially
different things.  So also, Cicero's analysis of Roman history leads him to a
*ratio* which is metaleptically posited as prior and immanent in nature.

Marx notes further that in time gold as money becomes the sole adequate form of exchange value (*Capital,* Part I, ch. 3):

> Circulation becomes the great social retort into which everything
> is thrown to come out crystallized gold.  Not even the bones of
> the saints, and still less are more delicate *res sacrosanctae extra
> commercium hominum* able to withstand this alchemy.  Just as
> every qualitative difference between commodities is extinguished
> in money, so money, on its side, like the radical leveler that it
> is, does away with all distinctions.

If the production of philosophical, scientific or political principles out of a
variety of specific cases is analogous to the establishment of gold as a transcendent value, Vergil's similes take us a step further in our economic comparison.  Both Cicero and Vergil "rewrite" history in order to make it conform to a principle.  But the task Cicero sets before himself is to identify that
*ratio*, to move from *logoi* to *Logos*.  Vergil sets himself the opposite task:
he already has the *logos* (the emperor); and he must show that everything is a
manifestation of that *logos*.  To continue our economic metaphor, Vergil
"invests" the *logos*, produces little Augustan colonies backward and forward
in history.  The *logos* here is not produced by exchange, but becomes established by a paradigmatic event: the victory of Augustus.  *Ex post facto* the

*logos* of the emperor is portrayed as fated, as grounded in the will of Jupiter. So too, Aeneas' victory is metaleptically represented as a *result* rather than as a cause. In Vergil, the *Logos* is the *datum*; in Cicero the *logoi* are the *data*. In both, however, there is a metaleptic reversal. Cicero takes the result of his *revocatio* and portrays it as the generative origin of Roman history. Vergil takes his *Logos* and portrays it as the result of divine will.

The Ciceronian and Vergilian functions of comparison may seem suspiciously similar to each other. There are good grounds for this suspicion. Both involve a transcendental principle which is in a sense outside of the productive process: which is both origin and *telos*. The distinctions drawn between Apollonius, Cicero and Vergil are actually oversimplified, but such simplifications have a certain heuristic value. We can, for example, see that the "transcendental" function of comparison continues a certain development incipient in Apollonius. If Apollonius recognizes the heterogeneity of the human world and exploits exchange in order to make those heterogeneities comparable, Cicero and Vergil seek to totalize human culture on a higher level of organization. It is no accident that two Romans provide us with excellent examples of this "universalizing" function, for both the late republic and the empire were remarkable success stories in "homogenization." The provinces of Rome became "Romanized" to a degree unprecedented in the relatively autonomous sectors of the Hellenistic empires. However various the components that the Romans assimilated, the result was a truly "universal" culture; and the immense cultural capital Rome accumulated during its heyday became the generative model for European civilization for centuries to come.

# DANTE

## Typology and Narrative

In the first canto of the *Inferno*, the pilgrim begins to ascend the holy mountain only to be driven back by a she-wolf. The pilgrim's situation is then described in the following way (55-58):

E qual è quei che volontieri acquista,
  e giugne 'l tempo che perder lo face,
  che 'n tutt' i suoi pendier piange e s'attrista;
tal mi fece la bestia sanza pace.

And like one who rejoices in his gains
  and when the time comes that makes him a loser
  has all his thoughts turned to sadness and lamentation;
such did the beast without peace make me.

Charles Singleton comments on this peculiar passage:[1]

This figure amounts to a pseudo-simile, common enough in the poem: the "one" of the first term of the comparison is actually not distinguishable from the "other" of the second term, except that the former is given as the generic instance and the latter as the particular. The wayfarer here is precisely such a one, in that he eagerly advances up the slope until he encounters the beast.

What Singleton observes is that there is no exchange in this "simile," and the result is an entirely opaque figure: without the code-switching of simile and metaphor, no new ideas are generated; no meaning is produced. This curious passage does not provoke any further comment from Singleton except that such "pseudo-similes" are common in the *Divine Comedy*. This and other like passages, however, present an obstacle to our analysis of the epic simile as a device emblematic of various models of signification; for it does not seem possible to evolve any such model from these "exchangeless" similes. It seems that, like the pilgrim, we have made a false start and will have to take an alternate route by identifying a model of signification elsewhere in the poem and then come back to this passage.

Another simile describes the pilgrim's feelings after emerging from the savage wood (*Inf.* I, 22-27):

> E come quei che con lena affanata
> uscito fuor del pelago alla riva
> si vogve all'acqua perigliosa e guata,
> così l'animo mio, ch'ancor fuggiva,
> si volse a retro a remirar lo passo
> che non lasciò già mai persona viva.

> And as he who with laboring breath
> has escaped from the deep to the shore
> turns to the perilous waters and gazes,
> so my mind, which was still in flight
> turned back to look again at the pass
> which never yet let any go alive.

As Singleton has pointed out, this simile is inspired by the biblical episode of the exodus, one of the key moments in salvation history. The "flight" (*fuggiva*), which is a "crossing over" (*passo*) to reach a "desert strand" (29: *piaggia deserta*) evokes the details of the crossing of the Red Sea by the Jews fleeing from Egypt. Singleton further notes that the flight from Egypt was an "established and familiar 'figure' of conversion." In the moral landscape of *Inferno* I, he concludes, the pilgrim's escape from the forest is an escape from sinfulness through God's grace, like the redemption of the Jews from slavery.[2] In his discussion of this simile, Singleton is interested in the thematics of conversion rather than in a model of signification. He nevertheless alludes to such a model with the word "figure," by which he refers to what Erich Auerbach calls "figural prophecy," what Dante himself terms the "allegory of the theologians," but what is better known as biblical typology.[3]

Biblical typology refers to the interpretation of various events of salvation history as prefigurations of other events of salvation history. Most often, it refers to the view of the New Testament as the fulfillment of the promises "figured" in the Old Testament, but the view of history underlying biblical typology played a major role in Christianity's understanding of its relationship to classical antiquity as well as to the Old Testament Jews. In his Letter to Can Grande, Dante gives a classic example of this type of exegesis:[4]

> Qui modus tractandi, ut melius pateat, potest considerari in hiis versibus: "In exitu Israel de Aegypto, domus Iacob de populo barbaro, facta est Iudaea sanctificatio eius, Israel potestas eius" [Ps. 113]. Nam si ad litteram solam inspiciamus, significatur nobis exitus filiorum Israel de Aegypto, tempore Moysis; si ad allegoricam, nobis significatur nostra redemptio facta per Christum; si ad moralem sensum, significatur nobis conversio animae de luctu et miseria peccati ad statum gratiae; si ad anagogicum, significatur exitus animae sanctae ab huius corruptionis servitute ad aeternae gloriae libertatem.

> This mode of writing can be exemplified in the following verses: "When Israel came up from the land of Egypt, when the house of Jacob came up from a barbarous land, Judah became his sanctuary, Israel his dominion." For if we look only at the letter, the exodus of the Jews in the time of Moses is signified; if we look at the mystical meaning, it is our redemption through Christ; the moral meaning is the conversion of the soul from sin to the state of grace; the anagogical meaning is our escape from the slavery of corruption to the freedom of eternal glory.

The exodus, that central moment of Israel's history, is here viewed as a real event with its own significance for the Jews *tempore Moysis*; but at the same time, it is a sign pointing to other events central to Christian history: the redemption, conversion and eternal glory. The exodus can be a real event with its own significance in its own context and, at the same time, can signify other events because the world is a divine text, God's book: "Auctor sacrae Scripturae est Deus," says Aquinas, "in cuius potestate est ut non solum voces ad significandum accomodet, sed etiam res ipsas."[5] In his article entitled "figura," Auerbach outlines the model of signification which underlines such a view of history:[6]

> Figural prophecy implies the interpretation of one worldly event through another; the first signifies the second, the second fulfills

the first. Both remain historical events; yet both, looked at in this way, have something provisional and incomplete about them; they point to one another and both point to something in the future, something still to come, which will be the actual, real, and definitive event. This is true not only of the Old Testament prefiguration, which points forward to the Incarnation and the proclamation of the gospel, but also of these latter events, for they too are not the ultimate fulfillment, but themselves are a promise of the end of time and the true kingdom of God. Thus history, with all its concrete force, remains forever a figure, cloaked and needful of interpretation, since even the general direction of interpretation is given through faith. In this light the history of no epoch ever has the practical self-sufficiency which, from the standpoint of primitive man and of modern science, resides in the accomplished fact; all history, rather, remains open and questionable, points to something still concealed, and the tentativeness of events in the figural interpretation is fundamentally different from the tentativeness of events in the modern view of historical development. In the modern view, the provisional event is treated as a step in an unbroken horizontal process; in the figural system, the interpretation is always sought from above; events are seen not in their unbroken relation to one another, but torn apart, individually, each in relation to something other which is promised and not yet present. Whereas in the modern view the event is always self-sufficient and secure, while the interpretation is fundamentally incomplete, in the figural interpretation the fact is subordinated to an interpretation which is fully secured to begin with: the interpretation aligns itself with an ideal model situated in the future and is thus far only promised. This model situated in the future and imitated in the figures...recalls Platonistic notions. It carries us still further. For every model, though incomplete as history, is already fulfilled in God and has existed from all eternity in His providence. The figures in which He cloaked it, and the incarnation in which He revealed their meaning, are therefore prophecies of something that has always been, but which will remain veiled for men until the day when they behold the saviour *revelata facie*, with the senses as well as in spirit.

I have quoted this remarkable passage at length because it raises a number of issues related to typology. Some things here are already familiar to us. That the interpretation of events is "sought from above," that this interpretation is "fully secured to begin with," and "aligns itself with an ideal model of history" (richtet sich aus nach einem Urbild des Geschehens), does indeed recall

Platonistic notions. It also recalls the Vergilian model of signification wherein Augustus is viewed as the cynosure of history, so that past events can be seen as signifiers pointing to him. Vergil's mode of text production is in harmony with this model, being a matter of reproducing the model of culture in the past.

There is clearly a sense in which Vergil's metaleptic "reading" of history as a process leading up to Augustus is similar to the "reading" of Old Testament events as a stage in salvation history preliminary to its fulfillment in Christ, the interpretant of history. But the Archimedean point for Vergil is a present situation, the victory of Augustus. The model of signification is established there by an exercise of power. The Christian, on the other hand, is situated between a past which is still tentative, "open and questionable," and a future which is "thus far only promised" and "will remain veiled for men until they behold the saviour *revelata facie.*" This raises the question, in what sense is the interpretation "fully secured to begin with."

Auerbach recognizes that the *Urbild* has a dual existence. On the one hand, it is already fulfilled in God, for whom everything is present, for whom *praescientia* is simply *scientia*. Humans, on the other hand, who experience everything as articulated in time, know divine meaning only in terms of historical categories: promise and fulfillment. At the end of time, when Christ comes to finally fulfill history, divine meaning will be available to us as presence. Until then we know God only in his historical manifestations, the events of salvation history which are "cloaked and needful of interpretation." The mediation between these two perspectives, the means by which the interpretation becomes secured, Auerbach notes, is "given through faith." How then does one acquire faith?

The inspired texts of the Christian tradition provide a mode of access to divine meaning, but they too, being articulated and subject to the heterogenizing influence of time, cannot contain divine meaning. In order to move from *figura* to *veritas*, it is necessary to receive divine illumination "from above," the gift of faith which is the conversion experience. August figures of the early church were afforded this gift of wisdom, and these figures are the pillars of what became the institutionalization of the conversion experience, the Church. The medieval Church stands in a relation to meaning similar to that of Augustus for the Romans. By an exercise of power (at least in Vergil's version), Augustus became the guarantor of meaning: he established a model of signification. So also, by the exercise of its authority, the Church governs the production of meaning, preserving and maintaining that which has been "handed down." Guided by the Holy Spirit, the teaching magisterium establishes a canon of inspired texts and secures their interpretation on the basis of ancient testimony.[7] This does not mean that personal revelations become extinct, but rather that the Church provides the framework within which they occur and are understood.

The mediation that the Church provides between God and his people, however, is communal. It assures us that, in general, everything is unfolding as it should. The situation can be compared to a drama in which the Church is the stage manager and God is the author. The Christian finds himself hurled into the middle of this text and is called upon to play out his role. Although the outline of the plot is known to all, no one is exactly sure what his role is. The Church can provide a more and more complex stage apparatus, but it too is ignorant of the outcome with regard to each individual. Although the interpretation of history as a whole is fully secured in the Church's teaching, interpretation as it relates to day-to-day living is anything but secure. The first canto of the *Divine Comedy* articulates this existential situation. The pilgrim finds himself lost in sinfulness and ignorance; but he finds hope of divine illumination when he sees the sun over the top of the blessed mountain. In terms of the exodus imagery, the lighted mountaintop suggests Mt. Sinai, which Moses climbed to see God face-to-face. But the pilgrim finds that not everyone is granted direct access to divine wisdom. He is driven back down the mountain by a *lupa*. Then Vergil appears and tells the pilgrim that there is another road he must take to find the illumination that he seeks; and after this prologue, the *Divine Comedy* begins.

A number of interesting points can be derived from this view of the prologue. To begin with, this scene has implications for the relationship between knowledge and narrative. Whatever the allegorical identity of the *lupa*, it is clear that had she not intervened, we would have no *Divine Comedy*. Had the pilgrim reached the top of the mountain, he would have achieved that supra-temporal perspective, the *kairos*, from which one sees as God sees. Past and future would have collapsed into a single vision of divine meaning. The seeking after divine knowledge is the movement toward the moment when all movement ceases: in human terms, the fullness of meaning in the divine presence is silence. When St. Paul was caught up into heaven, he heard "unspeakable words," not fit for man to utter (2 Cor. 12:4). So in the opening lines of the *Paradiso*, Dante notes that he has seen things in the highest heaven "which whoso descends from up there has neither the knowledge nor the power to relate." Narrative and human language collapse in the face of divine meaning. The figural model of signification creates a serious problem for the narrative poet; there is only one "narrative" which it is capable of producing: the narrative of God which is salvation history.

Whether the first canto of the *Inferno* represents general or specific events in Dante's personal experience or not, it is possible to see in it a representation of the narrative problematics of the *Divine Comedy*. Dante seeks to disclose in his poem divine significance and he therefore adopts as his model of signification the divine plan. But given this, he can do no more than reiterate that which has been handed down; he can do no more than quote God's book. The typological simile of lines 22-27 does in fact cite the event of salvation history which, in conjunction with its fulfillment in Christ, reveals in a general way God's plan for mankind. But this is not enough. Since mankind has not yet reached the top of the mountain, does not yet see from the *eschaton*, the interpretative perspective which would reveal to any one person *his or her* role in the unfolding drama is still lacking.

Although some have interpreted the *lupa* to be the papal Curia,[8] it is not necessary to see in the first canto's portrayal of the Christian's existential situation an attack on the mediating role of the Church, but rather a realization of the limits of that role. Although comforted and chastened by the Church, each person must still make his or her own way to divine wisdom. The *Confessions* of Augustine, a work which witnesses to God's salvific plan, ends in the following way (13, 38):

> But You who are Goodness itself and lack no goodness are forever at rest, since You are your own repose. What man can teach another this? What angel can teach it to another angel? What angel can teach it to a man? It must be asked of You, sought from You, knocked for of You. Thus, thus it will be received, thus it will be found, thus the door will be opened.

The *Confessions* is a book about the gift of faith and divine illumination; but, however powerful it is as a witness and as an inspiration, the very nature of the knowledge celebrated there makes it impossible to be articulated in human language, lies beyond the pale of narrative. What then of the rest of us who are denied direct access to the top of the mountain? How are we to find personal confirmation of our faith?

It is at this moment of *aporia* when the pilgrim encounters Vergil, who tells him of "another way" to achieve his desire. The textual implication of this scene is that although the model of signification of the *Comedy* is that of typology, the mode of text production is different from that model. In the final chapter of "figura" Auerbach asserts that the figural structure predominates the *Divine Comedy*, but he does not fully face up to the problem this poses for writing (67):

> The *Comedy* is a vision which regards and proclaims the figural truth as already fulfilled, and what constitutes its distinctive character is precisely that, fully in the spirit of figural interpretation, it attaches the truth perceived in the vision to historical, earthly events.

It is true that the *Comedy*'s portrayal of the afterlife claims to be an account from the perspective of the *eschaton*, an account in which signifiers are aligned to their signifieds. But the *Comedy* is not produced *by* a vision, it is the production *of* a vision. Had the pilgrim reached the top of the mountain, *then* he would have had a vision--but then he would have had nothing to tell us. It is only after this attempt fails that it becomes necessary to try another route and write the *Divine Comedy*.

What this means is that the authorial voice who is ostensibly reporting what he saw from the perspective of the end of the poem is, in fact, created along the way. The situation of the poet is the literary analogue of the Christian trying to feel his way to the *eschaton* from which he can know his role in God's plan. "It is Dante's fiction," notes Freccero, "that the author's existence precedes that of the poem, as though the experience had been concluded before the poem were begun. In reality, however, the experience of the pilgrim and the creation of the authorial voice take place at the same time, in the writing of the poem."[9] The fiction of the poem is that it produces meaning according to the typological model of signification, as God does, with the interpretation fully secured to begin with. But a text in the process of being written is just as "insecure" as the Christian trying to ascertain God's will as he or she lives from day to day.

The next task is to identify the mode of text production of Dante's poem; but already we can state in a preliminary fashion the role of the pseudo-simile with which we began. The fact that it lies between the failed attempt at direct access to divine knowledge and the appearance of Vergil suggests that it functions as a hinge between the model of signification and the mode of text production. The pseudo-simile is the perfect adjunct to the *aporia* of the pilgrim; for, like the figural model itself, the pseudo-simile is a form of meaning production which, in this case, fails to produce meaning.

We all know that meaning is up there on top of the brightly lit mountain, but somehow for the pilgrim it has fizzled.

## Abduction and *ratio difficilis*

The *Divine Comedy* poses the problem of its own production in a way that brings into sharp focus the dialectic between codes and messages. Let us reconsider briefly the "history" of the simile as it has been set forth above. When Apollonius uses epic similes in the *Argonautica*, he is, in a sense, "reading" Homer's similes. Homer had said "they are like wolves"; in his imitations, Apollonius asks, "in what way are they like wolves?" The posing of this question involves a particular aspect of the labor of sign production: *code making*.[10] The interpretation of Homer by Apollonius consists of the constitution of sememes into formal models so that they can become functives in a correlation. A correlation is the code which establishes equivalences between the pertinent features of two sememes by exchange.

Cicero's text can be seen as a further reading which takes as its starting point the production of codes. Given the constitution of sememes into models and the code which correlates them into a sign function, the Ciceronian analyst elaborates a subcode which authenticates the exchange process. Apollonius indicates how wolves are like men; Cicero accepts this analysis and adds that they are alike in this way *because they are* συγγενῶν: because they are generated by the same underlying *Logos*.[11] As an interpretative process, the Ciceronian function is comparable to induction wherein one produces from examples (*paradeigmata*) a more general statement of relationships (*ratio, logos*). This we have seen to be Cicero's conception of the republic; and although the *Ratio* is produced by Cicero's analysis of history (is the *telos* of his inductive process), he nevertheless posits it as immanent in nature, as the origin of the historical process. This metaleptic reversal is possible precisely because the *Ratio* itself lies outside of the process of production. The *Ratio* is timeless and constant, its temporal manifestations being only *simulacra*.

The *Aeneid* portrays Augustus as the *telos* of a historical process, a *telos* which is represented as existing all along in the will of Jupiter. This portrayal, as we have seen, is also metaleptic, since it is Augustus' victory which is in fact the generator of the productive process: a process which "recognizes" Augustus in the past and future. Whereas Cicero *produces* inductively a *Logos* which is then posited as prior, Vergil's *Logos* is given to begin with and then posited as a result. In both cases, the principle of intelligibility lies outside of the process of production; in both cases, "lateral" exchange has been thrust into the background making the focus of interest a *law*, whether generative or teleological. Production occurs either "down" from or "up" toward a law which is static and transcendent.

The *Divine Comedy* problematizes the relationship between law and production and can serve as a critique of the dichotomy outlined above. In the first canto the existence of a transcendent *Logos* is posited only to be represented as inaccessible. Production in the *Comedy* does not occur in respect to a transcendent law, but in its absence--in fact it occurs because of its absence. The fiction of the *Divine Comedy* is that there are two Dantes: one who is a reader on his way to the *Logos*, the other who is an author and who, by virtue of a prior revelation, is reproducing the *Logos*. But as the first canto suggests, the *Logos* is neither the starting point of a deductive process, nor the *telos* of an inductive process, but the instrument of what Eco calls an *abductive* process.[12]

Unlike deduction, which moves "down" from a general proposition to a result, or induction, which moves "up" from a number of cases to a general proposition, abduction is a kind of inferential procedure in which hypotheses are advanced to account for uncoded circumstances and complex contents. Faced with uncoded circumstances,

> the interpreter is obliged to recognize that the message does not rely on previous codes and yet that it must be understandable; if it is so, non-explicit conventions must exist; if not yet in existence, they have to exist (or to be posited). Their apparent absence postulates their necessity (Eco, 129).

Abduction can take two forms, which Eco calls undercoding and overcoding. Undercoding proceeds by hypothesis from non-existent codes to potential codes. Overcoding proceeds by hypothesis from existing codes to more analytic subcodes. In both cases, abduction

> represents the first step of a metalinguistic operation destined to enrich a code.... A consistently interpreted ambiguous uncoded context gives rise, if accepted by society, to a convention, and thus to a coded coupling. That context becomes step by step a ready made sentence, just as a metaphor, which at first has to be abductionally interpreted, becomes step-by-step a catachresis (Eco, 132-33).

Eco's notion of abduction summarizes the various aspects of sign production which we have identified as different functions of the epic simile. Undercoding, the movement from non-existent to potential codes, is what makes up the Apollonian function; overcoding, the movement from existing codes to a subcode, the Ciceronian. The hardening of a subcode into an accepted convention so that it is perceived as governing the code from which it was originally derived is the Vergilian function. Eco's discussion of abduction also makes it clear that the separation of these types of sign production is rather artificial and that examples of "pure" undercoding or overcoding occur rarely, if ever (Eco thus proposes the term "extra-coding" to cover both movements at once), and that the most conventional cliché is still an open form potentially able to be invigorated by a novel reading. The nature of abduction is a back and forth affair in which hypotheses are advanced, tested and modified. When Cicero claims that the *ratio* of the republic is grounded in nature, or when Vergil claims that Augustus' victory was fated, we recognize these as attempts to anchor the process of unlimited semiosis in some non-semiotic *primum mobile.*

What is interesting about the *Divine Comedy* is that although the existence of a *primum mobile* is certainly posited, it is nevertheless rejected as a text-constitutive force. As the poem begins, the poet has not yet had a revelation: he is both pilgrim and author, subject and object, reader and writer. What this means is that the process of interpretation is simultaneously the process of production. Despite the fiction that the *Divine Comedy* is produced in respect to a transcendental law, by an interpretation which is "secured to begin with," it is rather a case of radical invention, in which expressions must be established according to a content which does not yet exist as such. It is thus a case of rule-changing creativity (abduction) as opposed to a case of rule-governed creativity (induction, deduction). The semiotic analogue of this opposition in Eco's theory of sign production is *ratio difficilis* vs. *ratio facilis.*

The terms *ratio difficilis* and *ratio facilis* derive their names from the fact that all expressions are produced according to a type; i.e., they are tokens of a type. The relationship between an expression-type and an expression-token is the sign-function's type/token *ratio.* We have a case of *ratio facilis* "when an expression-token is accorded to an expression-type, duly recorded by an expression system and, as such, foreseen by a given code" (Eco, 183). The production of phonemes, for example, is ruled by a *ratio facilis*, since certain pertinent features are prescribed by the phonological system used as an expressive system for a language in order to produce a token. One type of *ratio difficilis* occurs when an expression-token is directly accorded to its content because the corresponding expression-type does not yet exist (Eco, 188):

> The sign producer has a fairly clear idea of *what* he would like to "say," but he does not know *how* to say it; and he cannot know *how* to do so until he has discovered *precisely what* to say. The lack of a definite content-type makes it impossible to find an expression-type, while the lack of an appropriate expression device makes the content vague and inarticulable.

The situation described here by Eco is precisely the "existential situation" of the Christian and the textual problematic articulated in the first canto of the *Divine Comedy*. The relationship between God and man is, from the standpoint of fallen man, a *ratio difficilis*. Although God's "book" exists completely written in His mind, for the ordinary Christian who has not received divine illumination, it is a discourse which as yet has no satisfactory interpretants. The theological analogue of this crux is the mystery of salvation, in which the Church's tradition has done a balancing act between Pelagianism and Jansenism. Does God save men or do they save themselves? Is there room for free will within a doctrine of predestination? Is man justified by faith or works? If faith is a gift, does anything man does or does not do cause this gift to be given or withheld? All these questions can be summarized in what appears to be a tautology: is grace gratuitous? For our study of the simile, the question can be posed thus: is there exchange between God and man (Pelagianism) or not (Jansenism)? The point here is not that there is an apparent contradiction which must be resolved; rather there is a real contradiction, which for the Christian is a theological mystery, a matter of faith. For the poet, however, it is a contradiction that he must occult in some way: it is an *aporia* out of which he must, if nothing else, simulate an escape. Language, of course, does work; communication does occur; we have, after all, the *Divine Comedy*. How does it all happen?

Since *ratio difficilis* involves the proposal of a correlation not fixed by convention, it may be straight away noted that such sign production may possibly fail: it may be received as noise. To ensure its success, a correlation produced by *ratio difficilis* must be based on something else. But what could this "something else" be if it is not a convention? How does a code come into being? The problem remains puzzling so long as one considers the disposition of the functives of a correlation into the role of expression-form or content-form as in some sense prior to the apportioning function of the code constitutive of the sign-function. In fact we should assert that the coding operation which does the apportioning also establishes the two functives in the role of expression or content.

Let us consider an example. When a beginning language teacher points to an object, such as a window, and says "fenestra," we have a case of *ratio difficilis*, the proposal of a new (to the students, that is) correlation. In this case, the window is the expression-form and the word "fenestra" is the content-form. This new correlation has good prospects for being accepted, because it is based on the conventions of "mentioning" (Eco, 163-65) and because of the contextual cues (the expectation of the students that they will learn Latin words in a Latin class). A related example of *ratio difficilis*, and one which is found in the *Comedy*, is allegory. An allegorical text establishes a network of relationships among various conventional units (animals, gods and goddesses, etc.) so that these conventional content-forms become expression-forms. The units are manipulated in such a way that signals to the addressee that the rule organizing the discourse is not the usual one governing these units (that is, it is not "about" gods and goddesses) but some other non-explicit rule being articulated for the first time.[13] There is always the possibility that the reader will not "catch on" and will view the text as a scandalous tale about pagan gods and goddesses. As it happened, certain allegorical correlations (such as Athena = wisdom), at one time produced by a *ratio difficilis*, became in western literature accepted as conventions. By Dante's time, in fact, a number of allegorical codes had become catachreses.

The point of these examples is a proposition fundamental to a "differentialist" view of signification: all language is figurative. Every *ratio facilis* was at one time a *ratio difficilis*; and every *ratio difficilis*, in order to be understood, must be based on some other convention. If *ratio difficilis* must establish correlations between expressive units and content units which do not exist as such, what do these units exist as? An answer suggested by the above examples is that they exist as functives of other correlations. In the first example, the referent of the pointing gesture (the window) becomes the functive of a new correlation in the role of expressive unit; and the Latin expressive unit *fenestra* becomes a functive of that correlation in the role of content unit. In the second example, the content "Athena" has become the expressive form for another element in the sememe of "Athena" (for she was traditionally associated with wisdom) by what rhetoric came to name a metonymy. It can now be seen that the situation of the pilgrim in *Inferno* I is not a peculiar case of sign production, but rather the regular conditions under which signification and communication occur. Abduction is not *one* way to interpret complex texts, but *the* way in which they are interpreted; and the problem of "inspiration" for Dante is a variant of a more general one: how does one write a poem which does not yet exist? What the notion of abduction takes into account is that sign production involves a dialectic between codes and messages (Eco, 139-42).

## Typology and Homology

We are now in a better position to understand how the pilgrim finds a "way out" of his dilemma in the first canto. Immediately after the pseudo-simile, he encounters Vergil, not so much a shade, or a man, or even the ful-fillment of the *figura* of Vergil, but a text (79-87):

> "Or se' tu quel Virgilio e quella fonte
> che spandi di parlar sì largo fiume?"
> rispuos' io lui con vergognosa fronte.
> "O delli altri poeti onore e lume,
> vagliami 'l lungo studio e 'l grande amore
> che m' ha fatto cercar lo tuo volume.
> Tu se' lo mio maestro e 'l mio autore,
> tu se' solo colui da cu' io tolsi
> lo bello stilo che m' ha fatto onore."

> "Art thou then that Vergil and that fount
> which pours forth so broad a stream of speech?"
> replied I with bashful front to him.
> "O honor and light of the other poets!
> May the long study avail me and the great love,
> which have made me search thy volume!
> Thou art my master and my author;
> thou alone art he from whom I took
> the fair style that has done me honor."

As a text, Vergil has many things to offer Dante as he begins his own narra-tive. Book Four of the *Aeneid* was, for the Middle Ages, a portrait of pas-sion overcome; Aeneas was a man who renounced individual desire for a providential destiny. Book Six was a highly overcoded *katabasis* into the afterworld, the outline of which is still recognizable in the *Comedy*. Most important, perhaps, Vergil offered a content-form that Dante could use as an expression-form for the "Kingdom of God": the ideal form of government represented in the *Aeneid* as the empire under Augustus.[14] Vergil's words about paradise in the first canto are a paradigm of this portrayal by means of imperial imagery (124-29):

> "chè quello *imperador* che là su *regna*,
>   perch' io fu' ribellante alla sua legge,
>   non vuol che 'n sua *città* per me si venga.
> *In tutte parti impera* e quivi *regge*;
>   quivi è la sua città e *l'alto seggio*:
>   oh felice colui cu' ivi elegge!"

> "For that *emperor who reigns* there above
>   because I was rebellious to His law,
>   wills it not that through me any one should come into His *city*.
> *In all parts He governs* and there *He reigns*:
>   there is His city and *His lofty throne*.
> O happy the man He chooses to go there!"

In the *De Monarchia*, Dante suggests there is a homology between the kingdoms of God and man, and the Roman empire is there singled out as the clearest manifestation of the monarchial ideal.  In the *Comedy*, the poet who celebrated the golden age of Rome, himself an unwitting messianic poet in his fourth *Eclogue*, comes to the aid of Dante to mediate his portrayal of the Kingdom of God.

This homology, however, is not without problems.  Earth and afterworld are homologous in the sense that everything is produced by one and the same *Logos*:  the will of God.  This is the claim of typology, that everything in this life is connected to and fulfilled in the afterlife.  Earth and heaven are *not* homologous in the sense that there is no exchange between them:  the relationship is not reciprocal.  One is subject to the heterogenizing influence of time; the other is timeless.  One is *figura*; the other is *veritas*.  The *logos* of earthly life cannot be understood in *comparison* to the afterlife, but only as the former is subsumed and fulfilled in the latter.  The assertion of the *De Monarchia* that there is a mandate from God for a temporal order with a temporal goal in some sense independent of (and therefore possibly homologous in the second sense to) the eternal order and the eternal goal of man assumes that this world has its own *logos*.  This leads in the direction of Pelagianism.

Indeed, in Augustine, the Doctor of Grace, we find a quite different view of the relationship between the "city of God" and the "earthly city." They are not, for Augustine, homologous but antinomous, for "a man cannot serve two masters." Again we are faced with contradictory claims that do not seem reconcilable and both of which have good authority in the words of Christ. For there are parables (*parabolai*) in which Christ ostensibly compares the kingdom of God to various earthly things; but when asked the purpose of the parables, indeed in the same passage, he denies that they actually produce meaning at all (Mark 4:11-12):

> To you has been given the secret of the kingdom of God, but for those outside everything is in parables; so that they may indeed see but not perceive, and may indeed hear but not understand; lest they should turn again and be forgiven.

The point, again, is not to resolve this contradiction by valorizing one or the other position, but rather to note that this contradiction is Dante's problem in the *Comedy*; he has, on the one hand, a signification system which leads to silence (typology) and on the other, one which cannot produce divine meaning (the homology of comparison).

Since valorizing one or the other of these two types of meaning production would dissolve the text, the solution of the *Divine Comedy* is to move forward in a way that vacillates between them. The *Comedy* claims to be a representation in human, time-bound terms of the divine and eternal. Since this is impossible, what it does is precipitate divine meaning indirectly. The dialectic between the pilgrim and the authorial voice is the dialectic between homology and typology. The pilgrim moves along, inspecting signs and producing hypotheses about their significance. The presence of the authorial voice authenticates these hypotheses as one who has already made it to the top. But the authorial voice, of course, has not made it to the top and is only hypostasized along the way. This is the characteristic movement of abduction: the hypothetical reconstruction of the process by which an initially unreadable text is produced. The pilgrim's "progress" is from signs to sign-systems; the authorial voice moves from sign-systems to signs. The former produces, for example, immortal bodies as analogues for the dead souls in hell; the latter recognizes that, however absurd this is as representation, it is true "typologically."

The typological model thus, in a sense, "leans" on the model of exchange, for typology is of itself incapable of producing a narrative.[15] The structure of exchange, on the other hand, is expert at producing isotopies and symmetries by which things can be seen as related to one another. Once this is done, typology can step in with its claim that all things are bound together by one *Logos*, that the net result of all exchange is zero. Everything in the *Comedy* must be represented in terms of exchange in order to be represented at all; but against this representational imperative is the typological claim that everything is abiding presence. Thus, whatever is introduced into the poem must produce something else to "balance it out," so that the result will be that homeostasis which is characteristic of the supra-temporal perspective.

A particularly interesting example of this process is the *lupa* in canto I of the *Inferno*. The she-wolf has traditionally been taken to be the allegorical figure of *cupiditas*, which we learn in the *De Monarchia* is "especially contrary to justice" (I, 11: *notandum est quod iustitiae maxime contrarietur cupiditas*). In fact, the universal temporal monarch for whom Dante argues will be just because, ruling and possessing everything, he will have nothing to covet:

> Ubi ergo non est quod possit optari, impossibile est ibi cupiditatem esse...sed Monarchum non habet quod possit optare...ex quo sequitur, quod Monarchum sincerissimum inter mortales iustitiae possit esse subjectum.

> Where there is nothing which could be desired, there avarice is impossible...but the monarch has nothing which he could desire...from which, it follows that the Monarch would possess justice most fully among mortals.

The *lupa*, it seems, is exchange gone mad, for she "has intercourse with many" and is "never sated" (97-101):

> e ha natura sì malvagia e ria,
> che mai non empie la bramosa voglia,
> e dopo 'l pasto ha più fame che pria.
> Molti son li animali a cui s'ammoglia,
> e più saranno ancora.

> And she has a nature so vicious and malignant
> that her greedy appetite is never sated,

and after food she is hungrier than before.
Many are the creatures with which she has intercourse
and there will be more to come.

Now the claim of typology is that everything is part of the divine plan. From the supra-temporal perspective of God, everything is in its place and signifying in the way that God wills it. How can human language, based on the structure of exchange, give an account of this claim? It does so by producing something to neutralize the *lupa*, something which has no appetite at all (100-4):

> Molti son li animali a cui s'ammoglia,
>   e più saranno ancora, infin che 'l Veltro
>   verrà, che la farà morir con doglia.
> Questi non ciberà terra nè peltro,
>   ma sapienza, amore e virtute.

> Many are the creatures with which she has intercourse
>   and there will be more to come, until the hound
>   comes that shall bring her to miserable death.
> He shall not feed on land or pelf
>   but on wisdom, love and virtue.

The *veltro*,[16] as a male domesticated version of the *lupa*, is produced by what Riffaterre would call the conversion of a descriptive system. But the operation of such a conversion does not result in an antinomy which marks off culture from non-culture, as it did in Homer, but rather in a *concordia discors*. In the perspective which typology ascribes to God, the pair is an unchanging and complementary unity. The *lupa* is not anti-culture or even non-culture, but already, in the eyes of God, "culture." The relationship between the *lupa* and the *veltro* is, in human terms, a negative homology (female--male, wild--domesticated, appetite--no appetite); but homology is an articulated version of what for God is just "*Logos*." The *Comedy* tries to pro-duce ("lead forth") in narrative form the homeostasis that typology claims to be the true nature of all things. But the "true" articulation of this homeostasis is silence;[17] divine meaning cannot be "produced" for it is immanent. Since Dante cannot produce the homeostatic vision of God, he instead establishes symmetries: if you come across a *lupa*, look around for a *veltro*. The *Comedy* uses the only resources available to language, the exchange of "figurative" language; but exchange is always, so to speak, "under erasure" in the *Divine Comedy*, always recognized as inadequate to the task.

The *Comedy* is a vast *momento mori* proclaiming that what men do in this life is "typologically" related to their fate in the afterlife. But, as we learn in the *Letter to Can Grande*, the *Comedy* does not produce this relationship logically (according to a *logos*), but *rhetorically* (*Epistle* X, 16):

> Genus vero philosophiae sub quo hic (sc. the *Comedy*) in toto et parte proceditur, est morale negotium, sive ethica. quia non ad speculandum, sed ad opus incoeptum est totum. Nam si in aliquo loco vel passu pertractatur ad modum speculativi negotii, hoc non est gratia speculativi negotii, sed gratia operis.

> The part of philosophy under which the whole work moves forward is that of moral duty or ethics. For the whole work was begun not for the sake of speculation, but for the sake of effecting change. So if here or there something is introduced in the mode of speculation, this is not for speculation's sake, but for the sake of influencing the reader.

What these sentences tell us is that the *Comedy* does not concern itself with causes and effects as they relate to the *Logos*, but causes as they relate to effects of persuasion. Dante is not concerned whether his picture of the afterworld is "true" in an objective sense (*ad speculandum*); but whether he represents the claim of typology that this world will be judged in the next persuasively (*ad opus*). The difference between the latter and the former is the difference between making it to the top of the *dilettoso monte* and writing the *Divine Comedy*. It is the difference between having a vision of the *Logos* and persuading others that there is a *Logos*. Since the correlation between life and afterlife is a *ratio difficilis*, the portrayal in the *Comedy* "leans," as it has often been noted, on rhetorical conventions. Lovers who are "carried away" by the "winds of passion," as the saying goes, are literally blown around by winds in hell (*Inf.* 5). A. C. Charity calls this operation of the *contrapasso* "figural realism," an apt name. For if man's earthly life is a *figura* which is fulfilled in the next life, the souls in the *Comedy* are reifications of figures of speech. In this way the associations and relationships of language make the *ratio difficilis* persuasive as typological truth.

## Propulsion and the *Divine Comedy*

If we return to the pseudo-simile of canto I, the significance of its juxtaposition with the typological simile can now be seen. The exodus simile projects a pattern of action which leads to the silent reception of meaning. The pilgrim should, as this simile suggests, make it to the top of the mountain, like Moses, and see Truth face-to-face. But this does not work; meaning is not available to the pilgrim in this way. But if he does not receive illumination "from above," the alternative, working one's way "up" by the exchange of the simile, it is recognized, does not work either. The pseudo-simile does not produce any more meaning for the pilgrim than did the typological one. The rescue mission of Vergil, we have suggested, implies that although divine meaning is not available in either of these two ways, poetry has the power to do the next best thing: produce a persuasive argument for the existence of divine Meaning.

The second canto of *Inferno* provides a sort of symmetry to the first canto, and a solution to the textual problematics of the Comedy is there proposed. As the pilgrim begins, he suddenly has a moment of self-doubt, described by a pseudo-simile (II, 37-42):

> E qual è quei che disvuol ciò che volle
>   e per novi pensier cangia proposta,
>   sì che dal cominciar tutto si tolle
> tal mi fec' io in quella oscura costa,
>   perchè, pensando, consumai la 'mpressa
>   che fu nel cominciar cotanto tosta.

> And like one who unwills what he has willed
>   and with new thoughts changes his resolve,
>   so that he quite gives up the thing he had begun,
> such did I become on that dark slope,
>   for by thinking on it I rendered null the undertaking
>   that had been so suddenly embarked upon.

Vergil responds by telling the pilgrim that *tre donne benedette* (124) have acted from on high so that his text production could move forward. These three ladies recall the *tre fieri* which block the pilgrim's ascent in canto I.[18] Just as those three beasts, who allegorically sum up man's fallen nature, block the pilgrim's access to the *Logos*, so these three ladies give Dante the "word" to go forward with his poem. After Dante hears of this heavenly aid, there follows the first "epic" simile of the poem (127-30):

> Quali i fioretti, dal notturno gelo
>   chinati e chiusi, poi che 'l sol li 'mbianca

si drizzan tutti aperti in loro stello,
tal mi fec' io di mia virtute stanca.

As little flowers, by chill of night
bent down and closed, when the sun brightens them,
straighten and all unfold upon their stems
such from my faint strength did I become.

This simile of self constitution is clearly a counterpoint to the *aporia* of the preceding pseudo-simile (*di mia virtute stanca*). What mediates this "conversion," however, is not divine illumination, but the persuasive power of love poetry. The fact that the "word" is given through three *donne* and that the whole passage recalls the *Vita Nuova*[19] indicates that the *Comedy* will achieve its end rhetorically (*ad opus*), not theologically (*ad speculandum*); that it will be enthymemic, not syllogistic; that it will move the reader, not prove things to him. Only in this way can exchange become part of a discourse which can be "understood" only by faith.

This opposition between what *is* and what is *persuasive* comes to a climax in the last canto of the *Paradiso*. As the pilgrim/author tries to see/remember the vision of God, words, as we would expect, fail him (*Par.* XXXIII, 55-63):

Da quinci innanzi il mio veder fu maggio
che 'l parlar nostro, ch'a tal vista cede,
e cede la memoria a tanto oltraggio.
Qual è colui che somnïando vede,
che dopo il sogno la passione impressa
rimane, e l'altro alla mente non riede,
cotal son io, chè quasi tutta cessa
mia visione, ed ancor mi distilla
nel core il dolce che nacque da essa.

From that moment on my vision was greater
than our speech, which fails at such a sight,
and memory too fails at such excess.
Like him that sees in a dream
and after the dream the passion wrought by it remains
but the rest returns not to mind
Such am I; for my vision almost wholly fades
and still there drops in my heart
the sweetness that was born of it.

The ultimate experience of the *Comedy*, the moment toward which the poem has been converging, just as we get to it, slips away. The pilgrim cannot see it and the author cannot remember it. All that remains is the *conviction* that something happened, the effect of that something. And although conviction is an object of faith, effects of persuasion are the objects of poetry.

In the *Divine Comedy*, the epic simile plays a role that, for the most part, has not been central since Homer. As we noted above, Homer's similes were *propulsive*; that is, what for his imitators was basically a *formal* device, productive insofar as it related to organizing and producing meaning as a model, Homer's similes were text-formative elements which propelled the narrative forward in various ways, particularly when the proairesis became inadequate for one reason or another. It is not surprising that Dante's similes should rejuvenate this Homeric function more explicitly than his predecessors, for clearly Dante's narrative dilemma is also one in which the "logic of action" (proairesis) is constantly problematic. As in Homer, the simile helps Dante to "get the story told." The existential situation of the Christian (how to do the will of God, how to live an "authentic" existence) is the same problem as that of the poet (how do you write a poem which has not yet been written); that is, when you sit down in front of a blank piece of paper, what propulsive mechanism can get you started and get you through to the end. The anxiety of the pilgrim who does not find divine illumination is the anxiety of the poet who has not found "inspiration." The textual production of a *veltro* from a *lupa* does not rely on revelation, but on a semiotic mechanism made possible by the propulsion inherent in sign systems structured according to an inferential model.

The function of the simile in the *Comedy* shows that the poem is not produced *by* a vision (or any objective correlative of a vision), but is the production *of* a vision; or perhaps more accurately, the *Comedy* is production *aimed toward* a vision. Language in the *Comedy* is "on the way" toward something. Language can move forward and the faith of the pilgrim is that it is moving toward something, although that something cannot be articulated. It is a small wonder that the Romantics, who were so fascinated with the notions of transcendence and inspiration, were attracted to Dante, the poet whose text poses in such a poignant way the problem of poetic *creation*: creation understood here as production *ex nihilo*.

# MILTON

Samuel Johnson once called *Paradise Lost* a grand testament to dead ideas. It is a fitting image for our last example of the epic tradition, for we can find in this poem monuments of various models of signification and textual functions identified in the texts considered so far. *Paradise Lost* can serve both as a summary and as a privileged locus for confronting in a more general way the key problems raised by our analyses. Eco's view of communication and signification as a dialectic between codes and messages implies an inherent dynamism in language going in two directions: on the one hand, an impulse toward totality and closure, and on the other, a persistent mutability, characterized by displacement and deferral.[1] The epics we have considered, generally taken to be homogeneous monuments to national identity or to a heroic ethic, have turned out to be more like battlegrounds where the impulse towards closure and totality confronts the mobility and openendedness of unlimited semiosis. The scope of *Paradise Lost* is nothing less than the "Global Semantic Universe" (as Eco calls it) and Milton's attempt to pursue "with no middle flight" things "unattempted yet in prose or rhyme," raises explicitly the issue of "epic totality" by thematizing the problem of origins. *Paradise Lost* relates the generation of the post-lapsarian world from the pre-lapsarian one: it is a continuous narrative which centralizes the very moment of discontinuity. Language in *Paradise Lost* seems to have forgotten its fallen nature while narrating its own fall. In the preface to Book Nine, the narrator contrasts the hackneyed themes of previous epics with his own "higher argument," which is "sufficient of itself to raise that name" (i.e., heroic). But fallen language, despite its impulse to autonomy and totality, cannot raise itself up to the immanence of divine language, cannot produce the plenitude. The remarkable thing about Milton's similes is that they are *not* emblematic of a model of signification which organizes *Paradise Lost*; rather, they are fragmentary remains of other models of signification. Collected here, they are always already produced elsewhere: always, in a sense, dead ideas.

## Homer

The very first simile of *Paradise Lost* describing the size of Satan is a very "Homeric" moment in the text (1, 196-209):

> In bulk as huge
> As whom the Fables name of monstrous size,
> *Titanian*, or *Earth-born*, that warr'd on *Jove*,
> *Briareos* or *Typhon*, whom the Den
> By ancient *Tarsus* held, or that Sea-beast
> *Leviathan*, which God of all his works
> Created hugest that swim th' Ocean stream:
> Him haply slumb'ring on the *Norway* foam
> The Pilot of some small night-founder'd Skiff,
> Deeming some Island, oft, as Seamen tell,
> With fixed anchor in his scaly rind
> Moors by his side under the Lee, while Night
> Invests the Sea, and wished Morn delays:
> So stretcht out huge in length the Arch-fiend lay.

The simile is framed at beginning and end with the ostensible *tertium comparationis* ("in bulk as huge...so stretcht out huge"), but clearly we have here an initial attempt to produce a set of interpretants for Satan, an attempt to produce an opposition between good and evil, culture and non-culture, etc. The simile thus resembles thematically and functionally the Typhoeus simile of Book 2 of the *Iliad*. There, as elsewhere in the *Iliad*, the social rupture caused by the conflict of Achilles and Agamemnon is "interpreted" by being placed against the background of the struggles of Zeus to establish cosmic order. The Homeric model of culture, in which the notion of cultural activity is produced in opposition to an isomorphically constructed negative image of "anti-cultural activity," introduces the paradigm of Zeus and Typhoeus as an interpretant of the action of the *Iliad*. The cosmic and mythological code, that is, becomes applied to a particular narrative circumstance. This exemplifies the way that, as the text propels itself forward, inevitably producing heterogeneities and ruptures, already constituted cultural codes are invoked to resolve or finesse those heterogeneities and ruptures.

This does not mean that the *Iliad* is a mere repetition of already constituted codes; if the relationship between code and message is truly dialectical, then the process of rectifying heterogeneities and ruptures can itself be an agent in restructuring codes. The coding of Achilles' unusual behavior as "wolfish," for example, reaffirms culture's distinction between proper and improper behavior. At the same time, the fact that a great hero who is beloved of Zeus acts wolfishly in a particular situation is a solution which must put into question at some level the definition of proper behavior. This can be seen as the beginning of the articulation of a new definition of culture. The *Iliad* is generally taken to be a text which is the product of a staunchly conservative oral tradition and reflective of a staunchly conservative and aristocratic ideology, a point of view with considerable corroboration in the poem. Nevertheless, the similes themselves are emblematic of the way in which a propulsive poetics can produce unforeseen results and create, at least on a small scale, new configurations of codes.

Milton's simile, however, does not represent a similar investment in a dialectic of code and message. The monsters named here are all traditional representations of the figure of Satan. Although Milton apparently takes us outside of the world of the poem to a world which "Fables name" and of which "Seamen tell," we remain at all times within one world, the world of human discourse, where Titans, Briaereos, Typhon and Leviathan are already identified with Satan. Since Satan is an already constituted master code of evil, what we have is a tautology which says only that Satan is like Satan.

*Paradise Lost* is a poem about origins, and especially about the "cause" (*PL* 1, 29) of the post-lapsarian world. But cultural definition does not *emerge* from this simile: it is simply restated. The line between culture and non-culture is not drawn in this simile; for this simile, and indeed the whole poem, already presumes the existence of that line. The production of such a simile here where the text poses for the first time the question, what is Satan like, imitates *formally* Homer's Typhoeus simile, but it only gives the impression that meaning is being produced. The kind of meaning available in Milton's simile is the kind dictionaries are full of: a series of namings which cannot transcend its own process of continual deferral to achieve a closure and fullness of meaning. We are left with a series of fragmentary texts produced by other models of signification, rather than a model of signification organizing meaning in a way adequate to Milton's project.

Apollonius

After the fall, Adam and Eve recognize their nakedness and contrive to cover themselves (*PL* 9, 1098-1118):

> So counsell'd hee, and both together went
> Into the thickest Wood, there soon they chose
> The Figtree, not that kind for Fruit renown'd,
> But such as at this day to *Indians* known
> In *Malabar* or *Decan* spreads her Arms
> Branching so broad and long, that in the ground
> The bended Twigs take root, and Daughters grow
> About the Mother Tree, a Pillar'd shade
> High overarch't, and echoing Walks between;
> There oft the *Indian* Herdsman shunning heat
> Shelters in cool, and tends his pasturing Herds
> At Loopholes cut through the thickest shade:  Those Leaves
> They gather'd, broad as *Amazonian* Targe,
> And with what skill they had, together sew'd,
> To gird thir waist, vain Covering if to hide
> Thir guilt and dreaded shame; O how unlike
> To that first naked Glory.  Such of late
> *Columbus* found th' *American* so girt
> With feather'd Cincture, naked else and wild
> Among the Trees on Isles and woody Shores.

The passage resembles Apollonius' use of the simile for code-making: "giving names to things without names," as Aristotle says.  In Apollonius, the epic simile is no longer a text-constitutive device designed to propel a text through a narrative complication according to already constituted cultural codes, but rather to conceptualize "analogically" new areas of thought, to expand the world of discourse outward toward new frontiers.  We saw above, for example, how Apollonius made use of comparison in the *Argonautica* to produce the inner world of man's feelings as a model, a microcosm structured in terms of the world outside man.  The key to the similes of Apollonius, therefore, and indeed to the poetics of Apollonius as a whole, is structure and form.  There the simile has become a rhetorical form, a mode of address capable of setting up a system of exchange between different things, and in this way of articulating a discourse about new things.  As the Argonauts travel to the very limits of the world, the heterogeneous institutions and objects that they encounter are formalized by a dialectical exchange, a process which generates "new ways of seeing."

Milton's passage also involves the likening of strange "other" cultures to the situation of Adam and Eve. Clearly there is an attempt here to evoke exotic and extraordinary images: a non-European fig tree which grows in a bizarre way, savages who live in trees, Amazonian targe, etc. The result is, however, once again a pseudo-simile, since the Indian and American natives are not "other genera"; they are themselves "Adam's seed," a species of the genus. This simile, in fact, shows clearly the incongruity of an Apollonian model for Milton's purposes. The geographical movement of a quest narrative is the perfect vehicle for Apollonius; for it makes possible a bracketing out of temporality in favor of spatial *comparata*: inside and outside, us and them. In *Paradise Lost*, however, there is no "outside" to be referred to: there is only our world "inside." If Apollonius is trying to encounter that which is "outside," Milton is trying to *contain* everything "inside." Hence he must replace the spatial opposition with a temporal one: then and now. But from a temporal perspective, Milton's *comparata* are merely repetitions. In fact, western Europe tended to see the technologically naive peoples of the New World as repetitions of their own "primitive" beginnings: as living in a "state of nature." Milton's similes cannot raise the issue of value anew, cannot produce new codes, because it takes for granted a historical framework, a teleology, in which everything has already received its "proper" value. Such a framework nullifies the possibility of sallying forth to find something not already named and recognized, something that could be really new.

## Cicero

In Book Four of *Paradise Lost*, Eden is described as it unfolds before the eyes of Satan. Milton tries to evoke in this passage a sense of nature prior to the fall and hence prior to death and decay. He attempts to capture the true *Logos* of divine creation, the original and ultimate pattern of beauty and order now lost to man through sin. The description of Eden is, in short, the most privileged example of the Ciceronian function of the simile. Unlike Apollonius, both Cicero and Vergil attempt to contain language within a coherent system, to reduce its propulsive power in respect to a transcendent code which is prior to all messages. The "lateral" proliferation of codes which is characteristic of Apollonius is now replaced by a "vertical" hierarchizing of codes. Cicero thus assumes the existence of a "law of nature," which is the transcendent master code. The argument of the *Republic* is thus that the dynamic processes of nature are ruled by an immanent *Ratio*, and Cicero relates the history of the Roman state as a progressive instantiation of this "natural" ideal. The further abstraction of the exchange process in order to produce a transcendent model (*Ratio, Logos*) has been compared above to the establishment of money, to the process of induction and overcoding. The common element in all of these is the establishment of a transcendental value or law which is the *telos* of the production process.

Milton, however, faces a different epistemological problem when portraying in fallen, contingent language that full and immediate presence that Eden comprises. For Cicero, temporality presents no problem; since history is a series of continuous manifestations of the *Logos*, segments of that continuum can be, theoretically, extracted at random and compared to each other in order to discover inductively the immanent principle continuously at work. For Milton, this is not the case. The fall marks a discontinuity in history so that nature and society after the fall are qualitatively different from nature and society before the fall. This discontinuity renders impossible the inductive discovery of the *Ratio* of paradise from a post-lapsarian perspective (4, 268-85):

> Not that fair field
> Of *Enna*, where *Proserpin* gath'ring flowers
> Herself a fairer Flow'r by gloomy *Dis*
> Was gather'd, which cost *Ceres* all that pain
> To seek her through the world; nor that sweet Grove
> Of *Daphne* by *Orontes*, and th' inspir'd
> *Castalian* Spring might with this Paradise
> Of *Eden* strive; nor that *Nysean* Isle
> Girt with the River *Triton*, where old *Cham*,
> Whom Gentiles *Ammon* call and *Lybian Jove*,
> Hid *Amalthea* and her Florid Son
> Young *Bacchus*, from his Stepdame Rhea's eye;
> Nor where *Abassin* Kings thir issue Guard,
> Mount *Amara*, though this by some suppos'd
> True Paradise under the *Ethiop* Line
> By *Nilus* head, enclosed with shining Rock,
> A whole day's journey high, but wide remote
> From this *Assyrian* Garden.

The original *Ratio* of nature can be conceived of, since the fall, only as something "other" than the present. The *amoeni loci* listed in this simile are all products of the pastoral tradition and are constituted as an imaginary return to some original (and now lost) goodness. The topos of the *amoenus locus* is usually based on the opposition of city and country, the former being the locus of conflict, contradiction and alienation, the latter being the negative image of the city. The idealized pastoral setting, where one lives in harmony with nature and one's fellow man, can only be imagined from the city, since it is constituted entirely as the absence of the conflicts and contradictions of real society.[2] Such a representation amounts to a negation of a negation. To describe the present as degraded presumes it to be a negation of an original harmony, something that the present has been degraded *from*. The representation of an *amoenus locus* reverses that degradation by rendering absent all that is reprehensible, all that is "fallen," about the present.

Milton explicitly states in the above similes that the *Ratio* of paradise cannot be inductively discovered by comparison ("Not that fair field...Nor that Sweet Grove," etc.). That is, he recognizes that the true and original paradise is qualitatively different from the literary paradises of fallen language. But these similes conclude Milton's own description of Eden which lies firmly in this same tradition of double negation. One can cite, for example, the devaluation of artifice in 4, 241-43:

> Flow'rs worthy of Paradise which not nice Art
> In Beds and curious Knots, but Nature boon
> Poured fourth profuse on Hill and Dale and Plain.

Many scholars have noted in Milton's paradise an underlying ambivalence, a potential and implicit evil.[3] This is not, however, a proleptic anticipation of the fall; rather, since Eden is a metaleptic negation of a negation, it lacks a *ratio* of its own. Since Milton's Eden is without an intrinsic mechanism of its own which could dispose various aspects of the representation into a unified system, it is essentially unorganized and always liable to internal contradiction. The description is a juxtaposition of fragments of other texts whose inclusion is determined by virtue of being negations of negative elements from other (not necessarily mutually compatible) descriptive systems. The *amoenus locus*, after all, existed in the literary tradition both as a foil to urban conflict and as a place of ignoble sloth where the hero forgets his mission.[4]

The ethical ambiguity of an *amoenus locus* is a direct result of its negativity, its lack of a *ratio*. Thus, for example, pain must be absent from Eden, but idleness is anathema to Puritan ethics. The result is a most un-Ciceronian antinomy between nature and culture (*PL* 4, 618-33):

> Man hath his daily work of body or mind
> Appointed, which declares his Dignity,
> And the regard of Heav'n on all his ways:
> While other animals unactive range,
> And of thir doings God takes no account.
> Tomorrow ere fresh Morning streak the East
> With first approach of light, we must be ris'n,
> And at our pleasant labor, to reform
> yon flow'ry Arbors, yonder Alleys green,
> Our walk at noon, with branches overgrown,
> That mock our scant manuring, and require
> More hands than ours to lop their wanton growth.

"Pleasant labor" is, strictly speaking, an oxymoron, for labor is an effect of the fall. For a Christian it can have positive value only in the sense that it is the means by which we repair the effects of the fall. Indeed, in the contrast of the behavior of men and animals, together with the portrayal of nature as "wanton" and in need of cultivation, this passage resembles the *Aeneid*, where man must impose organization on a disorganized environment. Milton's representation of Eden is "pseudo-Ciceronian"; it does not reveal the *ratio* of paradise, but collects a series of highly overcoded clichès from traditional conceptions of the *amoenus locus*.

## Vergil

The description of paradise is an important example because it involves the juxtaposition of products of incompatible models of signification, a sure indication that those models are not functioning to organize the text. It is not that texts must have a single model of signification which arranges everything into an organic whole, for we have paid attention all along to the contradictions and heterogeneities present in each of the texts discussed. The point is, rather, that a single model of signification will be made to seem to be the dominant model, and traces of the attempts to do so will be legible to a certain degree. What is lacking in *Paradise Lost* is any trace of this struggle. In the very moments which often epitomize such a struggle, the similes, there is a lack of the tension which characterizes the similes of Milton's predecessors. Instead we have tautology or an explicit undercutting of the productive process.

In Book 4 of *Paradise Lost* Satan is compared to a wolf, an almost inevitable simile given the persistent representation of wolves as the "outsider" in the epic predecessors of Milton (183-93):

> As when a prowling Wolf,
> Whom hunger drives to seek new haunt for prey
> Watching where Shepherds pen thir Flocks at eve
> In hurdl'd Cotes amid the field secure,
> Leaps o'er the fence with ease into the Fold:
> Or as a Thief bent to unhoard the cash
> Of some rich Burgher, whose substantial doors,
> Cross-barr'd and bolted fast, fear no assault,
> In at the window climbs, or o'er the tiles:
> So clomb this first grand Thief into God's Fold:
> So since into his Church lewd Hirelings climb.

Of the images of "wolfishness" that we have encountered from Homer to Dante, Milton's simile seems closest to Vergil's, for whom the opposition between culture and non-culture was defined as *organized* vs. *disorganized*. When Aeneas is compared to a hungry wolf (*Aen.* 2, 355-58), the implication is that he acts spontaneously, "naturally," and hence his actions are retrograde with respect to the claims of culture. Nature, for Vergil, is disorganized raw material in need of civilizing influences to have value. The movement of Milton's similes from comparing Satan first to a wolf and then to a thief implies that breaking and entering is acting "wolfish." This simile seems to evolve out of nature a model of evil, just as Vergil evolved out of nature a pattern of "non-cultural" activity. Being a thief, it is implied, is like being a wolf; and since the wolf is simply following his natural impulse (hunger), Satan is evil because he is incapable of resisting "natural impulses."

The ironies of such an implication are manifest. Wolves are marked as the image of rapacity because their actions are like those of thieves, not the other way around; and people steal not because it is natural but because it is Satanic, and we all partake of the Satanic since the fall. That this simile is actually a pseudo-simile is made clear by its apodosis:

> Or as a thief....
> So clomb this first grand Thief into God's Fold.

Satan is not *like* a thief, he *is* a thief; and the thief of the simile as well as the lewd Hirelings are like Satan; and then, last of all, the wolf is marked by culture as "like a thief." If the simile cannot be understood as an antithesis between nature and culture, it can neither be seen as a "Homeric" projection of negativity onto Satan, since Satan is a more generic image of anti-culture than the wolf. Nor can it be seen as the reification of a crucial moment in the psychological drama of Satan, for there is no dialectical tension between Satan, on the one hand, and wolves, thieves and false prelates on the other. What we have, in fact, is a collection of overcoded images of Satanic behavior, but Satan is not "like" them in terms of any particular model of signification. That is, the image of Satan is not *organized* into a *logos* in this simile. We have here not a productive device, but products.

### Dante

The *Divine Comedy* is in certain obvious ways closer to *Paradise Lost* than any of the other works we have considered; but in other ways it is utterly different. In describing the devils in Book I of *Paradise Lost*, Milton evokes the exodus event in a passage with numerous connections to the *Divine Comedy* (I, 301-12):

> His Legions, Angel Forms, who lay intranst
> Thick as Autumnal Leaves that strow the Brooks
> In *Vallombrosa*, where th' *Etrurian* shades
> High overarcht inbow'r; or scatterd sedge
> Afloat, when with fierce Winds *Orion* arm'd
> Hath vext the Red Sea Coast, whose waves o'erthrew
> *Busiris* and his *Memphian* Chivalry,
> While with perfidious hatred they pursu'd
> The Sojourners of *Goshen*, who beheld
> From the safe shore thir floating Carcasses
> And broken Chariot Wheels; so thick bestrown
> Abject and lost lay these, covering the flood.

The image of "the Sojourners of Goshen" looking back over the Red Sea from the safe shore recalls the typological simile of *Inferno* 1, 22-27. But in Dante's simile, it is the experience of the pilgrim which is compared to the exodus crossing; and the typological model of signification is evoked there to situate that personal experience. The typological model, moreover, as a trajectory of significance for the pilgrim's situation, is immediately scuttled by his inability to reach the top of the lighted mountain. The typological model only works for someone who has had a revelation, someone who has achieved the Augustinian *kairos*; and it is precisely this type of vision that the first canto indicates the pilgrim has *not* had. At the same time, it is impossible to "work your way up" inductively, because of the qualitative difference between human and divine discourse. It is this aporia out of which the writing of the *Divine Comedy* proceeds, a writing which is not an articulation of the *Logos*, but a personal witness to its activity. By writing a spiritual autobiography, Dante places himself in a sound Christian tradition. In such a discourse, where subject and object are fused, revelation and discovery become the poles of a dialectic which neither produces nor is produced by the *Logos*, but constitutes the self as a witness to the *Logos*. A personal witness can only hope to be effective *ad opus*, for it is surely of little value *ad speculandum*.

Milton sets out, like Dante, to produce divine meaning, to say the cause of the post-lapsarian world and in this way to "assert Eternal Providence and justify the ways of God to men" (*PL* 1, 25-6). But Milton enters his poem most often as the traditional amanuensis of the muse (*PL* 1, 6-36; 3, 19, 37-38, 51-55; 9, 20-24, 47).[5] He does not put himself forward as authentication for his own discourse; rather, his "higher Argument" is "sufficient of itself" to make *Paradise Lost* a heroic poem (9, 43). But the very event which is the subject of the poem conflicts with this purpose of producing an unmediated version of the divine plan. Thus, for example, Milton's allusion to the exodus event makes a link between Satan and one of his most famous earthly manifestations: the Pharaoh. Since the Pharaoh is traditionally a *vera daemonis figura* the text tells us that Satan is like one of his manifestations: *veritas* is like a *figura*, to use Auerbach's terms. This is, of course, hardly a productive use of typology, but there is more at issue here.

Cicero, Vergil and Dante all produce a "history." Cicero views history as the dynamic interplay of forces ruled by an immanent *ratio*. His selection and relation of events is aimed at discovering that underlying first principle (*revocatio ad rationem*). For Vergil, the *ratio* of history is given: it is Augustus; and Vergil's selection and relation of events is aimed at imposing that model of the past on the future. For Dante, the *ratio* of history is neither fully revealed nor comprehensible; and Dante claims neither to know it nor how to come to know it. Dante confronts history with *a* history, his own. Although the content of that experience is ultimately incommunicable and unrepeatable, it is nevertheless a witness to God's activity in history. It makes a claim that history does have divine significance.

Milton does not *produce* a history, he collects fragments of other histories. In all the instances cited above, it is not the productive device which is imitated or put to use; rather, it is the products of those devices in other texts which are restated in *Paradise Lost*. Milton's poem is indeed a "grand testament to dead ideas," for *Paradise Lost* does not have a productive device of its own to create live ideas. At the same time, part of the "grandness" of Milton's poem lies in the fact that it contains practically everything. How is it that a text which lacks a model of signification can not only be produced, but can go on encyclopaedically including everything within it, and then be followed by a sequel? To rephrase the question, what propels *Paradise Lost* forward?

## Propulsion and *Paradise Lost*

The peculiar status of the language of Paradise Lost has not escaped the notice of Milton's readers. Samuel Johnson's criticism of the logical incongruities of *Paradise Lost* is well known.[6] T. S. Eliot noted the "conventional and artificial" character of Milton's poetry and accused him of writing English "like a dead language." Eliot's complaint of a "dissociation of sensibility" in Milton's language became a sort of catch word in Milton scholarship, and his contention that there is a fundamental dislocation between the "inner meaning" of his verse and the "poetic surface" became the terms of a considerable debate about the virtues of Milton's poetry.[7] Stanley Fish, for example, maintains that the dislocation of which Eliot speaks is strategic and that the "coherence and psychological plausibility of the poem are to be found in the relationship between its effects and the mind of the reader."[8] Another tack is taken by such scholars as John Steadman, who suggests that Milton consciously undercuts the representational functions of language to debunk the ethical and aesthetic values of traditional epics, and ultimately, in order to write an "anti-epic."[9]

Christopher Grose, with special attention to the similes and other types of discursive shifts, argues that Milton strategically separates himself from the fictive narrator in order to separate the "true poem" from the mere technical performance. For example, in the first simile of *Paradise Lost* (1,

196-210, cited above), Milton the man presents us with a narrator/poet in the midst of a perceptual dilemma, "confronted with a crisis in the poem's community of knowledge...pretending to cast about for an appropriate alternative likeness" to Satan.[10] Apart from this staged performance by a helpless narrator, Grose suggests, something else happens in this simile: "What emerges as it were spontaneously from this improvised performance is an emblematic scene which clearly has little to do with size" (151). This simile, together with its accompanying commentary (*PL* 1, 209-220),

> serves to clarify what may be called the poetic moment's historical outcome, its "event", and suggests that the function of Milton's simile is to do so, even where it pretends to amplify such simpler (and more sensuous) likenesses as the hugeness or magnificence of Satan.... The poet at such times, we might say, is a public man, sharing with the reader his difficulties in the face of the poem's mysteries. No vision or flight of fancy cuts him off from his audience, taking him either into himself or (alternatively) above the poles and toward the Holy Light. He is most clearly one of us; and as a stylist he is most clearly time-bound, most evidently at the mercy of his own unpremeditated process of speech.
>
> All of this, however, is less complicated than the facts of the poem itself. As we have seen, the unpremeditated "error" of simile often wanders into a circumstance which establishes the ironies of a narrative scene; "low" as they may seem stylistically, *as forms of perception* they bring us closer than does the "purer" narrative (narrative without the directive commentary) to the highest kind of awareness in the poem, contained ultimately in God's "prospect high" (see *Paradise Lost* 3, 77).[11]

In this passage, Grose opposes two forms of validation (that of the witness and that of the prophet) to the "unpremeditated process of speech."[12] The phrase is a particularly felicitous one, for it recognizes in Milton's verse a mobility of its own, an internal propulsion. Grose further says that this "process of speech," because it is *staged* in *Paradise Lost*, makes the poem "sincere and its words lucky" (17):

> To stage the poem's origins, and, so to speak, its emergence from them, would provide the poet's equivalent of the preacher's logical scaffolding, and thus the process of speech--including the speaker--which could somehow validate whatever true acts the true poem might effect (12).

In the terms set out above, Grose's point can be summarized something like this: Milton, as a Christian and an iconoclast, thematizes, as did Dante, the inadequacies of fallen speech by presenting a "character" struggling helplessly to grasp the *Logos*. In opposition to this "low" guise of the poet, another perspective emerges as an effect of the poem's discursive process; it is not, however, the perspective of the witnessing self constituted by the experience which lies behind the writing of the poem, but the perspective of a true poet/prophet which merges with God's "prospect high." The very scrupulousness with which Milton underscores the inadequacies of the merely technical performance of his narrative produces, as it were, an alternative mode of seeing which transcends that performance.

Significantly, Grose documents his approach to *Paradise Lost* with discussions of Milton's works centered on his desire to become England's poet/prophet, as well as with discussion of Milton's Ramist handbook of logic. Clearly the problem of producing a true and sincere poetry was a major preoccupation of Milton, all the more acute because of his Ramism and Puritan suspicion of "image-making." Language in *Paradise Lost* only *seems* to have forgotten its own fallen nature while narrating its own fall; at a closer look, it seems more correct to say that Milton is constantly aware of the nature of language, but determined to transcend it in some way. If readers of *Paradise Lost* have perceived in it something other than the poem "intends to pursue," it is not because Milton was naive about the possibilities of "lik'ning spiritual to corporal forms."

If Dante splits the self into pilgrim and author, Milton empties himself into his fictive narrator. If the figure of the helpless narrator/poet is staged in *Paradise Lost*, the figure who is doing the staging is totally unrealized in the poem. If Milton strategically relies on his audience's expectations as readers to constitute the true poet behind his multiple guises (and the true poem behind its multiple guises), the history of Miltonic scholarship shows that the true poet and the true poem can be realized in more than one way. The history of interpretations of *Paradise Lost*, in fact, is a testimony to that most insidious aspect of language; its tendency to masquerade as *substance*. In his attempt to produce "the meaning, not the name" (*Paradise Lost* 7, 6), the substance, not the play of differences, Milton provides us with a poem which can contain and accommodate everything which has taken on the appearance of linguistic substance. The "true poem" is an absence around which human discourse can be encyclopaedically proliferated; just as the "true poet" is an absence around which a variety of conventional identities alternatively appear.

If both Dante and Milton explicitly eschew logic for rhetoric, it is clear that a different kind of persuasive argument animates each poem. Dante requires us to leap from his own experience to one of our own; Milton requires us to leap from our own linguistic universe into the divine universe of signification. What propels the *Divine Comedy* forward is the abductive dialectic between fictive author and fictive pilgrim, between the enormous static structures of the afterworld's completeness and the probing tentativeness of the pilgrim's search for personal meaning; and the similes of the *Divine Comedy* seem to act as a hinge between these two textual economies. What propels *Paradise Lost* forward is language's inexhaustible "interpretability" or "readability," its capacity for unlimited displacement and deferral. T. S. Eliot once compared Milton's verse to the Great Wall of China.[13] It is a most fitting image for the reading process as it is established in *Paradise Lost*: a virtually unending "lateral" movement from text to text, from interpretant to interpretant, convincing the reader of the reality of a distant yet ever deferred horizon. As readers, we can extend and continue the "process of speech," adding commentary and citing multiple resonances; but any attempt to ground *Paradise Lost* into a unified totality can be opposed with other equally well-grounded (or equally ungrounded) unities.

Grose's notion of the transcendent perspective of the poem, therefore, must be thought of in a different way. *Paradise Lost* is not a poem in which readers are allowed momentary glimpses of "God's prospect high"; nor is there an equivalent of a "logical scaffolding" constructed here which could somehow validate various effects of the poem. The "vision" of *Paradise Lost* is fixed on nothing but the world of names. The scrupulousness of which Grose speaks does not lead out of figurative language; rather, it empties language of any denotative power whatsoever. Milton exploits the play of differences which animates the aesthetic language of his predecessors so completely that the productive possibilities of language are completely circumscribed. Milton's poem totalizes language not as a figure of the real, but as *figurality itself*. The productive possibilities of exchange are shown to be infinite, but monotonal. All rhetorical elements are in the end equal; and rhetoric is all that human language can achieve.

*Paradise Lost* is indeed without a model of signification; but it levels all the products of other models of signification, shows them to be only rep resentation and deferral. The translation of a fragment from another text into *Paradise Lost* allows the model of signification which is operating in it to play itself out, to yield up its claim to being anything other than rhetoric parading as authentic discourse. In the analyses of Milton's similes above, I repeatedly made the point that a model of signification was being invoked, but that it was not functioning in *Paradise Lost*. The same point can be made in the other direction. Those models of signification *do* function in their respective texts precisely because of a certain blindness to their own rhetoricity. Milton's text illuminates the blind spots in each of those models by juxtaposing and intermingling them. In the space created by *Paradise Lost*, these models of signification are unmasked as having only a certain sectoral validity, as only working by the exclusion of certain things from view.[14]

For is it not the case that every model of signification we have identified from Homer on is able to function by means of a certain arbitrary *mastery*? Is it not the case that these texts attempt, by strategies of exclusion and containment, to occult the groundlessness of language, to reduce unlimited semiosis to a closed system, to make sure that language propels in a certain way? Thus, for example, when we say that Vergil, Cicero and Dante all produce a history, we should also note that those histories are possible by virtue of some sort of finesse with respect to the problem of temporality. Many critics of the *Aeneid* have called attention to the persistent tension and ambivalence which lie just beneath the smooth Vergilian surface, sometimes reading the poem as the exact opposite of its stated purpose. Similarly, Cicero's assumption that nature's laws have guided the evolution of Rome's history requires him to forget a great number of individual things about Rome (e.g., the preceding century) and about nature (e.g., hurricanes). Moreover, in Cicero and Vergil the *Logos* leads a double and contradictory existence: in each case, it is eternally present and immanent and at the same time in the process of being constructed. The *Divine Comedy* sidesteps the problem of temporality by shifting focus to the individual, whose experience is unrepeatable and unexchangeable; and thus is unable to be "situated" in a temporal scheme. Even in the limiting case, that of Apollonius, one can see that the whole prospect of sallying forth beyond the frontiers of culture presupposes a valorization of the "inside." That is, the best-intentioned attempts to counter ethnocentrism with evidence that others are more like us than is thought tends to highlight the ways in which *they* are like *us*.

*Paradise Lost* is not, therefore, a figure or simulacrum of the "true poem" in the sense that Grose suggests. It is, rather, figurality as such: language shown to be always figurative, always only connotative, always able to produce and reproduce only itself. In *Paradise Lost* similes and other such figures of speech are seamlessly continuous with the rest of the narrative. To put it in the terms we have used above, language in *Paradise Lost* is pure propulsion. The strategy of circumscribing language as rhetoric does not, however, lead only to a collapse in aporia; for the non-rhetorical, the denotative, the fully immanent discourse of God is, if not present, conspicuous by its absence. If language cannot produce divine discourse, its enclosure as mere rhetoric calls out for an absent closure. The totality of exchange is the only side of the coin we see; but, it is implied, there must be another side. Milton stands with his back to Being, seeing only a world of motion and representation, but assured that behind him, unseen, lies a world of permanence and presence. If the Romantics found Milton a heavy burden to bear, his project was essential to their own. For they too recognized that language was a vicious circle of displacement and deferral. But their solution was to turn their gaze away from the marketplace of verbal exchange and gaze into the unknown and unknowable world which for Milton is always absent to men.

# APOLOG

In Heliodorus' *Aethiopica*, Calasiris, an old priest, is narrating to Cnemon, another character, the circumstances of the meeting of the two young lovers of the romance (3, 1-2):

> "When the procession and the consecration were concluded..."
> "But they have not been concluded, father," interrupted Cnemon, "for your discourse has not yet made me a spectator, and I am completely overcome by eagerness to hear and see the festivity with my own eyes. But you evade me, like the man in the story who came after the party was over; you open your theater and shut it in the same instant." "I have no wish to trouble you, Cnemon," said Calasiris, "with matters extraneous to our subject. I was proceeding to the relevant parts of the story (τὰ καιριώτερα)."

The unusual wording of Cnemon's interruption calls attention to the productive aspect of discourse, the fact that language makes, not merely represents. If Milton provides our story of the epic simile with a certain closure, this closure is not a function of literary history as such so much as a function of what I have included as "relevant" (καιρός) to the story I have made. It may be objected that the history of the epic simile does not end with Milton, or that vast gaps have been left. These objections are based on some notion of what is essential to a good story (or a good history), on some idea of what is central and what is peripheral, on what is relevant and what is extraneous. Although these are not categories that one can easily eschew, nor would it be entirely desirable to do so, they should at least be recognized for the problems they are.

In fact, the previous pages have provided several possible ways to answer the objection that something essential has been left out, or something else has been given an uneven treatment. For example, I could answer in a Homeric manner by citing excellent authorities and precedents for limiting discussion in the way that I have; or I could answer in an Apollonian manner, and promise that subsequent installments will deal with other episodes of the simile; or I could take a Ciceronian view, and assert that the examples I give constitute a typology which exhausts all the possibilities, and that any anomalies are only apparent; or I could answer in a Vergilian manner that any similes which fall outside of the explanatory power of my scheme are not really similes at all; or I could give my personal reasons for choosing the ones that I have rather than others (Dante); or I could aver that human finitude has prevented me from accomplishing the impossible task of including every simile, and that I have, nevertheless, fought the good fight (Milton). But one of the main points of this book has been how various versions of epic totality are illusory. It has not been my intention to be complete, to master once and for all the subject of the epic simile, or even necessarily to be fair.

The term I would use for the above chapters is *sequence of interpretants*. The use of this term recognizes the fact that the authors Homer, Apollonius, Cicero, Vergil, Dante and Milton make up a *series*, a set of connected terms; but at the same time, it does not imply that this series constitutes a sequence of essential functions in some master narrative, whether economic, philosophical or anthropological. Although references to such narratives have been made at times, and indeed it is difficult to resist them, a semiotic analysis should give us something different than a mere recoding of clichés from literary history. My focus on the similes as indicative of a model of signification for various texts has been *strategic* in the sense that it implies a critique of the tendency of "essentialist" interpretative strategies to reify various factors of textual organization into a hierarchy of "levels" of narrative; for the simile is traditionally held to be a marginal and merely ornamental feature in such hierarchies. The epic simile, to cite another story, has been *repressed* since Aristotle's valorization of plot as the "soul" of narrative. The preceding account of narrative semiotics in the epic tradition from Homer to Milton can no doubt be accused of repressing other things; but if semiotics is to take its place as one form of *social practice*, it is in the attempt "to demonstrate how much broader than most ideologies have recognized is the format of the semantic universe" (Eco, 298). I would like to conclude, therefore, with some summary notes about how I hope to have modified the *communis opinio* about similes.

The most commonsense notion of simile is that it allows us to say things that otherwise could not be said well or could not be said at all. At the heart of this notion is the sense that similes are *productive*. If one takes an instrumental and undialectical view of language, such as that underlying Aristotle's *Rhetoric*, then this productive capacity is finding a novel *means of expression* for some as yet unnamed content, a process which can improve the persuasiveness of an argument with respect both to content (clarity) and to expression (urbanity). I have set out in this study with the assumption that similes have a much broader range of productive possibilities, an assumption which, as I have repeatedly asserted, rejects the instrumental view of language so closely linked to essentialist interpretive strategies. In my discussion of Homer, I said that shifts of discursive mode can be seen as indications of a problem or blockage for the proairetic mode, as places where for one reason or another it was no longer possible to let the action "speak for itself." More generally, similes can be seen to be places where something is being *done* in a discourse, places where latently figurative language had to be replaced by patently figurative language.

This kind of shift can, of course, mean many things. It could be that a new content is being articulated for the first time, more or less in the manner that Aristotle describes, and that the simile does indeed produce clarity. It could also be the case that a simile is a smoke screen to cover up an infelicity in the continuity of a discourse: not to articulate new content, but to give the *effect* of the articulation of content. I would venture to say that there are few if any cases where either of these two functions is entirely absent. That is, similes always have an expressive component, and they are also always part of the glue that holds a discourse together; although, as the case of *Paradise Lost* shows, this hardly distinguishes similes from any other class of linguistic features. The story of the simile which has been given above is not so much the history of a form, as it is a series of examples of these two polar characteristics interacting in various texts, texts which are thereby trying to do certain things.

It might be tempting to see the simile in the *Iliad* as a sort of original and proper use of the simile in contrast to Homer's more decadent predecessors; or, alternatively, to see the sequence from Homer on as a sort of progressive evolution of forms toward some more "modern" use of the simile. The semiotic notion of a sequence of interpretants does not rely on any such scheme of development. What is foregrounded by this notion is the *artificial* character of human language (as opposed to an account of its "nature"). That is, human language has no nature which can be cultivated or perverted; no origin to which it can be false or true; no overall goal that it can achieve or fail to achieve. Instead, it is a mixture of possibilities, functions and characteristics which are created, exploited and suppressed at various times by various people trying to exercise influence over their world. A semiotic analysis notes the way that certain incipient functions are more fully exploited later, the way certain functions disappear or are redirected elsewhere, and also the way wholly new and unrepeatable functions appear: all a consequence of innumerable pressures internal and external to language. That language, like other human institutions, is systemic is a fundamental premise of semiotics; another premise is that human systems such as language are heterogeneous, open-ended, incomplete and self-contradictory. This means that texts are always full of ambiguities and capable of numerous contradictory meanings; it means that texts are always in danger of falling apart. In all of the examples I have chosen, I have tried to show not only how similes help hold a text together, but also how they mark threadbare seams about to pop open. If in each case I have foregrounded this process of "fastening together" (καίρωσις) at the expense of the seduction of the narrative as a whole, I trust that there is some way in which my remarks will not be "irrelevant" (ἀπὸ καιροῦ).

# NOTES

## Introduction

1. For the discussion of the similes by the rhetorical tradition, see M. H. McCall, *Ancient Rhetorical Theories of Simile and Comparison* (Cambridge, 1969). For antiquity's views on Homer's similes, we have Adolf Clausing's *Kritik und Exegese der homerischen Gleichnisse im Altertum* (Parchim, 1913). These matters will be taken up in more detail below in the discussion of Apollonius. I do not mean to say that the ancient critics sought no further justification for the similes than mere ornamentation. Many scholia attribute broadly defined functions for various similes, such as auxesis, emphasis, etc., but these functions are themselves perceived as ornamental in respect to the narrative. Modern scholarship has likewise often proposed various "ornamental uses" for the simile: (1) the presentation of the generic alongside the individual: Kurt Riezler, "Das homerische Gleichnis und der Anfang der Philosophie," *Antike* 12 (1936), 253-71; W. Schadewaldt, "Die homerische Gleichniswelt und die kretisch-mykenische Kunst," in *Von Homers Welt und Werk* (Leipzig, 1944), 130-54; P. Vivante, "On the Representation of Reality in Homer," *Arion* 5 (1966), 149-90. (2) Creation of atmosphere: H. Fraenkel, *Die homerischen Gleichnisse* (Göttingen, 1921). (3) Imagistic continuity: Carroll Moulton, *Similes in the Homeric Poems*, Hypomnema 49 (Göttingen, 1977); Martin Mueller, *The Iliad* (London, 1984), 108-124. (4) Characterization and foreshadowing: T. Krischer, *Formale Konventionen der homerischen Epik* (Munich, 1971); S. E. Basset, *Poetry of Homer*, Sather Classical Lectures 15 (Berkeley, 1938), 164-72; M. Coffey, "The Function of the Homeric Simile," *AJPh* 78 (1957), 113-32. (5) Incorporation of the past into the present: F. Müller, "Das homerische Gleichnis," *NJAB* 4 (1941), 175-83. (6) Allusion to antecedent literary traditions: Philip Damon *Modes of Analogy in Ancient and Medieval Verse*, University of California Publications in Classical Philology 15, No. 6 (Berkeley, 1965).

2. For Hellenistic criticism on Homer, see R. Pfeiffer, *History of Classical Scholarship From the Beginnings to the End of the Hellenistic Age* (Oxford, 1968); Howard Clarke, *Homer's Readers* (Newark, 1981).

3. Convenient summaries of the criticism of this period can be found in

M. P. Nilsson, *Homer and Mycenae* (London, 1933; repr. 1968); J. A. Davison, "The Homeric Question," in *A Companion to Homer*, ed. A. Wace and F. Stubbings (London, 1962). Most helpful for the analyst position is Peter von der Mühll, *Kritische Hypomnema zur Ilias* (Basel, 1952). For examples of unitarian criticism of the similes, see J. T. Sheppard, "Traces of the Rhapsode," *JHS* 42 (1922), 220-37; A. Shewan, "Suspected Flaws in Homeric Similes," *CP* 6 (1911), 271-81; and, of course, Fraenkel, *Die homerischen Gleichnisse*. See note 7 below for analyst works on the simile.

4. Milman Parry, *The Making of Homeric Verse*, ed. Adam Parry (Oxford, 1971). A. B. Lord develops the notion of a "semi-autonomous" pattern or "theme" in *Singer of Tales* (Cambridge, 1960), 69-98. This notion will be rethought in a semiotic context below.

5. W. Hansen, *The Conference Sequence*, University of California Publications in Classical Philology 8 (Berkeley, 1972); G. S. Kirk, *Songs of Homer* (Cambridge, 1962); D. Page, *The Homeric Odyssey* (Oxford, 1955).

6. B. Fenik, *Typical Battle Scenes in the Iliad*, Hermes Einzelschriften 21 (Wiesbaden, 1968). Neo-analytic critics presume the unity of the poems, but usually take the position that Homer was a literate poet who substantially transformed traditional oral sources. See, for example, W. Kullmann, "Zur Methode der Neoanalyse in der Homerforschung," *Wiener Studien* NF 15 (1981), 5-42; and "Oral Poetry Theory and Neoanalysis," *GRBS* 25.4 (Winter, 1984), 307-23.

7. W. C. Scott, *The Oral Nature of the Homeric Simile*, Mnemosyne Supplementband 28 (Leiden, 1964). D. J. N. Lee, *The Similes of the Iliad and the Odyssey Compared*, Australian Hum. Res. Council Monograph 10 (Melbourne, 1964). G. P. Shipp, *Studies in the Language of Homer* (Cambridge, 1953; 2nd ed., 1972).

8. Michael Nagler, *Spontaneity and Tradition* (Berkeley, 1974), 28. Hereafter cited as *Spontaneity*.

9. For a discussion of relativist and universalist theories of language, see George Steiner, *After Babel* (Oxford, 1975), 49-109.

10. For Humboldt's term and Chomsky's articulation of the "rationalist" or "nativist" position in language acquisition, see Chomsky, "Review of B. F. Skinner's *Verbal Behavior*," reprinted in *The Structure of Language*, ed. J. Fodor and J. Katz (Englewood Cliffs, 1963), 384-89. The comparison of the Indian theory of meaning to generative transformational grammar is inevitable and suggested by Nagler himself ( *Spontaneity*, 19).

11. *Spontaneity*, 198. James Redfield, *Nature and Culture in the Iliad* (Chicago, 1975), 219. Cedric Whitman, *Homer and the Heroic Tradition* (Cambridge, 1965), 219. F. Jameson notes that readings which make appeals to the "universal truth" of poetry provide organizations of the text which "find their proper use in the staging of the fundamental problems of a narrative text" and "in the evaluation of the narrative solution, or sequence of solutions, invoked for this purpose" (*The Political Unconscious* [Ithaca, 1981], 256). This can be so even with militantly ahistorical analyses such as that of T. McCary, *Childlike Achilles* (New York, 1982), who sees the "thematic core" of the poem as a "formative stage in the development of every male child" (95).

12. Whitman, *Homer*, 240. The full sentence is, "The universal limitation of death which causes human beings to restrain their passions, and

Achilles' disregard of that limitation, is what allows him to carry his passions so far and become more like a god than a man."

13. This little overview of semiotics is based on lectures by Wlad Godzich at the University of Minnesota. See his review of U. Eco, *A Theory of Semiotics* (Bloomington, 1976), in *Journal of the History of Music* (Winter, 1979), 117ff. The following discussion of the theory of codes is based almost entirely on Eco's book, hereafter cited as "Eco." Further elaboration of Eco's theory can be found in *The Role of the Reader* (Bloomington, 1979) and *Semiotics and the Philosophy of Language* (Bloomington, 1984).

14. The terms "seme" and "sememe" were introduced by A. J. Greimas, *Sémantique Structurale* (Paris, 1966), with a slightly different meaning than Eco's. See Eco, 93-94.

15. Noam Chomsky, *Aspects of a Theory of Syntax* (Cambridge, 1965), 157ff.

16. C. S. Peirce, *Collected Papers* (Cambridge, 1931-58), I, 339.

17. It will not be possible to give much space to the numerous varieties of reading theory, and what follows here is a strategic selection aimed at foregrounding issues pertinent to the approach to be outlined below. Culler's chapter on reading theory in *On Deconstruction* (Ithaca, 1983), is most useful for identifying the key problems. So-called "reader-response criticism," examples of which are collected in *Reader-Response Criticism*, ed. Jane Tompkins (Baltimore, 1980), tends to focus on how various readers, or groups of readers (women, students, social classes) transcend or skew the function of the addressee, however that function is objectified.

18. Norman Holland, *Five Readers Reading* (New Haven, 1977).

19. Stanley Fish, *Self-Consuming Artifacts* (Berkeley, 1972).

20. Fish has abandoned the notion of the informed reader in his more recent work. In *Is There a Text in This Class?* (Cambridge, 1981), Fish notes the importance of "reading strategies" which are the product of shared assumptions of an "interpretive community." These interpretive strategies "are the shape of reading" and hence "give texts their shape, making them rather than, as is usually assumed, arising from them" (13). That Fish's notion of interpretive communities is still a valorization of the addressee is evident from the fact that the reading strategies are themselves not subject to analysis. Since they exist "prior to the act of reading and therefore determine the shape of what is read *rather than the other way around*" (14, my emphasis), there is no dialectic between text and reader. See Terry Eagleton, *Literary Theory: An Introduction* (Minneapolis, 1983), 85-89.

21. *Structuralist Poetics* (Ithaca, 1975), 112. The Frye quote is from *Anatomy of Criticism* (Princeton, 1971), 17. Culler has moved away from this position, but the idea of a "literary competence" analogous to linguistic competence has persisted in various forms. See, for example, E. Spolsky and E. Shauber, "Stalking a Generative Poetics," *NLH* 12, No. 3 (Spring, 1981), 397-413; and S. H. Olsen, "The 'Meaning' of a Literary Work," *NLH* 14, No. 1 (Autumn, 1982), 13-31, with discussion by C. Belsey, 176.

22. N. Chomsky, "Formal Discussion," reprinted in Chomsky, *Selected Readings*, ed. J. Allen and P. van Buren (London, 1971), 130-1.

23. George Steiner, *After Babel* (Oxford, 1975), 107.

24. U. Eco, *The Role of the Reader* (Bloomington, 1979), 11. I have un-

derscored the words *textually established* to emphasize that the interpretant is not the interpreter.

25. M. Riffaterre, *The Semiotics of Poetry* (Bloomington, 1978), 1-6. See also his earlier article, "Paragram and Significance," *Semiotexte* I, No. 2 (Fall, 1974), 72-87.

26. The term "hypogram," or Riffaterre's earlier term "paragram," derives from Saussure's theory of the anagram. Saussure had toyed with the idea that the verses of ancient poetry represented by phonic imitation the names having importance in each passage. In this theory the verse would be phonic proliferations (anagrams or paragrams) of the names of gods or heroes. Saussure was never sufficiently satisfied with his idea to publish it; indeed, as Riffaterre notes, such a notion does not take into account the ordinary experience of reading a poem. For Riffaterre, Saussure's genius was "to understand that the text's center is outside of the text, not behind it, hidden away, as seekers after the writer's real intent are fond of thinking; its true nature lies in the text's consistent formal reference to and repetition of what it is about, despite continuous variations in the telling of the story built around that 'it'" ("Paragram and Significance," 12). This "it" which a poem is about was for Saussure a phonic sequence, but for Riffaterre this "it" consists of the "lexical transformations of a semantic given" ("Paragram and Significance," 73). For discussion of the relevant passages from Saussure's notebooks, see P. Wunderli, *Ferdinand de Saussure und die Anagramme* (Tubingen, 1972).

27. *Poems of Emily Dickinson,* ed. T. H. Thompson (Cambridge, 1955), 768. This example was given by Professor William Beauchamp of Southern Methodist University in a lecture at the University of Minnesota. He has kindly given me permission to reproduce his analysis.

28. For the term see *Semiotics of Poetry*, 25-26 *et passim*; see also the discussion of seme and sememe above, p. 10.

29. "Theme" is defined by Riffaterre as a "culture-marked hypogram" (39); that is, a repeatedly poeticized hypogram. The word "theme" has itself been repeatedly "poeticized" and hence has a descriptive system entailing essentialist notions of disembodied ideas (Lord, Nagler, etc.). For this reason the term "subcode" will be developed below for repeatedly poeticized hypograms in the context of narrative, a term which will emphasize their operational status.

30. For the notion of descriptive system, which will be exemplified below, pp. 25ff., see *Semiotics of Poetry*, 39ff.

31. Speaking specifically of a pedagogical situation, Bourdieu and Passeron, *Reproduction in Education, Society and Culture* (London, 1977), argue that this is the one irreducible and inevitable characteristic of communication. More generally, see M. Foucault, *Discipline and Punish* (New York, 1979).

32. Eco uses the term "textual strategy" for the notion of the sender in textual studies; and this is what will be meant by the term "poet" or "author" in the discussion below. A communicational model emphasizes the dialectical relationship between reader, writer and text; meaning is *produced* in this dialectic. It does not reside in any one of these terms.

33. Fredric Jameson, *The Political Unconscious* (Ithaca, 1981), offers numerous examples of this sort of methodological progression. See also Terry Eagleton's call for a recasting of literary studies as "cultural studies" in *Literary*

*Theory* (Minneapolis, 1983).

34.   Hence the rise of the "aesthetic crisis" in Homeric studies, the suspicion that critics are deceiving themselves by attributing meaning to various aspects of Homer's expression actually determined by metrical constraints. Parry's theory has attracted a number of attacks with varying degrees of *ira et studium* for being the "Darwin of Homer" (H. T. Wade-Gerry). A "soft" Parry school has tried to modify the oral theory to make more room for the aesthetic use of formulaic diction. For a summary of the literature, see J. Holoka, "Homer's Originality: A Survey," *CW* 12 (1973), 257-93.

35.   Berkeley Peabody, *Winged Word* (Albany, 1976), 176-94, argues that text production in Homer and Hesiod proceeds from "phonic cores" which preserve traditional "information cores." This unusual hypothesis should be compared to Saussure's theory of the anagram (note 26 above). G. Nagy, *Best of the Achaeans* (Baltimore, 1979), who also produces many interesting results, nevertheless bases his analysis on a very stable tradition of meaning stretching back to its Indo-european "roots." Peabody and Nagy are both more explicitly "intertextual" than Nagler, but all three see meaning as produced by substance (*sphota*, information cores, roots) rather than by difference.

# Homer

1.   Walter Leaf, ed., *The Iliad*, 2nd ed. (New York, 1902), ad loc.

2.   Ulrich von Wilamowitz-Moellendorf, *Die Ilias und Homer* (Berlin, 1920), 125.

3.   Herman Fraenkel, *Die homerischen Gleichnisse*, 74-75.

4.   For these notions of the functions of Homer's similes, see the works cited in note 1 of the Introduction.

5.   Walter Arend, *Die typischen Szenen bei Homer* (Berlin, 1933), 64-78.

6.   For the "conversion of a descriptive system" see *Semiotics of Poetry*, 63-75.

7.   The adverb ἀγεληδόν (160), "in a herd-like fashion," suggests a pell-mell motion in contrast to the rigorously ordered procedures of the heroes and the hierarchy implied by their ritual propriety. Cf. A 448: ἑξείης ἔστησαν ἐΰδμητον περὶ βωμόν, "They stood *in order* around the altar."

8.   If we changed the accent to the antepenult, we would have the only Homeric example of an adjective found in later Greek (ἀραῖος from ἀρά), which means *in bono* "prayed to" (cf. Ζεὺς ἀραῖος) and *in malo* "cursed," a particularly pregnant association.

9.   A 469, B 432, I 92, I 222, Λ 780, Ω 628, α 150, γ 473, θ 72, θ 485, μ 308, ο 303, ο 143, ο 501, ξ 454, π 55, ρ 99, ψ 57, ω 489.

10.   See Arend's discussion of this passage as well as the suitors' varied feasting habits, *Die typischen Szenen*, 67-68. See also his discussion of the lexical inversions of meal language in the Cyclops episode of the *Odyssey*, 75.

11.   Bruno Snell, *The Discovery of the Mind*, tr. T. G. Rosenmeyer (New York, 1960), 9.

12.   It is not specifically called a meal; the children are hidden in a "hollow place" in the earth, but the notion of reingestion is clear enough. Cf.

Kronos' explicit consuming of his children in the next phase of the succession myth, *Theogony*, 458-59.

13. Neither Chantraine, *Dictionaire etymologique de la langue gréque* (Paris, 1968), nor Frisk, *Grieshisches etymologisches Wörterbuch* (Heidelberg, 1973), see any etymological connection between στένω and στείνω, although Autentrieth does in *A Homeric Dictionary*, tr. R. P. Keep (Norman, 1958). But *Theogony*, 159-60, suggests at least a folk etymology.

14. Vladimir Propp, *The Morphology of the Folktale*, tr. L. Scott, 2nd ed. (Austin, 1968).

15. That is, they are not universal. While there is no doubt about the heuristic value of a formalist analysis such as that of Propp, the generalization of such a "morphology" to all narratives everywhere, or even all fairy tales everywhere, falls back on essentialism. See T. Todorov, *Introduction to Poetics*, tr. R. Howard (Minneapolis, 1981), 48.

16. Cf. the opening words of Odysseus to Achilles in the embassy scene (I 225): δαιτὸς μὲν ἐΐσης οὐκ ἐπιδευεῖς, "you have no lack of a fair portion."

17. Cedric Whitman, *Homer and the Heroic Tradition* (New York, 1958), 206.

18. See Charles P. Segal, *The Theme of the Mutilation of the Corpses in the Iliad* (Leiden, 1971).

19. Achilles has been variously condemned or praised for holding out so long. See, for example, A. L. Motto "*Ise Dais*: The Honor of Achilles," *Arethusa* 2.2 (Fall, 1969), 109-25; Peter W. Rose, "How Conservative is the *Iliad?*" *Pacific Coast Philology* 13 (1978), 86-93. The value of his actions relative to the other Greeks, however, is clearly negative; and it is this intra-textual perspective with which we are concerned at present. But see below, pp. 71ff.

20. See J. I. Armstrong, "The Arming Motif in the *Iliad*," *AJPh* 79 (1958), 337-54.

21. The first critic to suggest that the plot of the major action of the *Iliad* is the Διὸς βουλή was, I believe, Schadewaldt, *Iliasstudien*, 3rd ed. (Darmstadt, 1966), 110. The extension of Riffaterre's term *matrix* to mean the plot of a narrative is only approximate. The "will of Zeus" is hardly the single unifying element of the *Iliad*, but it does seem to be the most important such plot feature.

22. Helmut Erbse, *Scholia*, III, 275: πῶς γὰρ ἄνανδρος ὁ εἰργασμένος τοσαῦτα; "How can such an unmanly thing be compared to someone who has just accomplished what Agamemnon has?" This indicates the traditional concern, largely as a result of the rhetorical tradition, that the *ethos* of simile and narrative should be related. See Clausing, *Kritik*, 77-82.

23. This does not mean that the rest of the simile is fortuitous. As the scholiast points out, there is a lexical expansion of the painfulness (Erbse, III, 275): πάντα δὲ ὀδυνηρὰ ἔλαβε τὰ ὀνόματα, τὸ ὀξυ (269), τὸ δριμύ (270), τὸ πικρόν (271), ἐπιτείνων τὰς ὀδύνας. "All the names describe the painfulness: the sharpness, the piercing, the bitterness, expanding the notion of wounds." For "expansion" (ἐπιτείνων), see *Semiotics of Poetry*, 47-63.

24. Note that the woodsman is overdetermined in the simile by the frequent comparison of a fallen hero to a fallen tree (e.g. Δ 482, E 590, N 389, Π 482).

25. On the peculiarity of the fighting in this scene, especially Hector's fighting of the "right side," see von der Mühll, 197-98.

26. The *teichomachia* seems to be almost an afterthought to deal with the wall built back in Book 7, as the initial 33 lines of Book 12 suggest. It consists mainly of a seesaw battle in which Hector and Aias do not confront each other. The end of the episode (when Hector smashes the wall), with its ἴσα μάχη resolved by Zeus' intervention and accompanied by a balance simile (M 432-37), recalls the other moments in Θ 66 and Λ 84 when Zeus "tips" the scales in the Trojans' favor (cf. esp. the golden scales of Θ 69). The essay of Norman Austin, "The Function of Digressions in the *Iliad*," *GRBS* 7 (1966), 295-312, should remind us that "digression" is not viewed in the same way by Homer as by his post-Aristotelian critics.

27. Note the ὄφρα...τόφρα diction of O 318-22.

28. *Winged Word*, 231-33.

29. *Formale Konventionen der homerischen Epik*, 62.

30. Cf. Π 770-1, where these words are repeated at that "equal battle."

31. See Leaf's comment, *The Iliad*, ad loc. For the "gnomic" character of the passage, see Ernst Ahrens, *Gnomen in griechischer Dichtung* (Halle, 1937), 33.

32. Hans Trumpy, *Kriegerische Fachausdrüke im griechischen Epos* (Basel, 1950), 140.

33. Eris is twice described in the *Iliad* as ἄμοτον μεμαυῖα, "raging insatiably" ( Δ 440, E 518). The epithet θυμοβόρος, "gnawing on the *thymos*," is applied only to Eris (six times). Nagy, *The Best of the Achaeans*, 130-32, discusses further the δαίς/ἔρις nexus.

34. Eco, *The Role of the Reader* (Bloomington, 1979), 15.

35. Cedric Whitman, *Homer and the Heroic Tradition*, 249-84. Cf. Karl Reinhardt, *Die Ilias und ihr Dichter* (Göttingen, 1961), 210:

> Kann die Einheit nicht auch eine Art von Ganzen sein, dass man ein bewegtes Ganzes nennen möchte?  In dem verschiedenen Ringe, gleich exzentrischen Kreisen auseinander hervorgehend, einander überschneidend einander zuwachsend sich einer über den anderen legen.  So dass zu einem zugrunde liegenden Entwurf oder Grundstock Neues nacheinander hinzukam, das teils aus ihm selber sich entwickelte, teils von aussen durch die Umstände hinzugetragen wurde, um mit dem Hauptstamm, mehr oder weniger, zu verwachsen.

To call this "Ganze" an "Einheit" is a rather harsh extension of the meaning of that word.  Notopoulos adopts the term "inorganic unity" to describe Homeric narrative ("Parataxis and Homer," *TAPA* 80 [1949], 9-10). Both of these oxymorons show how value laden the notion of "unity" is when applied to literary works.

36. *Winged Word*, 176-215. Peabody does not, of course, omit discussion of other levels of linguistic organization, but his assumption that narrative is a late development which enters the tradition as explication of non-narrative material does not seem the most likely possibility.

37. Such a notion is exemplified in social criticism which defines the "problematic" of any theoretical approach as the questions that govern its mode of social inquiry, but also the questions *not* asked, and the relationship

between them. See Louis Althusser, *For Marx*, 66-67. For a specifically literary example of such criticism, see Paul de Man, *Blindness and Insight* (Minneapolis, 1983).

38. See, for example, A. Parry, "The Language of Achilles," *TAPA* 87 (1956), 1-7; J. A. Russo, "How and What Does Homer Communicate? The Medium and the Message of Homeric Verse," *CJ* 71.4 (1976), 289-99; L. Versenyi, *Man's Measure* (Buffalo, 1974), 32-42.

39. See von der Mühll, 189-90.

40. G. Nagy, *The Best of the Achaeans*, 15ff. Thus, a common form of insult is to question a man's genealogy (e.g., Π 33-35).

41. Cf. the other occurrence of ἀπηλεγέως in the same phrase in *Odyssey* 1, 373, where Telemachus addresses himself bluntly to the suitors. See also other uses of ἀλέγω with the negative in such phrases as θεῶν ὄπιν οὐκ ἀλέγοντες, "disregarding the watchful eyes of the gods" (Π 388).

42. Adam Parry, "The Language of Achilles," *TAPA* 87 (1956), 1-7, makes a similar claim about Achilles' inability to articulate his "meaning," but obscures the point by attributing the difficulty to the constraints of oral poetry. The difficulty of saying something new for the first time is not peculiar to oral poetry, since all communication relies on conventions. See the discussion of *ratio difficilis* below in the Dante chapter. Related discussions of the peculiarity of Achilles' speech include D. Claus, "*Aidos* in the Language of Achilles," *TAPA* 105 (1975), 13-28; S. Scully, "The Language of Achilles: The Ὀχθήσας Formula." *TAPA* 114 (1984), 11-27; S. Nimis, The Language of Achilles: Construction vs. Representation," *CW.* 79.4 (March-April, 1986), 217-25.

43. Note the parallel between Priam's "wallowing" in dung and Achilles' "tossing from side to side" in Ω 5.

44. Cf. Υ 222-24 where Achilles is compared to a father weeping for a son, another identification between Achilles and Priam.

45. Note also Achilles' groaning in Σ 315-6, expanded into a simile of a lion groaning.

46. See *Iliad* 14, 125, where ἀκούω with the accusative means "understand" (cf. *LSJ* s.v. II.3). For μῦθος meaning "unspoken thought or purpose," see *LSJ* s.v. 5.

47. As in Β 433-34; γ 473-74; cf. Ι 92-94; Ι 222-25; Λ 778-80; Θ 485-86; ο 304-4, ο 501-2, π 55-56; ρ 99-100; ω 489-90.

48. Peter W. Rose, "How Conservative is the *Iliad*?" *PCP* 13 (1978), 86-93, outlines the ideological apparatus of Agamemnon's authority and sketches briefly the *Iliad*'s implicit critique of various symbolic forms of that authority (scepters, divine birth formulae, etc.). Professor Rose has kindly shown me drafts of work in progress which develop these ideas more fully.

49. Of the many discussions of gift-exchange in a traditional society, I have found most useful that of P. Bourdieu, *Outline of a Theory of Practice* (Cambridge, 1977), 177-97. Bourdieu uses the term "misrecognition" (*méconnaisance*) to describe the process by which power relations are perceived not for what they objectively are, but in a way which renders them legitimate in the eyes of the beholder. See also W. Donlan, "The Politics of Generosity in Homer," *Helios* 10.2 (1982), 1-15; Bjørn Quiller, "The Dynamics of Homeric Society," *Symbolae Osloenses* 56 (1981), 109-55.

50. Nagler notes that the phrase ἔνθα καὶ ἔνθα (B 90) often suggests fruitless activity (*Spontaneity*, 170 n.), a point well supported by this bee simile. Note other occurrences in similes of Book 2: 397, 462, 476, and most significantly, 779.

51. These two Hesiodic stories, as West notes, are variations of each other. I will therefore use details of the Titanomachy as evidence for the traditional representation of the Typhonomachy. See West's notes on these stories, *Theogony*, (Oxford, 1966), 336-38, 379-83.

52. The other "groaning" of the earth is in *Theogony* 159, for which see above, p. 31.

53. In the Typhonomachy, M. L. West reconstructs one manuscript's reading for κονάβησε in *Theogony* 840 to σμαρ]αγησε. See West, "More Notes on the Text of Hesiod," *CQ* 12 (1962), 180.

54. West notes that in Homer Okeanos seems to have taken over the role of primeval father from Ouranos (*Theogony*, 23). Cf. Ξ 201: 'Ωκεανόν τε, θεῶν γένεσιν.

55. T. B. L. Webster, *From Mycenae to Homer* (New York, 1964), 64-90. West, *Theogony*, 19: "This succession myth has parallels in oriental mythology which are so striking that a connection is uncontestable."

56. See West's commentary on *Theo.* 706 and 846.

57. Cf. *Erga* 505-11; *Theo.* 706, 846, and West's notes there.

58. The phrase παντοίων ἀνέμων is repeated in a passage of the *Erga* (618-22) which recalls the evil winds of the *Theogony*. Cf. also P 56 and ε 293.

59. See Nagler's discussion of this key passage, *Spontaneity*, 156-57.

60. B. Fenik. *Typical Battle Scenes of the Iliad*, 20; W. C. Scott, *The Oral Nature of the Homeric Simile*, 87. T. Krischer, *Formale Konventionen der homerischen Epik*, 49-52 and 61-66.

61. E.g., B 455-56, Δ 422-27, Λ 155-57, Λ 305-9, N 795-800, Π 765-70, O 380-83, P 737-39, Y 490-92.

62. The term *proairesis* is used by Aristotle to indicate a logic of action as it applies to a represented character ("inclination" or "code of behavior" *AP* 1454a) in terms of class, sex, etc., but this places too much importance on the referent. In a semiotic context, we say that a logic of action is determined by genre rules for "verisimilitude" or, in a more radically innovative case, are constructed in a text; in any case it is based on a *discourse*. See Roland Barthes' discussion of proairetic codes in *S/Z*, tr. R. Miller (New York, 1974).

63. I regret to say that this analogy is not my own invention, but that of Wlad Godzich. In the original ABC Monday Night Football broadcast, Frank Gifford gave the play-by-play (proairesis), Don Meredith regularly discussed the instant replays, explaining what "really" happened, and Howard Cosell performed a third narrative function to be discussed below.

64. See Leaf and von der Mühll on this passage for enumerations of its many difficulties.

65. The relationship of Zeus and the gods to "fate" has long been debated. See B. C. Dietrich, *Death, Fate and the Gods* (London, 1965), 179-93, for a survey. Reinhardt suggests that the prevarication of Zeus in Π 432ff. and Y 168ff. reflects the portrayal of Zeus in the *Aithiopis*, the work he argues is the source for the *Patrokleia* and the slaying of Hector (*Die Ilias und ihr Dichter*,

382-90). If this is indeed a case of intertextual "noise," it is still a question of determining what motivated the intrusion of a contradictory portrayal. Note that although the deaths of Sarpedon and Hector are said to be "established long ago," they were actually established by Zeus himself in O 65-67.

66. Especially useful is Jack Goody, *The Domestication of the Savage Mind* (Cambridge, 1977).

67. For this important problem, see Pierre Bourdieu, *Outline of a Theory of Practice* (Cambridge, 1977).

## Apollonius

1. See Juri Lotman and B. A. Uspensky, "On the Semiotic Mechanism of Culture," *NLH* 9, No. 2 (Winter, 1978), 211-33, for these points about the relationship of culture and non-culture.

2. Whitman writes (*Homer*, 161): "Few things are more subtle in the *Iliad* than the way this 'good-for-nothing,' the social and physical antitype of Achilles, reiterates the resentment of the hero (sc. Achilles): the theme of the second Book is Delusion, and the truth can appear only in the mouth of a Thersites." Whitman sees the opposition of Achilles and the rest of the Greeks as the opposition of absolute value and relative value. We should say, however, that two truths are juxtaposed here: that of culture (Odysseus) and that of anti-culture (Thersites), and Achilles is aligned with the latter.

3. *Histories* 3, 38. The interpretation of the Pindaric fragment has been disputed, but Herodotus' meaning is clear enough. Cf. J. L. Meyers, "Herodotus and Anthropology," in *Classics and Anthropology*, ed. R. R. Marett (New York, 1966), 157.

4. J. R. Goody, *The Domestication of the Savage Mind* (Cambridge, 1967), 52-73. Eric Havelock, *Preface to Plato* (Cambridge, 1963), and H. Fraenkel, *Early Greek Poetry and Philosophy* (Oxford, 1967), ch. 7, make related observations.

5. Besides *The Domestication of the Savage Mind*, see J. Goody and Ian Watt, "The Consequences of Literacy" in *Literacy in Traditional Societies*, ed. J. Goody (Cambridge, 1968), 27-68; and Eric Havelock, *The Literate Revolution and Its Cultural Consequences* (Princeton, 1982); and his *Preface to Plato*. Havelock's notion that the use of writing "released psychic energy" is, however, rather vague. In the end it is best to speak of a conjuncture of causes. Alfred Sohn-Rethel, *Intellectual and Manual Labor*, (New York, 1978), for example, argues that the abstraction of use-value into exchange-value, which gives rise to the money-form, was the key factor in the rise of abstract thinking; while Bourdieu, *Outline of a Theory of Practice*, 233, notes that the concentration of diverse populations is a significant factor.

6. Marsh McCall, Jr., *Ancient Rhetorical Theories of Comparison and Simile*, 52.

7. This passage is of considerable interest for the relationship between metaphor and simile. See J. Derrida, "White Mythology" in *The Margins of Philosophy*, tr. A. Bass (Chicago, 1982), 207-71. For a semiotic critique of idealist theories of metaphor, see U. Eco, *The Role of the Reader*, ch. 2; and *Semiotics and the Philosophy of Language*, ch. 3.

8. *Rhetoric* 3, 10, 1411a 7 also makes this point.

9. Adolf Clausing, *Kritik und Exegese der homerischen Gleichnisse im Altertum* (Parchim, 1913), 66-67.

10. Both Clausing, *Kritik*, 28-59, and J. F. Carspecken, "Apollonius Rhodius and the Homeric Epic," *YClS* 13 (1952), 58-99, make these points and give ample illustrations.

11. Carspecken, "Apollonius" (above note), 67.

12. T. M. Andersson, *Early Epic Scenery* (Ithaca, 1976), 37, calls Homer's scenic technique "symbolical, not descriptive," which is to say that Homer's scenes do not cohere "mimetically." See Nagler's discussion of ι 9, 491 in *Spontaneity*, 35-36.

13. Fraenkel makes this point repeatedly, *Noten zu den Argonautika des Apollonios* (Munich, 1968): 32 n. 15; 173 n. 54; 430 n. 180.

14. Note that explicit examples of "analogizing" in Homer, such as Polydamas' interpretation of the omen in M 200-9 or Phoenix's "paradigm" of Meleager in the embassy scene, are most unsymmetrical. See Fraenkel's discussion of the former in *Die homerischen Gleichnisse*, 3-4; and von der Mühll, *Hypomnema*, 176, for the latter.

15. The seminal text is Snell, *The Discovery of the Mind* (New York, 1960). See also E. R. Dodds, *The Greeks and the Irrational* (Berkeley, 1951), ch. 1; and Fraenkel, *Early Greek Poetry and Philosophy*.

16. C. R. Beye, *Epic and Romance in the* Argonautica *of Apollonius* (Carbondale, 1982), 79:

> "Apollonius is not writing as a spokesman for a community. To the contrary, this is a private narrative about private people.... Apollonius does not ask us to admire Jason or consider him a specimen of the community's values. He asks us to believe in Jason, and in that Apollonius is successful."

Similar judgments are given by Carspecken, 88-89, and W. D. Anderson, "Notes on the Simile in Homer and His Successors," *CJ* 53 (1957), 83-84. I thus cannot agree with Brooks Otis, *Virgil* (Oxford, 1964), 40, when he lumps together Homer and Apollonius as representative of the "objective" style in comparison to the "subjective" style of Vergil.

17. Fraenkel, *Noten*, 162-63; "Apollonius Rhodius as Narrator in *Argonautica* 2. 1-140," *TAPA* 83 (1952), 144-55. See also his discussion of *Argo.* 3, 775-89 in *Noten* ad loc.

18. Clausing, *Kritik*, 28-59.

19. For a survey of the content of Apollonius' similes, see M. Schellert, *De Apollonii Rhodii comparationibus* (Halle, 1885); or E. G. Wilkins, "A Classification of the Similes of the *Argonautica* of Apollonius of Rhodes," *CW* 14.21 (April 11, 1921), 162-66.

20. See the discussion of B 144-9 (above, p. 82), and of Λ 558-62 (above, p. 52).

21. See Max Pohlenz, *Die Stoa* (Göttingen, 1964), 81ff.

22. J. M. Rist, *Stoic Philosophy* (Cambridge, 1962), 198-200. The early Stoa was heavily influenced by the Cynics, who wished to liberate men by eradicating all cultural institutions (see Rist, 54-80, and Lesky, *History of Greek Literature*, 669-70).

23. Besides the works cited above in note 15, see A. W. H. Adkins, *Merit and Responsibility* (Oxford, 1960); J. Russo and B. Simon, "Homeric Psychol-

ogy and the Oral Epic Tradition," *JHI* 29 (1968), 483-98. Others, such as Norman Austin, *Archery at the Dark of the Moon* (Berkeley, 1975), 81-129, have criticized this view as a form of primitivism. Austin argues that the similes, in particular, are one of Homer's means of representing psychological events (115-17). This view, taken by Fraenkel, Riezler, and others (see note 1 of the Introduction) is, however, based on the assumption that comparison *functions* pretty much the same way in all texts in all times. So Austin can assert, for example, that Homer's similes attempt to "make visible the human order by finding correspondences between it and the order of nature" (176), iterating here the orthodox view of simile since Aristotle. The least that can be said is that there is a difference in degree between Homer and Apollonius with regard to the amount of agency that each attributes to individuals. One index of this is the relatively superfluous divine machinery in the *Argonautica* (see Lesky, *History of Greek Literature*, 734). For a most radical assertion of the historical nature of human consciousness, see Julian Jaynes, *The Origin of Consciousness in the Breakdown of the Bicameral Mind* (Boston, 1976).

24.  See E. Phinney, "Hellenistic Painting and the Style of Apollonius," *CJ* 62 (1967), 145-49.

25.  For the role of the similes in constructing character, see J. Clark, "The Medea Similes of Apollonius' *Argonautica*," *CJ* 68 (1973), 310-15.

26.  *The Novel Before the Novel* (Chicago, 1977), 15. See also C. M. Bowra, *Pindar* (Oxford, 1964), 137-42.

27.  See, for example, Carspecken, 110-25; G. Lawall, "Apollonius' *Argonautica*: Jason as Anti-hero," *YClS* 19 (1966), 119-69; M. Hadas, "The Tradition of the Feeble Jason," *CP* 31 (1939), 166-68; C. R. Beye, *Epic and Romance in the Argonautica of Apollonius* (Carbondale, 1982), 77-99; T. M. Klein, "Apollonius' Jason, Hero and Scoundrel," *QUCC* 42 (1983), 115-26.

28.  See Erwin Rohde, *Der griechische Roman und seine Vorläüfer*, 2nd ed. (Leipzig, 1900), 22-23; W. W. Tarn, *Hellenistic Civilization*, 3rd ed., tr. G. T. Griffith (London, 1952), 278; Albert Cook, *The Classic Line* (Bloomington, 1966), 187-88. Heiserman, *The Novel Before the Novel*, 11-29.

# Vergil

1.  The former, the more traditional reading, can be seen in critics like V. Pöschl, *The Art of Vergil*, tr. Gerda Seligson (Ann Arbor, 1962); Brooks Otis, *Virgil* (Oxford, 1964). The latter can be seen in critics like W. R. Johnson, *Darkness Visible* (Berkeley, 1976); Mario di Cesare, *The Altar and the City* (New York, 1974); and in the essays by Adam Parry, R. A. Brooks and W. Clausen in *Virgil*, ed. Steele Commager (Englewood Cliffs, 1966). One of many attempts to mediate the two positions is H. C. Gotoff, "The Transformations of Mezentius," *TAPA* 114 (1984), 191-218.

2.  The idea that a constitution comprising a mixture of aristocracy, kingship and democracy might have certain advantages is at least as old as Plato's *Mnexenus* (238c-d) and is a peripatetic commonplace. Polybius, who is mentioned by name in *Republic* I, xxi, 34, gives essentially the same scheme as Cicero in Book Six of his *Histories*. For more on the background of the basic idea, see Kurt von Fritz, *The Theory of the Mixed Constitution in Antiquity*

(New York, 1954), 60-95; and F. W. Walbank, *Polybius* (Berkeley, 1972), ch. 5.

3.  It is, in fact, the *balance* among the three simple forms which is important, not the simple mixing, a point emphasized more by Cicero than by Polybius.  Cicero notes that other states had "mixed" constitutions, but that like the early Roman monarchy, they did not have a *balanced* mixture (*Rep*. II, xxiii, 42): "ita mixta fuerint et in hac (sc. Roma) civitate et in Lacedaemoniorum et in Karthaginiensium, ut *temperata nullo fuerint modo*."

4.  In his discussion of the origin of the city (*Rep*. II, 369b-c), Plato states that each man was unable to provide everything for himself.  This weakness led to the institution of a *metadosis*, a "reciprocal exchange," among men.  Government is the institutionalization of this exchange, and justice is simply a "proper" *metadosis* (*Rep*. IV, 433a-b).  Polybius (6, 2, 5) also cites man's weakness as the main cause for the rise of political institutions.  Cicero, like the Stoics, emphasizes a more positive principle, an innate political instinct (*Rep*. I, xxv, 39): "eius autem prima causa coeundi est non tam imbecillitas quam *naturalis quaedam hominum quasi congregatio*."  The two are not mutually exclusive, but each produces a different emphasis on the relationship of nature and culture.  For this tradition and its roots, see T. Cole, *Democritus and the Sources of Greek Anthropology*, American Philological Monographs 25 (1967).

5.  See Cicero's discussion of the *ratio* of Rome's site, possessing the advantages of both inland and coastal locations, but none of the disadvantages (*Rep*. II, v, 10).  See also the fragments of *Republic* III, xxii, 22-25, for the "natural" basis of justice and government.

6.  The Greek term is μεταβολή.  I have simplified somewhat the relationship among the primary forms; Polybius and Cicero also discuss the changes (*conversiones*, μεταβολαί) among the pairs (e.g. from tyranny to democracy), and this is the main concern of Plato.  Nevertheless, in all three authors there is the basic contrast between a cycle of revolutionary change among the simple forms, on the one hand, and a stable structure of exchange according to a *ratio* on the other.  Cicero is most clear on this point; Polybius less so.  See C. O. Brink and F. W. Walbank, "The Construction of the Sixth Book of Polybius," *CQ* 4 (1954), 97-122.

7.  Typical of this approach is W. S. Anderson, *The Art of the Aeneid* (Englewood Cliffs, 1969).  The similes are treated along these lines by R. A. Hornsby, *Patterns of Action in the Aeneid* (Iowa City, 1970).

8.  *Coorior* is used twice elsewhere in Vergil:  once for a storm's rising (*Geo*. 3, 478) and once for the wind's rising (*Aen*. 10, 405).  *Orior* is used typically of the sun's rising (*Aen*. 3, 277, etc.) or of a race of men "rising" from its ancestors (*Aen*. 1, 626, etc.).

9.  Otis, *Virgil* (Oxford, 1964), 155.

10.  Cf. especially *Geo*. 2, 61-62:
    scilicet omnibus est labor impendendus, et omnes
    cogendae in sulcum ac multa mercede domandae.
See also *Geo*. 2, 35-36, 47-52.  I thus cannot agree with Otis' evaluation of the second *Georgic* as showing man's happy cooperation with nature (*Virgil*, 163-64).

11. Otis, *Virgil*, 181-90.
12. See again Juri Lotman and B. Uspensky, "On the Semiotic Mechanism of Culture," *NLH* 9, No. 2 (Winter, 1978), 211-33, for this opposition.
13. Cf. *Georgics* 3, 244-46:
    amor omnibus idem
    tempore non alio *catulorum oblita* leana
    saevior erravit campis.
*Amor* is described as a natural impulse which must be overcome throughout the section of the *Georgics* (3, 209-83) from which this is taken.
14. Cf. Servius on *Aen.* 4, 69:
    furor enim est amor, in quo nihil est stabile: unde et Cupido puer inductier, quam instabilis et *infans*, qui *non potest fari*: unde post paulo (76) incipit effari etc.
Cf. also line 85 where Dido's *amor* is called *nefandum*, "unspeakable."
15. Cf. the utopia of *Eclogue* 4 (22-25):
    nec magnos metuent armenta leones;
    ipsa tibi blandos fundent cunabula flores
    occidet et serpens, et fallax herba veneni
    occidet.
Snakes and poisonous weeds, it seems, unlike the lions, are unassimilable.
16. The Homeric and Apollonian background for the Dido episode confirms this view. The Diana simile is much closer to *Od.* 6, 102-8 than to *Argo.* 3, 876-85; and, in fact, the last half of *Aeneid* 1 seems to draw most of its inspiration from Odysseus' Scherian episode (Knauer, *Aeneis und Homer* [Göttingen, 1964], 152-73). *Aeneid* 4, on the other hand, is closer to *Od.* 5, 1-262 (Knauer, 209-14), and *Argo.* 3 (Felix Ruetten, *De Vergilii studiis Apollonianis* [Münster, 1912], 66-76). Dido thus shifts from a Nausicaa interpretant to a Medea/Calypso interpretant; and the former is a much more attractive model than the barbaric Medea or Calypso the "Hider."
17. For the Homeric and Hesiodic background of the earth's groaning, see above, pp. 31-32, 76-79.
18. Cf. *Republic* III, xxii, 33; Polybius 6, 2, 5; Aristotle, *Politics* I, 1254a-b.
19. Cf. Θ 69 and see above, pp. 43ff.
20. Note that in the ensuing battle Turnus is compared to a *cervus* pursued by an Umbrian *canis venator* (749-55). The comparison of Aeneas to a dog is the only animal simile in the *Aeneid* which does not have some negative connotation; but then a *trained* hunting dog has been made part of culture.
21. See M. M. Bakhtin, *The Dialogic Imagination*, tr. Caryl Emerson and Michael Holquist (Austin, 1981), 34-35.
22. For a fuller discussion of this analogy, see Marc Shell, *The Economy of Literature* (Baltimore, 1978), who cites a substantial bibliography on the subject. A full-scale philosophical attempt to identify the relationship between the rise of abstract thought and abstract value (i.e., money) can be found in Alfred Sohn-Rethel, *Intellectual and Manual Labor* (New York, 1978).

## Dante

1. C. Singleton, ed., *The Divine Comedy* (Princeton, 1970), ad loc.

2. C. Singleton, "In exitu Israel de Aegypto" in *Twentieth Century Views on Dante*, ed. J. Freccero (Englewood Cliffs, 1965), 103-21.

3. E. Auerbach, "figura," in *Scenes form the Drama of European Literature*, tr. R. Manheim (Minneapolis, 1984), 11-76. Dante, *Convivio* II, 1. Of the many works on biblical typology, I have found A. C. Charity, *Events and their Afterlife* (Cambridge, 1966), to be the most useful.

4. *Epistle* X, 7, cited by Charity, *Events*, 201. My translation.

5. *Summa theologica* I, i, 10. For a discussion see Charity, *Events*, 173-8, who argues that *res ipsae* be translated as "historical events."

6. Auerbach, "figura," 58-59. Manheim's translation has been modified according to the German version in *Gesammelte Aufsätze zur romanischen Philologie* (Bern, 1967), 80-81.

7. The New Testament canon of 27 books was firmly established in the Latin West in three African synods of the fourth century through the influence of Augustine. But a large number of apocryphal works (e.g., the Gospel of Nicodemus), whose status was controversial, still circulated in Dante's time.

8. See the annotation ad loc. in *La Divina Commedia*, ed. G. A. Scartazzini (Bologna, 1881).

9. J. Freccero, "Medusa: The Letter and the Spirit," *Yearbook of Italian Studies* (1972), 2.

10. Eco, 153-55, 250-56, and the whole section on the "semiotic purport of the aesthetic text," 261-76.

11. See Aristotle, *Rhetoric* 3, 2, 1405a12, cited above, p. 136.

12. C. S. Peirce coined the term "abduction" in *Collected Papers*, II, 623-25. See Eco, 131-42, and his paper "The Theory of Signs and the Role of the Reader," *Bulletin of the Midwest Modern Language Association* 14, No. 1 (Spring, 1981), 43-45, and the discussion by Wlad Godzich which follows, 53-55.

13. This should be compared to Riffaterre's notion of "indirection"; see *Semiotics of Poetry*, 1-6.

14. See C. T. Davis, *Dante and the Idea of Rome* (Oxford, 1957).

15. Typological exegesis always "leans" on exchange in the sense that an analogy of some sort must be the basis for establishing an antithesis between *figura* and fulfillment. Hence Auerbach, "figura," 29: "The relation between the two events is revealed by an accord or similarity.... Often vague similarities in the structure of events or in their attendant circumstances suffice to make the *figura* recognizable." We would restate this as "suffice to make the *ratio difficilis* acceptable."

16. The *veltro* has been interpreted both politically (e.g., Singleton, ad loc.) and religiously (e.g., Sapegno, ad loc.). We should remember, however, that political and religious allegories are not two different "levels" of meaning, but two terms of a dialectic which constitutes both the political and the religious realms into models.

17. The "silence" of the divine presence is a major theme of the *Confessions*. See, for example, 9, 10; 10, 2; and J. Freccero, "The Laurel and the Fig Tree," *Diacritics* 2 (1972), 35-36.

18. Compare the *pelle macolata* of the *lonza* with the Virgin who was conceived *immaculata*. St. Lucy, whose martyrdom was a victory over haughtiness, balances off the *leone* (Scartazzini, ad loc.), and Beatrice, whose eyes

shine like the stars (II, 55), balances off the *lupa*, whose visage so terrifies the pilgrim (I, 53).

19.  Sapegno, ad loc.

## Milton

1.  See Eco, 125-29 for the inherently transitory character of the "Global Semantic Universe," and 139-42, for the dialectic of codes and messages.

2.  Note that Eden unfolds in Book Four of *Paradise Lost* before the eyes of Satan, to whom it is no longer available.  Cf. the similes comparing Satan and the devils to various "anti-pastoral" types:  a city dweller visiting the country (9, 446-54), merchants (2, 636-42), pioneers (1, 675-78), and sailors (4, 159-65).

3.  See Arnold Stein, *Answerable Style* (Minneapolis, 1953), 73; J. R. Knott, "Symbolic Landscapes in *Paradise Lost*," *Milton Studies* 2 (1970), 37-58; J. B. Broadbent, *Some Graver Subject* (London, 1960), 185; A. B. Giamatti, *The Earthly Paradise in Renaissance Epic* (Princeton, 1970), 295-351; John Steadman, *Epic and Tragic Structure in Paradise Lost* (Chicago, 1976), 20-28.

4.  The portrayal of an *amoenus locus* as a sensuous trap is exemplified in the *Odyssey* (Scheria and the islands of Circe and Calypso), imitated by Vergil (Carthage in *Aen.* 4), Ariosto (Alcina's island in *Orlando Furioso* 6), and many others.  See Giamatti, *The Earthly Paradise* (previous note).

5.  Milton's narrator has other faces as well. See Ann Ferry, *Milton's Epic Voice* (Cambridge, 1963); and Christopher Grose, *Milton's Epic Process* (New Haven, 1973), discussed below.

6.  Samuel Johnson, "Milton," in *Lives of the English Poets*, repr. with numerous other older critics of Milton in *Milton Criticism: Selections from Four Centuries*, ed. J. Thorpe (New York, 1966), 81-82.

7.  T. S. Eliot, *On Poetry and Poets* (New York, 1957), 162, 173.  The earlier stages of the Milton "controversy" have been made available in *Milton: The Critical Heritage*, ed. J. Shawcross, 2 vols. (New York, 1970-72).  The post-Eliot debate can be gleaned from R. M. Adams, *Ikon: John Milton and the Modern Critics* (Ithaca, 1955), among others.

8.  Stanley Fish, *Surprised by Sin* (New York, 1967), 2 n.  For a similar view which focuses on the similes, see Douglas Knight, "The Dramatic Center of *Paradise Lost*," *South Atlantic Quarterly* 63 (1964), 44-59.

9.  John Steadman, *Milton and the Renaissance Hero* (Oxford, 1967); *Milton's Epic Characters* (Chapel Hill, 1959); *Epic and Tragic Structures in Paradise Lost* (Chicago, 1976); T. J. B. Spencer, "*Paradise Lost*: the Anti-Epic," in *Approaches to Paradise Lost*, ed. C. A. Patrides (London, 1968), 81-98; M. di Cesare, "*Paradise Lost* and the Epic Tradition," *Milton Studies* 1 (1969), 31-50; S. P. Revard, "Milton's Critique of Heroic Warfare in *Paradise Lost* V and VI," *SEL* 7 (1967), 119-39; M. B. McNamee, *Honor and the Epic Hero* (New York, 1960).  With special reference to the similes, see C. M. Bowra, *From Vergil to Milton* (Oxford, 1949), esp. 228; Kingsley Widmer, "The Iconography of Renunciation:  The Miltonic Simile," in *Milton's Epic Poetry*, ed. C. A. Patrides (London, 1967), 121-31; D. P. Harding, *Studies in the Classical Background of Paradise Lost* (Urbana, 1962).

10.  Christopher Grose, *Milton's Epic Process* (New Haven, 1973), 151.

11. Grose, 154. A related view of the similes is taken by G. Hartman, "Milton's Counterplot," *ELH* 25 (1958), 1-12.

12. The phrase is a pastiche of *Paradise Lost* 7, 178 and 9, 24.

13. T. S. Eliot, *The Sacred Wood* (New York, 1930), 87. F. R. Leavis, *Revaluation* (London, 1936), 60, compares the composition of *Paradise Lost* to bricklaying. I do not cite these critics because I agree with their judgment that Milton is "bad" for poets to read, but because their response to the poetry of *Paradise Lost* recognizes an essential characteristic of the narrative organization. A more favorable estimation of this aspect of Milton's poetry can be found in C. S. Lewis, *Preface to* Paradise Lost (Lnodon, 1942), 43-45.

14. See Paul de Man, *Blindness and Insight* (Minneapolis, 1983); and the introduction by Wlad Godzich, xxvii-xxx. *Paradise Lost* can thus be seen to accomplish *within* the epic tradition the "novelization" of stylizations that Bakhtin, *The Dialogic Imagination*, argues is characteristic of the novel.

# REFERENCES

## Texts and Translations

The following editions and translations have been used throughout. The translations, however, have been frequently modified to reflect my interpretation. The translations are for the reader's aid only and do not of themselves constitute any evidence for the argument.

Allen, T. W., ed. *Homeri Opera*, 5 volumes. *Ilias*, 3rd edn. Oxford, 1920; *Odysseia*, 2nd edn. Oxford, 1917; *Hymni, Cyclus, Fragmenta...* Oxford, 1961.
Fraenkel, Hermann, ed. *Argonautica*. Oxford, 1961.
Freese, J. H., ed. and tr. *Aristotle: Art of Rhetoric*. London, 1975.
Hadas, Moses, tr. *Heliodorus' An Aethiopian Tale*. Ann Arbor, 1967.
Hughes, Merrit Y., ed. *Complete Poems and Major Prose of John Milton*. New York, 1957.
Kassel, R. *Aristotelis De arte poetica*. Oxford, 1965.
Keyes, C. W., ed. and tr. *Cicero's De re publica*. London, 1970.
Lattimore, R., tr. *The Iliad*. Chicago, 1951.
--------, tr. *The Odyssey*. New York, 1965.
Mandelbaum, A., tr. *The Aeneid of Virgil*. New York, 1961.
Mynors, R. A. B., ed. *Opera Vergilii*. Oxford, 1969.
Rieu, E. V., tr. *The Voyage of the Argo*. Bungay, 1959.
Schmidt, M. C., tr. *Hesiod and Theognis*. Bungay, 1959.
Sinclair, J. D., ed. and tr. *The Divine Comedy of Dante Alighieri*. New York, 1975.
Solmsen, F., ed. *Opera Hesiodi*. Oxford, 1970.
West, M. L., ed. *Iambi et Elegi Graeci*, 2 vols. Oxford, 1972.
LSJ = Liddell, H. G., and R. Scott, eds. *A Greek-English Lexicon*. 9th ed. Oxford, 1940.

## Critical Works

Adams, R. M. *Ikon: John Milton and the Modern Critics*. Ithaca, 1955.
Adkins, A. W. H. *Merit and Responsibility*. Oxford, 1960.
Ahrens, Ernest. *Gnomen in griechischen Epos*. Halle, 1937.
Althusser, Louis. *For Marx.*, tr. Ben Brewster. New York, 1969.
Anderson, W. D. "Notes on the Simile in Homer and his Successors." *Classical Journal* 53 (1957-58), 81-87, 127-33.
Anderson, W. S. *The Art of the Aeneid*. Englewood Cliffs, 1969.
Andersson, T. M. *Early Epic Scenery*. Ithaca, 1976.
Arend, Walter, *Die typischen Szenen bei Homer*. Berlin, 1933.
Armstrong, J. I. "The Arming Motif in the *Iliad*." *American Journal of Philology* 79 (1958), 337-54.
Auerbach, Erich. "*Figura*," in *Scenes from the Drama of European Literature*, tr. Ralph Manheim. Minneapolis, 1984.
-------- "*Figura*," in *Gesammelte Aufsätze zur romanischen Philologie*. Bern, 1967.
Austin, Norman. *Archery at the Dark of the Moon*. Berkeley, 1975.
Autentrieth, G. *A Homeric Dictionary*, tr. R. P. Keep. Norman, 1958.
Bakhtin, M. M. *The Dialogic Imagination*, ed. Michael Holquist, tr. Caryl Emerson and M. Holquist. Austin, 1981.
Barthes, Roland. *S/Z*, tr. R. Miller. New York, 1974.
Basset, S. E. *Poetry of Homer*, Sather Classical Lectures 15. Berkeley, 1938.
Belsey, Catherine. "Problems of Literary Theory: The Problem of Meaning." *New Literary History* 14, No. 1 (Autumn, 1982), 175-82.
Beye, C. R. *Epic and Romance in the* Argonautica *of Apollonius*. Carbondale, 1982.
Bourdieu, Pierre, and J.-C. Passeron. *Reproduction in Education, Society and Culture*. Sage Studies in Social and Educational Change 5, tr. R. Nice. London, 1977.
Bourdieu, P. *Outline of a Theory of Practice*, tr. R. Nice. Cambridge, 1977.
Bowra, C. M. *From Vergil to Milton*. Oxford, 1949.
-------- *Pindar*. Oxford, 1964.
Brink, C. O., and F. W. Wallbank. "The Construction of the Sixth Book of Polybius." *Classical Quarterly* 4 (1954), 97-122.
Broadbent, J. B. *Some Graver Subject*. London, 1960.
Brooks, R. A. "*Discolor Aura*: Reflections on the Golden Bough," in Steele Commager, ed., *Virgil* (Englewood Cliffs, 1966), pp. 143-63.
Carspecken, J. F. "Apollonius Rhodius and the Homeric Epic." *Yale Classical Studies* 13 (1952), 33-143.
diCesare, M. "*Paradise Lost* and the Epic Tradition." *Milton Studies* 1 (1969), 31-50.
--------. *The Altar and the City*. New York, 1974.
Chantraine, P. *Dictionaire etymologique de la langue grècque*. Paris, 1968.
Charity, A. C. *Events and their Afterlife*. Cambridge, 1966.
Chomsky, Noam. "Review of B. F. Skinner's *Verbal Behavior*, repr. in *The Structure of Language*, ed. J. Fodor and J. Katz (Englewood Cliffs, 1963), 384-89.

--------. *Aspects of the Theory of Syntax*. Cambridge, 1966.

--------. "Formal Discussion," repr. in *Selected Readings in Chomsky*, ed. J. Allen and P. van Buren. London, 1971.

Clark, J. "The Medea Simile of Apollonius' *Argonautica*." *Classical Philology* 68 (1973), 310-15.

Clarke, Howard. *Homer's Readers*. Newark, 1981.

Claus, D. "*Aidos* in the Language of Achilles." *TAPA* 105 (1975), 13-28.

Clausen, W. "An Interpretation of the *Aeneid*," in *Virgil*, ed. S. Commager (Englewood Cliffs, 1966), pp. 75-88.

Clausing, Adolf. *Kritik und Exegese der homerischen Gleichnisse im Altertum*. Parchim, 1913.

Coffey, M. "The Function of the Homeric Simile." *American Journal of Philology* 78 (1957), 113-32.

Cole, T. *Democritus and the Sources of Greek Anthropology*, American Philological Monographs 25 (1967).

Commager, Steele, ed. *Virgil*. Englewood Cliffs, 1976.

Cook, Albert. *The Classic Line*. Bloomington, 1966.

Culler, Jonathan. *Structuralist Poetics*. Ithaca, 1975.

--------. *On Deconstruction*. Ithaca, 1975.

Damon, Philip. *Modes of Analogy in Ancient and Medieval Verse*. University of California Publications in Classical Philology 15, No. 6. Berkeley, 1961.

Davis, C. T. *Dante and the Idea of Rome*. Oxford, 1947.

Davison, J. A. "The Homeric Question" in *A Companion to Homer*, ed. A. Wace and F. Stubbings (London, 1962), 234-65.

Derrida, Jacques. "White Mythology," in *Margins of Philosophy*, tr. A. Bass. Chicago, 1982.

Dietrich, B. C. *Death, Fate and the Gods*. London, 1965.

Dodds, E. R. *The Greeks and the Irrational*. Berkeley, 1951.

Donlan, Walter. "Reciprocities in Homer." *Classical World* 75, No. 3 (Feb., 1982), 137-75.

Eagleton, Terry. *Literary Theory: An Introduction*. Minneapolis, 1983.

Eco, Umberto. *A Theory of Semiotics*. Bloomington, 1976.

--------. *The Role of the Reader*. Bloomington, 1979.

--------. "The Theory of Signs and the Role of the Reader." *Bulletin of the Midwest Modern Language Association* 14, No. 1 (Spring, 1981), 35-45.

--------. *Semiotics and the Philosophy of Language*. Bloomington, 1984.

Eliot, T.S. *The Sacred Wood*. New York, 1930.

--------. *On Poetry and Poets*. New York, 1957.

Erbse, Helmut, ed. *Scholia Graeca in Homeri Iliadem*, 5 vols. Berlin, 1967-78.

Fenik, B. *Typical Battle Scenes in the Iliad*, Hermes Einzelschriften 21. Wiesbaden, 1968.

Ferry, Ann. *Milton's Epic Voice*. New Haven, 1973.

Fish, Stanley. *Surprised by Sin*. New York, 1967.

--------. *Self-Consuming Artifacts*. Berkeley, 1972.

--------. *Is There a Text in This Class?* Cambridge, 1981.

Foucault, M. *Discipline and Punish*. New York, 1979.

Fraenkel, Hermann. *Die homerischen Gleichnisse*. Göttingen, 1921.

--------. *Wege und Formen frügriecisches Denkens*. Munich, 1968.

--------. *Early Greek Literature and Philosophy*, tr. Moses Hadas. Oxford, 1973.

--------. *Noten zu den* Argonautica *des Apollonios*. Munich, 1978.

Freccero, J. "The Laurel and the Fig Tree." *Diacritics* 5 (Spring, 1975), 34-40.

--------. "Medusa: The Letter and the Spirit." *Yearbook of Italian Studies* I (1972), 1-18.

Fries, Carl. "Zur Gleichnissprache des Iliasdichters." *Philologische Wochenschrift* 55 (1935), 765-8.

Frisk, A. *Griechisches etymologisches Woerterbuch*. Heidelberg, 1973.

von Fritz, Max. *The Theory of the Mixed Constitution in Antiquity*. New York, 1954.

Frye, Northrop. *Anatomy of Criticism*. Princeton, 1971.

Giamatti, A. B. *The Earthly Paradise in Renaissance Epic*. Princeton, 1970.

Godzich, Wlad. "Review of U. Eco's *A Theory of Semiotics* and Jean J. Nattiez's *Fondemonts d'une semiologie de la musique*." *Journal of the History of Music* (Winter, 1979), 117-32.

--------. "Introduction" to P. de Man, *Blindness and Insight* (Minneapolis, 1983).

Goody, J., and Ian Watt. "The Consequences of Literacy" in *Literacy in Traditional Societies*, ed. J. Goody (Cambridge, 1968), 304-45.

Goody, J. R. *The Domestication of the Savage Mind*. Cambridge, 1977.

Gotoff, H. C. "The Transformatioons of Mezentius." *TAPA* 114 (1984), 191-218.

Greimas, A. J. *Sémantique structurale*. Paris, 1966.

Grose, Christopher. *Milton's Epic Process*. New Haven, 1973.

Hadas, M. "The Tradition of a Feeble Jason." *Classical Philology* 31 (1939), 166-68.

Hansen, W. *The Conference Sequence*, University of California Publications in Classical Philology 8. Berkeley, 1972.

Harding, D. P. *Studies in the Classical Background of Paradise Lost*. Urbana, 1962.

Hartman, G. "Milton's Counterplot," *ELH* 25 (1958), 1-12.

Havelock, Eric. *Preface to Plato*. Cambridge, 1962.

--------. *The Literate Revolution in Greece and its Cultural Consequences*. Princeton, 1982.

Heiserman, Arthur. *The Novel Before the Novel*. Chicago, 1977.

Holland, Norman. *Five Readers Reading*. New Haven, 1977.

Holoka, J. "Homer's Originality: A Survey." *Classical World* 12 (1973), 257-93.

Hornsby, R. A. *Patterns of Action in the Aeneid*. Iowa City, 1970.

Jameson, Fredric. *The Political Unconscious*. Ithaca, 1981.

Jaynes, Julian,. *The Origin of Consciousness in the Breakdown of the Bicameral Mind*. Boston, 1976.

Johnson, W. R. *Darkness Visible*. Berkeley, 1976.

Keyes, C. W., ed. and tr. *Cicero: De Re Publica*. London, 1977.

Kirk, G. S. *Songs of Homer*. Cambridge, 1962.

Klein, T. M. "Apollonius' Jason, Hero and Scoundrel," *QUCC* 42 (1983), 115-26.

Knauer, G. N. *Die Aeneis und Homer*, Hypomnemata 7. Göttingen, 1964.

Knight, Douglas. "The Dramatic Center of *Paradise Lost*." *South Atlantic*

*Quarterly* 63 (1964), 44-59.

Knott, J. R. "Symbolic Landscapes in *Paradise Lost.*" *Milton Studies* 2 (1970), 37-58.

Krischer, Tilmann. *Formale Konventionen der homerischen Epik.* Munich, 1971.

Kullmann, Wolfgang, "Zur Methode der Neoanalyse in der Homerforschung." *Weiner Studien* NF 15 (1981), 5-42.

--------. "Oral Poetry Theory amd Neoanalysis." *GRBS* 25.4 (Winter, 1984), 307-23.

Lawall, G. "Apollonius' *Argonautica*: Jason as Anti-hero." *Yale Classical Studies* 19 (1966), 119-69.

Leaf, Walter, ed. *The Iliad.* New York, 1900.

Leavis, F. R. *Revaluation.* London, 1936.

Lee, D. J. N. *The Similes of the Iliad and Odyssey Compared.* Australian Hum. Res. Council Monograph 10. Melbourne, 1964.

Lesky, Albin. *A History of Greek Literature,* 2nd edn., tr. James Willis and Cornelis de Heer. New York, 1966.

Lewis, C. S. *A Preface to* Paradise Lost. London, 1942.

Lord, A. B. *Singer of Tales.* Cambridge, 1961.

Lotman, Juri and B. A. Uspensky. "On the Semiotic Mechanism of Culture." *New Literary History* 9, No. 2 (Winter, 1978), 211-33.

McCall, Marsh H. *Ancient Rhetorical Theories of Simile and Comparison.* Cambridge, 1969.

McCary, T. *Childlike Achilles.* New York, 1982.

McNamee, M. B. *Honor and the Epic Hero.* New York, 1960.

Meyers, J. L. "Herodotus and Anthropology" in *Classics and Anthropology,* ed., R. R. Marett (New York, 1966), 150-63.

Motto, A. L., and J. R. Clark. "*Ise Dais*: The Honor of Achilles." *Arethusa* 2, No. 2 (Fall, 1969), 109-25.

Moulton, Carroll. *Similes in the Homeric Poems,* Hypomnema 49. Göttingen, 1977.

von der Mühll, Peter. *Kritische Hypomnema zur Ilias.* Basel, 1952.

Mueller, Martin. *The Iliad.* London, 1984.

Müller, F. "Das homerische Gleichnis." *Neue Jahrbücher fur antike und deutsche Bildung* 4 (1941), 175-83.

Nagler, Michael. *Spontaneity and Tradition.* Berkeley, 1974.

Nagy, Gregory. *The Best of the Achaeans.* Baltimore, 1979.

Nilsson, M. P. *Homer and Mycenae.* London, 1933.

Nimis, S. "The Language of Achilles: Construction vs. Representation." *Classical World* 79.4 (March-April, 1986), 217-25.

Notopoulos, J. A. "Parataxis and Homer." *TAPA* 80 (1949), 1-23.

Olsen, S. H. "The 'Meaning' of a Literary Work." *New Literary History* 14, No. 1 (Autumn, 1982), 13-31.

Otis, Brooks. *Virgil: A Study in Civilized Poetry.* Oxford, 1964.

Page, Denys. *The Homeric Odyssey.* Oxford, 1955.

Parry, Adam. "The Language of Achilles." *TAPA* 87 (1956), 1-7.

--------. "The Two Voices of Virgil's *Aeneid,*" in *Virgil,* ed. S. Commager (Englewood Cliffs, 1966), 107-123.

Parry, M. *The Making of Homeric Verse,* ed. Adam Parry. Oxford, 1971.

Patrides, C. A., ed. *Approaches to Paradise Lost*. London, 1968.
--------, ed. *Milton's Epic Poetry*. London, 1967.
Peabody, Berkeley. *Winged Word*. Albany, 1976.
Peirce, Charles S. *Collected Papers*. Cambridge, 1931-58.
Pfeiffer, Roland. *History of Classical Scholarship: From the Beginnings to the end of the Hellenistic Age*. Oxford, 1968.
Phinney, E. "Hellenistic Painting and the Style of Apollonius." *Classical Journal* 62 (1967), 145-49.
Pöschl, Victor. *The Art of the Aeneid*, tr. Gerda Seligson. Ann Arbor, 1962.
Pohlenz, Max. *Die Stoa*. Göttingen, 1964.
Propp, Vladimir. *The Morphology of the Folktale*, tr. L. Scott, 2nd edn. Austin, 1968.
Quiller, Bjørn. "The Dynamics of Homeric Society," *Symbolae Osloenses* 56 (1981), 109-55.
Redfield, J. M. *Nature and Culture in the Iliad*. Chicago, 1975.
Reinhardt, Karl. *Die Ilias und ihr Dichter*, ed. U. Hölscher. Göttingen, 1961.
Revard, S. P. "Milton's Critique of Heroic Warfare in *Paradise Lost* V and VI," *Studies in English Literature* 7 (1967), 119-39.
Riezler, Kurt. "Das homerische Gleichnis und der Anfang der Philosophie." *Die Antike* 12 (1936), 253-71.
Riffaterre, M. *The Semiotics of Poetry*. Bloomington, 1978.
--------. "Paragram and Significance." *Semiotexte* I, No. 2 (Fall, 1974), 72-87.
Rist, J. M. *Stoic Philosophy*. Cambridge, 1962.
Rohde, Erwin. *Der griechische Roman und seine Vorläufer*, 2nd edn. Leipzig, 1900.
Rose, Peter W. "How Conservative is the *Iliad*? *Pacific Coast Philology* 13 (1978), 86-93.
Rütten, Felix. *De Vergilii studiis Apollonianis*. Munster, 1912.
Russo, J. A. "How and What Does Homer Communicate? The Medium and the Message of Homeric Verse." *Classical Journal* 71.4 (1976), 289-99.
Russo, J. A., and B. Simon. "Homeric Psychology and the Oral Epic Tradition." *JHI* 29 (1968), 483-98.
Sapegno, Natalion, ed. *La Divina Commedia*. Firenze, 1977.
de Saussure, Ferdinand. *Course in General Linguistics*, tr. W. Baskin. New York, 1961.
Scartazzini, G. A., ed. *La Divina Commedia*. Bologna, 1881.
Schadewaldt, Wolfgang. "Die homerische Gleichnis und die kretisch-mykenische Kunst," in *Von Homers Welt und Werk*. Leipzig, 1944.
--------. *Iliasstudien*, 3rd edn. Darmstadt, 1966.
Schellert, M. *De Apollonii Rhodii comparationibus*. Halle, 1885.
Schlunk, R. R. *The Homeric Scholia and the Aeneid*. Ann Arbor, 1974.
Scott, W. C. *The Oral Nature of the Homeric Simile*. Mnemosyne Supplementband 28. Leiden, 1964.
Scully, Stephen. "The Language of Achilles: The 'Οχθησας Formula." *TAPA* 114 (1984), 11-27.
Segal, Charles P. *The Theme of the Mutilation of the Corpses in the Iliad*. Leiden, 1971.
Shawcross, John, ed. *Milton: The Critical Heritage*, 2 vols. New York, 1970-72.

Shell, Marc. *The Economy of Literature.* Baltimore, 1978.

Sheppard, J. T. "Traces of the Rhapsode." *Journal of Hellenistic Studies* 42 (1922), 220-37.

Shewan, A. "Suspected Flaws in Homeric Similes," *Classical Philology* 6 (1911), 271-81.

Shipp, George P. *Studies in the Language of Homer,* 2nd edn. Cambridge, 1972.

Singleton, C., ed. *The Divine Comedy,* Bollingen Series 80. Princeton, 1970.

--------. "In Exitu Israel de Aegypto" in *Dante,* ed., J. Freccero (Englewood Cliffs, 1965), 102-21.

Snell, Bruno. *The Discovery of the Mind,* tr. T. G. Rosenmeyer. New York, 1960.

Sohn-Rethel, A. *Intellectual and Manual Labor: A Critique of Epistemology.* New York, 1978.

Spencer, T. J. B. "*Paradise Lost*: The Anti-epic," in *Approaches to Paradise Lost,* ed., C.A. Patrides (London, 1968), 81-98.

Spolsky, E., and E. Shauber. "Stalking a Generative Poetics." *New Literary History* 12, No. 3 (Spring, 1981), 397-413.

Steadman, John. *Milton's Epic Characters.* Chapel Hill, 1959.

--------. *Milton and the Renaissance Hero.* Oxford, 1967.

--------. *Epic and Tragic Structure in Paradise Lost.* Chicago, 1976.

Stein, Arnold. *Answerable Style.* Minneapolis, 1953.

Steiner, George. *After Babel.* Oxford, 1975.

Tarn, W. W. *Hellenistic Civilization,* 3rd edn., tr. G. T. Griffith. London, 1952.

Thompson, T. H., ed. *Poems of Emily Dickinson.* Cambridge, 1961.

Thorpe, J., ed. *Milton Criticism: Selections from Four Centuries.* New York, 1966.

Todorov, Tzvetan. *Introduction to Poetics,* tr. R. Howard. Minneapolis, 1981.

Tompkins, Jane., ed. *Reader-Response Criticism.* Baltimore, 1980.

Trumpy, Hans. *Kriegerische Fachausdrüke im griechischen Epos.* Basel, 1950.

Versenyi, L. *Man's Measure.* Buffalo, 1974.

Vivante, Paul. "On the Representation of Reality in Homer." *Arion* 5 (1966), 149-90.

Wallbank, F. W. *Polybius.* Berkeley, 1972.

Wade-Gerry, H. T. *The Poet of the Iliad,* J. H. Gray Lecture for 1949. Cambridge, 1952.

Webster, T. B. L. *From Mycenae to Homer.* New York, 1964.

West, M. L. "Some More Notes on the Text of Hesiod." *Classical Quarterly* 12 (1962), 177-81.

--------. *Theogony.* Oxford, 1966.

Whaler, J. P. "The Miltonic Simile." *PMLA* 46 (1931), 1034-74.

Whitman, Cedric. *Homer and the Heroic Tradition.* New York, 1958.

Widmer, Kingsley. "The Iconography of Renunciation: The Miltonic Simile," in *Milton's Epic Poetry,* ed. C. A. Patrides (London, 1967), 121-31.

Wilamowitz-Moellendorf, Ulrich. *Die Ilias und Homer.* Berlin, 1920.

Wilkins, E. G. "A Classification of the Similes of the *Argonautica* of Apollonius of Rhodes." *Classical Weekly* 14.21 (April 11, 1921), 162-66.

Wunderli, P. *Ferdinand de Saussure und die Anagramme.* Tübingen, 1972.

# INDEX